Lost in Mu[sic]

'I think Giles Smith has nailed the pop tail on the pop donkey – I identified with every aspect of his troubled relationship with music' – Paddy McAloon, Prefab Sprout

'A chance for people who don't like pop music to find out what they're missing and for the rest of us to relive our past' – Andy Cox, Fine Young Cannibals

'Passionate, funny and obsessive to the edge of madness, *Lost In Music* is a book for anyone who has ever had a record player at the centre of their universe' – Tony Parsons

'Giles Smith is a wonderful writer: fluid, elegant, acute and very, very funny. *Lost In Music* is everything one had expected from his first book – and those of us who admire his work expected a lot' – Nick Hornby

'Smith might be unusual in the scale, the intensity and longevity of his pop obsession, but . . . if there's a shrewder or more readable account of its detours and hazards, I've never read it' – *Arena*

'What Giles Smith has done is tell his own, hilarious and moving story of a life spent in a search for the perfect record collection filing system . . . I cringed, I guffawed, I gritted my teeth. I wished I'd thought of writing it' – *Scotsman*

'Forget that impenetrable shrink-wrapped CD that has to be put in the fridge! You have enough Grace Jones albums! Get out there and put this book at number one, man – or you're as square as a cardboard box' – Patrick McCabe

Giles Smith was born in Colchester, Essex, in 1962. He joined the staff of the *Independent* newspaper in 1990. His writing has been published in *Q*, *Mojo*, the *New Yorker*, *Vogue* and the *Daily Star*. He lives in London.

Giles Smith

Lost in Music

A Pop Odyssey

PICADOR

First published 1995 by Picador

This edition published 1996 by Picador
an imprint of Macmillan General Books
25 Eccleston Place, London SW1W 9NF
and Basingstoke

Associated companies throughout the world

ISBN 0 330 33917 6

'Vine Street' by Randy Newman
© January Music Corp. USA. Warner Chappell Music Ltd, London W1Y 3FA.
Reproduced by permission of International Music Publications Ltd.
'A Windmill in Old Amsterdam' by Ted Dicks and Myles Rudge
© 1964, 1973 Westminster Music Ltd, London SW10 0SZ. International copyright secured.
All rights reserved. Used by permission.
'This is Pop' words and music by Andy Partridge
© 1978, reproduced by permission of EMI Virgin Music Ltd, London WC2H 0EA.

Author's note: the names of of some of the characters have been changed.

3 5 7 9 8 6 4 2

A CIP catalogue record for this book is available from
the British Library.

Phototypeset by Intype London Ltd
Printed and bound in Great Britain by Mackays of Chatham plc, Chatham, Kent

Acknowledgements

With thanks to: Ben Cairns, Tristan Davies, Diana Eden, Georgia Garrett, Nick Hornby, Anthony Lane, Cat Ledger, Charlie Meredith, Ian Parker, Tom Sutcliffe, Andrew Watson and Richard Williams. And thank you especially Sabine Durrant.

For my mother and father

That's a tape
That we made
But I'm sad to say
It never made the grade
That was me
Third guitar
I wonder where the others are

Randy Newman, 'Vine Street'

Introduction

In the spring of 1989, shortly after my twenty-seventh birth-day, as I stood in the sleet at a bus-stop in Colchester, it dawned on me that I had probably, all things considered, failed in my mission to become Sting. At least, for the time being. It was late afternoon, dark prematurely, and RCA Records in Germany had just ditched the Cleaners from Venus.

You may not have read about this at the time; there were disappointingly few angry headlines in the press, not many shocked editorials in the trade magazines. None at all, actu-ally. But the Cleaners from Venus was the band I was in, and for three and a half years this band had served as the very nerve-centre of my pop-stardom operation, my Become Sting campaign. There had been other bands before, but this was the one I really lavished my chips on, the one I really rode hard – all the way from our ignominious beginnings in an Essex industrial village, to our triumphant recording deal with RCA Germany (why Germany? Because nobody else would have us), right up until about 11.30 a.m. on this dis-consolate day, when someone important in Hamburg con-tacted our manager in London and said whatever the German is for 'You're fired'.

To be fair to RCA, things had gone slightly awry. Sales of the Cleaners from Venus's first album, *Going to England*, had been negligible yet, astonishingly, they had been undercut by sales of our second, *Town & Country*. The last time we had appeared live in Hamburg, (on the Town & Country Tour 1988), the chairman of the record company had walked out after three numbers, shaking his head despondently.

Furthermore, our manager was about to run away, our drummer was about to be deported to Japan and the singer, who wrote all the songs and whose band it was anyway, had stomped off in a huff ages ago to become a gardener.

Leaving me, just off the London train at North Station, waiting for a number 5 to take me up the hill to town, round the one-way system to Crouch Street and then out west down Lexden Road, left at the lights by MFI, and home to my mum's.

It was a shame because I really fancied Sting's job. Great pay: the *best* pay. Superb hours, too (because what does Sting actually *do* in the long months between albums and tours? He mucks about, I reckon). Homes in Hampstead and New York and Miami and Los Angeles (Barbra Streisand's old place, in fact). Not that I wanted to make records that sounded like his, but I was certainly on for the lifestyle. Concerts, fans. Pop music. Pop stardom.

Strictly speaking, of course, no vacancy for a Sting was ever advertised – though, as aspiring musicians tend to do, I read Sting's mere existence as an indication that the world needed Stings. In any case, the fact that no one had said so, let alone been looking at me as they said it, was really the least of the insuperable obstacles I wilfully ignored when I set out on Mission Big Time.

This book is the story of that voyage – one man's journey into the world of rock and then back to his mum's. And at the same time it's a book about what gets into people when pop gets hold of them. And, boy, can pop get a hold. It's pushy like that. You've really got to watch it. You invite pop into your house on a fairly casual basis and the next thing you know it's telling you what to wear and picking your friends.

Growing up in the 1970s, you were often told by your elders that pop's tyrannical rule over your life would not last.

Pop, they said, was just a phase you were going through, a kind of teenage mood. It would clear, like spots, as you entered your twenties to be smoothly replaced by an adult taste for classical music – orchestras, operas, the real thing, music which demanded more of you than a three-minute spasm of helpless assent and (the rumour was) gave you so much more in return.

But I've reached thirty-two and it still hasn't happened. Pop isn't only for young people any more and it isn't only made by them. Now it looks as though youth was just a phase pop went through. I've grown up with pop, and pop has grown up with me; and both of us are very different now from the way we were in 1970. And from time to time, a slight uneasiness creeps into our relationship which I would like to get to the bottom of.

About the records and artists covered in these pages. The book spans some twenty-five years of pop music but it does not pretend to offer any kind of overview. This is a personal account and perhaps it would be fairer to call it an under-view. I'm not suggesting these are the best things that happened in all that time. This is probably obvious from the fact that there's a chapter on Nik Kershaw, but it's as well to be clear.

Not that there aren't pieces of music here whose value as contributions to twentieth-century culture I would be prepared to argue until I was a very nasty shade of blue. It's just that, in my experience, a record collection is subject to some fairly arbitrary forces. It includes the record you bought because a friend told you to, or because you thought you liked it and you were mistaken, or because you thought it was another record altogether until you got it home but then you quite liked it anyway, or because it happened to be playing when something else, entirely unrelated to it, occurred, so your pleasure in it is only tangentially a musical one. With my own record collection, there are holes where great, seminal things ought to be; and there are things where I often wish there were holes, most acutely, most buttock-clenchingly, when people come round and start browsing and saying things like: 'You bought *this*?' or, 'Bloody hell – the Wombles!'

I've had my triumphs, I might say – my small share of those ginchy moments when your own tastes and some broader consensus on what is gifted and worthwhile coincide. But much of one's relationship with pop is circumstantial and happenstance and conducted against one's better judgement. In fact, I hold it to be one of pop's most winning gifts (and much underestimated in writing on the subject) that nothing can so smoothly persuade your better judgement to take the rest of the night off.

It seems only fair to warn, then, that these pages contain graphic descriptions of some truly horrible music and, appended to these descriptions, some passages of self-justification of a deplorably see-through nature. Readers with sensitive dispositions may wish to skip, for example, the chapter on 10cc. Also that one on Nik Kershaw. And to tread carefully during the chapters on Randy Crawford and Pink Floyd.

And to go nowhere near any of the chapters about the bands that I was in, from Pony through the Orphans of Babylon to the Cleaners from Venus. I really did think one of them might make it. I'd even started thinking about places in Colchester where they might erect the plaque, commemorating my early days – days when people hardly suspected, yet *somehow knew*, what would become of me. My parents' house was obviously a prime landmark candidate. Or perhaps above the door at one of the pubs or clubs, scenes of those tentative first steps on to the world's stage – the Oliver

Twist, the Embassy Suite, the Colne Lodge (now an old people's home). Or what about outside that little rehearsal room off Priory Street, which became a shop selling leotards?

Actually, no. The best place would be on the wall of the garage at John Taylor's house (not the John Taylor who ended up as bassist in Duran Duran, but another one), which is where it all started and, really, if I had known about some of the grief that lay ahead, where it all would have ended.

The band with no name

It is 1971, T. Rex are No. 2 in the charts with 'Jeepster' and I'm on lead guitar and vocals in the garage at John Taylor's house. I don't have a guitar, actually, but I do have a two-stringed ukulele, one of a pair found in the attic at home. I also have a pair of plastic sunglasses and a waistcoat, yanked out of a bundle of dressing-up stuff. I am nine and I think I just saw John Taylor's mum put her face up to one of the small square windows at the top of the garage doors, and I'm pretty sure she was laughing, but I'm not going to let that put me off.

My cousin Ian, who lives in the house at the end of John Taylor's garden, is behind me on drums – or rather on drum, hitting an old bust snare he pulled out of the trash in his father's shed. Phil, who's in our class, is over to the side on bass, except there's no bass so he's using the second of that pair of ukuleles. As for John Taylor, who is much smaller than the rest of us, he's on percussion. He's shaking some kind of bottle filled with sand or stones or God knows what.

I'm already a bit narked with John Taylor because in the scramble through the dressing-up clothes, he got the bullet belt – the big ex-army number. No bullets in it, but it's really wide and black and dangerous. Personally, I reckon the bullet belt is lead guitarist's gear. I mean, it's wasted on the per-cussionist. Who looks at the percussionist?

But the belt business is nothing compared with what John Taylor's doing right now. In fact, I'd be prepared to grant him unquestioned rights to the belt every time, from now and for ever, if he'd just pack up what he's doing, which is walking, while we're playing, in a huge clockwise circle, round behind the drum, up the side, across directly in front of me (in *front* of me!), down the other side, round the drum again . . . And he's doing this in big, clowny, exaggerated steps and every time his foot slaps down on the ground, he shakes the bottle. Plod, plod. Shake, shake.

I am incensed. What does he think that looks like? What does he think this is?

So midway through the second verse (or where the second verse would be if this song had any verses), just after he's gone by me on his stupid circuit for about the third time, I stop playing and turn on him.

'What are you doing?'

Because I think I *know* what he's doing: I think he's taking the mickey. Or he's trying to ruin everything. Or he's taking the mickey *and* trying to ruin everything. Or he's trying to steal the show like he stole the belt . . . Of course, he comes on all defensive.

'This is how I play it,' he says.

'It's not what they do,' I say.

'But I can't play it otherwise. It's how I do it.'

'It's not what they do,' I say again.

'It's my garage,' he says, irrefutably.

Well, I quit. Just took my ukulele, got out of there and never went back. Who needs these amateurs? I was looking for a *real* band.

The Beatles

If anyone ever asks me, 'What was the first record you bought?' I tell them proudly it was 'Let it Be' by the Beatles, which I got on its first release in 1970 when I was eight. And like, I think, pretty well everyone who tackles this 'first record' question (and I calculate that within a normally active social life, it's likely to come up three or four times annually), I am lying through my teeth. 'Let It Be' wasn't the first single I bought at all.

I've just been back through my singles and checked and there were other records which I had well before I owned 'Let It Be', records which I have somehow come to overlook with the years. And, I must say, the truth has come as something of a shock. I'm so used to connecting myself with the Beatles at their most anthemic that when the conversation comes round again and someone says, 'What was *your* first record?', I'm not even conscious of setting the other records aside; I never find myself beginning to say the name of one of them and then changing in a hurry to 'Let it Be'.

I am unable to pinpoint the precise moment when I began to indulge in this fiction, yet it seems clear to me that it must have been a thought-through decision. When you talk about your first record, you're saying something about how quick you were off the mark: you're indicating the place where you and pop music first really hit it off. And I must have realized at some point that I didn't want to start just anywhere. And it must have occurred to me at the same time that the affiliation between oneself and one's first record was too important to rest on something so insubstantial and arbitrary as the truth.

So I went ahead and fiddled with the history and, by a

peculiarly judicious telescoping of the past, I arrived at the single which marked the end of the Beatles, and not at 'A Windmill In Old Amsterdam' which was, if we're going to be literal about it, the first piece of vinyl I ever called my own. Yet splendid though Ronnie Hilton's mellow yet cheerful delivery is ('I saw a mouse/Where?/There on the stair/*Where* on the stair?' etc) this was not quite the statement I wanted to make about me and pop, as we were in the beginning.

For the same reason, I have tended not to offer up for consideration my entire album of songs from *The Jungle Book*, bought at Colchester Woolworth's and, again, acquired some years before John and Paul began completely ignoring each other.

A quick gripe about that *Jungle Book* album: it wasn't the film soundtrack by the original cast, I discovered when I got it on the deck, but a shoddy mock-up by second-rate sessioneers – a rogue Mowgli, a bogus Balou. It was like one of those cheap Top of the Pops albums, which were doing big business at the time and which used to feature a selection of the day's hits made by soundalikes who didn't. Except there was no woman in a tasselled suede bikini on the cover of my *Jungle Book* soundtrack, but rather a genuine-looking shot of the Colonel and his pals herding cheerfully through the undergrowth, which, in my naïvety, I took to signal the pukka, Disney-endorsed product. Not that it mattered in the end. By persistent playing over a five-day period, I managed to convince myself that this wanton fakery was equal to the real thing – a trick I was to attempt many years later, but with significantly less success, with records by Paul Young.

Anyway, in the crucial matter of my first record, somewhere along the line I have started performing a little shimmy and slipping forward a few purchases to 1970, where the

Beatles were right at the end of their tether and marking the occasion of their dissolution with 'Let It Be', this glazed, sway-along number, in which you can virtually hear them waving goodbye to the sixties, waving goodbye to us all. At the time, the *New Musical Express* called the song 'a cardboard tombstone', arguing that 'Let It Be' – which does, it must be said, contain more than its fair share of cod religiosity – was no fitting tribute to the Beatles, no suitable endnote for the band who, in so many ways, started it all. I take the point. There is no simpler way to measure how far the Beatles had travelled and how much they had lost along the way than to mark the distance from 'She Loves You', in which every second seems to count more vitally than the last, to the cyclical defeatism of 'Let It Be'.

A bum note for me to come in on, but a trenchant one with slightly thrilling morbid overtones: my first single, the Beatles' last. There's a story there – and, needless to say, it's a story which flatters me, which was the entire point of this 'Let It Be' illusion. It was my way of indicating that, though a child of the musically impoverished 1970s, I had at least some kind of grounding in the golden 1960s. It also allowed me to imply that, had I been a record-buyer in the 1960s, I would, clearly, have been connecting with the Beatles and not been the sort of saddy who thought Cliff Richard was more exciting.

To tell the truth, though, I haven't always been strictly loyal to 'Let It Be' as my first record. There was a substantial period, which ended only quite recently, when I told people that the first record I bought was 'Hey Jude'. There was, I'm fairly sure, nothing deliberately misleading about this; I wasn't intending to prove anything. Quite simply, out of a combination of forgetfulness and confusion, I stopped saying 'Let It Be' for a while and started saying 'Hey Jude'. (Hugely unlikely that this could have been the case: I was six when that song was released and probably not quite ready for Sparky and his magic piano on Ed 'Stewpot' Stewart's *Junior Choice*, let alone for 'Hey Jude' with its squally McCartney vocal and its infinitely circling fade-out.)

The problem is, once you have started tampering with the facts like this, once you've seen how, with a nip here and a tuck there, your musical past bursts gratifyingly into significance, there's potentially no end to it. In the early 1970s, for example, when my loyalty to the group T. Rex was at its blindest and fiercest, the first record I ever bought was 'Ride A White Swan'.

And then, at the height of the Jam's success in the late 1970s, and in a lame attempt on my part to suggest precocious Mod-leanings, 'Cindy Incidentally' by the Faces was the first record I ever bought, though, according to my elaborate numbering system (we will come to my elaborate numbering system later), it was the nineteenth. And just once, more recently than I would care to acknowledge, the first record I ever bought was Otis Redding's '(Sittin' On) The Dock Of The Bay' (1968). This was to impress a girl. Shameless: I never owned it at all. (Though my brother did, if that's any good.)

But after each of these truancies, I would always return, shame-faced but with the contentment of the homecomer, to 'Let It Be'.

So why can't I find my copy of it? I've been upstairs and gone through the box where my singles are and it's not there. And it's implausible that I have lost it or got rid of it somewhere in the intervening years. I should probably mention this early on: I do not sell, exchange or give away records that I have bought. These are not transactions I'm even prepared to contemplate. It seems to me that one's ownership of

records and the moral responsibilities and personal signifi-
cances involved are way too grave to allow for the kind of
flippant horse-trading that some people go in for. I *have* been
known to pass on to friends records of which I have, for
one reason or another, a duplicate copy, but even then only
grudgingly, in the spirit of someone granting a loan which he
expects to see repaid within the next five minutes. In every
other respect, with regard to the filing and maintenance of
records, related literature and all things pop, I combine the
characteristics of an archivist who fears for his job and a
badly paranoid squirrel.

Hence the decade's-worth of *Record Mirrors* and *NMEs*
(1977–87) currently representing an unrivalled fire hazard in
the attic at my mother's house; hence also my unbroken set of
Q magazines (about to exceed a hundred monthly copies as I
write, most of them in starchy good nick) and my having
retained a poorly Xeroxed list of tour dates handed out at a
Tom Robinson Bang gig I went to at Essex University in
1978.

Weighing the absence of a copy of 'Let It Be' against the
refined efficiency of my own storage systems, I am forced to
confront the disturbing possibility that not only is 'Let It Be'
not the first single I ever bought but that I never actually
bought it in the first place. Yet I can see it clearly – the dark
green apple pictured on the A-side middle, the halved apple
on the B-side – though I could be remembering that from any
Beatles record released on the Apple label. But what about
the plain white sleeve it came in, the black lettering, almost
too dark to be legible, at the single's centre? A fantasy, it
would appear. A self-installed myth.

So what *was* the first single I bought – I mean the first non-
nursery-based single, the first piece of pop proper? Returning
to the single box, I discover that the single boldly marked

'No. 1' in blue biro, is '(Dance With The) Guitar Man' by Duane Eddy and the Rebelettes, but I can discount that, firstly because it was a hit in November 1962, when I was nine months old, and secondly because I stole it at some point from one of my brothers. I know this because small boys are always in a hurry to write their names on things and on the green paper Columbia sleeve, just below where I wrote mine in earnest block capitals, I crossed out, but failed to obliterate, my brother's initials. A bad job by me, there – but a significantly better one than my brother did before me, as revealed in the distress marks on the B-side where he has tried to scuff out the centre label with his fingernail but where you can still read, clear as daylight, the proprietorial legend 'Ada Clark'. (I don't know who Ada Clark was, but I do know that she was robbed.)

When I finally came to install the numeric system, which would have been around 1972 or '73, just as soon as my collection had burgeoned to the degree where it needed strict control by cataloguing (i.e., when I had about four or five singles), I made Duane Eddy 'No. 1' on the grounds that it was the oldest – and, perhaps, also the most daringly acquired. (It remains to this day the only record I have ever appropriated in a heist.) As I go through the rest now, the numeric sequence is unbroken. There is no hole where 'Let It Be' may once have been. Frightening though it is to concede, all the evidence points to the fact that the first record I ever bought was 'Rosetta' by Georgie Fame and Alan Price from 1971.

Thinking about it, I feel sorry for anyone whose first single genuinely was 'She Loves You' or Elvis singing 'Heartbreak Hotel' or 'I Wish It Would Rain' by the Temptations or any other astonishing one-off pop moment, people who really were in the right place at the right time with their pulse beating at the right pace. Because we'll all nod slowly and heavily with approval when they tell us and say things like, 'Oh, really? Fan-tastic!' But who's going to believe them?

Of course, now that the single is debased currency, all but replaced by the CD and the cassette, perhaps the more poignant question is 'What was the *last* single you bought?' Do you remember? The last piece of 7-inch vinyl. Mine was 'Don't Dream It's Over' by Crowded House. Which works out OK, because I would argue that that was their finest song so far, what with that little tripped-up chorus line ('Hey now'), the way the bass guitar prods the last verse along and that overall feeling in the drummer's dragged pace and the singer's slur that the whole song is being seen through early-morning eyes. And there wouldn't be much risk of social estrangement involved in nominating 'Don't Dream It's Over' as positively your last 7-inch buy, the one you went out on, because most people like Crowded House anyway.

But how long before I'm making that one up? How long before I'm bolting together a story to suit the times?

Well, no time at all, in fact. For as I now recall, when I bought 'Don't Dream It's Over' I also bought 'Building A Bridge To Your Heart' by Wax. I was in Tower Records in London, about to take the underground to Liverpool Street for a train, and it was quite late at night and I was mildly drunk, which is not a condition in which you should ever shop for records unless you are prepared to accept the risk that you will come out of there with about seventy pounds' worth of old Carly Simon albums. Or, failing that, a single by Wax.

Wax were a short-lived duo formed by Andrew Gold (he of the sublime 'Never Let Her Slip Away' and the abysmal 'Thank You For Being A Friend') and Graham Gouldman, the one with the fuzzy hair from 10cc. I'd heard 'Building A

Bridge To Your Heart' a couple of times on the radio and had developed, rather guiltily, a fondness for the chorus. What with the drink and the suspension of reality that comes from being in a record shop late at night, this fondness became a raging urge to spend money. And I suppose 'Building A Bridge To Your Heart' *is* kind of satisfying, in the way that truly soulless pop music so often can be. But as an epilogue to the story of my life as a buyer of 7-inch vinyl singles . . . well, I don't think it has quite the substance or the legs. I'll opt for Crowded House, I think.

So my first single turns out to be a record I never bought, and I arrive at my last single by sweeping another equal claimant under the carpet. Appalling. But many of my dealings with pop music turn out to have been like this. The opportunities for self-invention which pop offers seem nearly limitless. And I've been leaping at them from the word go.

T. Rex

Every Saturday morning, shopping reluctantly in Colchester town centre with my parents, I kept an eye open for Marc Bolan of T. Rex. Not that Marc Bolan lived in Colchester. He came from Hackney and he had no connection that I knew of with the town, or any reason to be shopping there on a Saturday, when the place got pretty busy what with the market. But I kept my eyes peeled, just in case.

I didn't bother too much upstairs in Jacklin's where, at eleven o'clock, we had coffee and individually wrapped chocolate digestives; Jacklin's had dark panelled walls, middle-aged waitresses in starchy black and white uniforms and a display of Rotary Club pennants from around Britain. No place for Bolan, really, with his corkscrew hair, his glitter-painted cheekbones, his shiny silver jacket and satin trousers. (That's what he wore on the telly; I assumed that's what he wore all the time.) More likely to see him near Wright's the butcher's or in the vicinity of Woolworth's on the High Street, or walking down the road which runs past the back door of Boots the Chemist, which is where I always had to stand with my father while my mother went in briefly to shop alone.

Week in, week out I looked, and week in, week out he failed to show. But I wasn't discouraged. Come the summer of 1971, Marc Bolan was by no means the only pop star I hadn't seen in Colchester High Street. Others included Rod Stewart, Noddy Holder of Slade and that man with the sideburns out of Mungo Jerry. Then again, these others could have slipped by without me noticing because, following 'Hot Love' and 'Get It On', Bolan was the only one I was really looking for. I had no questions for him, nothing that I urgently needed to say. An autograph would have been nice, I suppose. I wasn't asking him to put on a concert, or anything. I just wanted to see him.

But Colchester wasn't a good town for that. It wasn't the kind of place pop stars came to, or came from. Look it up in Pete Frame's tremendous *Rock Gazetteer of Great Britain*, the ultimate pop geography book and a mine of indispensable information; like the fact that Rick Astley used to work at Parkside Garden Centre, Newton Le Willows, and Midsomer Norton is the birthplace of Anita Harris. The *Gazetteer*'s big and cheerful message is that pop archaeology is anywhere and everywhere. Just disturb the soil slightly with your foot and there they are – traces of pop. But not really in Colchester, Essex.

Under 'Colchester', you'll learn that Twink, later the drummer with the Pretty Things, had his first band here – the Fairies. The *Gazetteer* carries a picture of him captioned 'Twink trashes a drumkit on TV'. You will also discover that the sleeve for Fairport Convention's *What We Did On Our Holidays* album is a photograph of a chalk drawing on a blackboard, taken in a dressing room at Essex University, which lies on the outskirts of Colchester. My copy of the book was published in 1989, too early to record the group Blur, most of whose members are Colcestrians, though all of them moved to London and affected Cockney accents as soon as they were old enough to shave. So in the third and final entry, the town is 'home of eighties hopefuls, Modern English'. I love that 'hopefuls'.

It doesn't get much better when you look up a few places in the district: Kevin Rowland of Dexy's Midnight Runners once had a summer job washing up at Butlin's in Clacton-on-Sea. And Clacton is where Sade grew up, although, as Mr Frame is careful to mention, she was born in Nigeria. Also,

'Yes made their début well away from the public glare at East Mersea Youth club in 1968.' The first time I read that sentence, some sort of local protectiveness bridled inside me and I thought: How patronizing. What about the public of East Mersea? Don't they have a glare worth anything? But then I thought about East Mersea and the author's got a point.

I don't mean to quibble, but Mr Frame does sell Colchester a little short. He doesn't mention that Steve Harley, of Cockney Rebel, worked briefly on the local newspaper and lived in a small flat above the bakery on Sheregate Steps. (Was this the original 'up' referred to in the song 'Come Up And See Me (Make Me Smile)'? I like to think so.) And he doesn't indicate that local guitarist Steve Linton once auditioned for Thin Lizzy who kept him waiting a whole week before informing him they'd given the job to Gary Moore.

Nor does Mr Frame include a story one of my brothers told me: that, on their way to a show in Ipswich in the mid-1960s, the Beatles stopped for chewing gum at the newsagent at the end of our road. (I never believed this tale: it had the ring of other tales employed by my brothers to wind me up. I've used it a lot since, though, pointing out the newsagent to visitors.) And the *Gazetteer* is silent about the time I saw Ray Cooper, the percussionist who works with Elton John and Eric Clapton among others, run into Gunton's, the delicatessen in Crouch Street.

But, true enough, there is no 'Colchester Sound', no 'Colne Beat'. A little to the south and we could have been part of the Canvey Island R&B explosion: Dr Feelgood! Wilko Johnson! A little to the left and down a bit and we could have joined in with Basildon's 1980s synthesizer happening: Depeche Mode! Yazoo! And just sixty miles to the west and we would have been in London: Nearly Everyone! But, no, we were in

Colchester: the town voted, during the 1980s, the most boring place in Britain by listeners to *The Terry Wogan Show* on Radio 2, and they should know; the town where an awful lot happened in Roman times, but not much since, except the abolition of early-closing on Thursdays; the town where, aged nine, I walked around looking for Marc Bolan.

T. Rex never played in Colchester, but they did appear at the Weeley Pop Festival in August 1971, just as my Bolan interest was really catching fire after the low-slung groove of 'Hot Love', which I witnessed on *Top of the Pops*, and after 'Get It On', which was the same thing, basically, played at a different pace and which I got my mother to buy me from Harper's Music Store, thus redeeming one of those Saturday mornings.

Weeley is to the east of Colchester on the way to Clacton. There's not much there except fields and a few quiet cottages, which made it the perfect place for a weekend of live rock and substance abuse. 'T. Rex,' said the posters in town. 'Lindisfarne, The Faces, Rory Gallagher, Caravan, Colosseum, Barclay James Harvest, Mott the Hoople, Curved Air . . .'

I didn't even bother to ask my parents if I could go. I was only recently the beneficiary of a number of rights relating to unaccompanied cycling. To suggest that I might now set off for three uncertain nights under canvas in the company of 30,000 rock fans would have been pushing my luck. And these were the days when a rock festival was a rock festival: with chainsaw-toting Hell's Angels, continuous nudity and shockingly poor-quality drugs. I base this statement on vague recollections of some of the stories printed in the local paper in the run-up to Weeley and discussed at home. All of the stories featured 'angry villagers' and may have contained exaggerations. Even so, you can bet there was a distinction between the flavour of Weeley '71 and today's Glastonbury

Festivals which, ever more pre-packaged and accessible, have quietened down into a vaguely alternative shopping weekend with live coverage on Channel 4.

At home, that Weeley weekend was agony – and the anticipation of it, too, with the free, cut-out-and-keep festival guide in the paper, the week beforehand. So near and so far. And yet I figured if I couldn't go and see Bolan, I could at least catch him on the way past.

'To get to Weeley from London,' I said to my father, more than once, 'you have to go through Colchester, don't you?'

'Yes. Why?'

'Nothing.'

I had a very clear picture of the Bolan I would see, stopped at the traffic lights on London Road, bound for Weeley. He was in the passenger seat of a Ford Escort van, with a load of instruments clustered behind him. None of the rest of the band was there, just Bolan – with the glitter under his eyes and the silver jacket and the satin trousers. So, on the first day of the festival, I cycled down to the main road which, before they built the bypass, fed the traffic from London round the edge of the town. And I leaned my bike up against the Nat West bank and waited for most of the afternoon. No sign of him, though. Typical Colchester.

In those days it was either T. Rex or it was Slade. The whole history of pop seemed to have boiled down to this crucial axis. Actually, *history* seemed to have boiled down to this crucial axis. The industrial unrest of the early 1970s? It was just background hum during the Slade versus T. Rex chart wars of 1972/73; 'Mama We're All Crazy Now' versus 'Children Of The Revolution'; 'Cum On Feel The Noize' versus '20th Century Boy'; 'Skweeze Me, Please Me' versus 'The Groover'.

After the boy/girl distinction, Slade or T. Rex was about

the easiest way to divide the people I knew at school. Slade had Noddy Holder, as whiskery as a Victorian factory-owner, the wearer of a top hat with reflective discs set into it, his voice a sulphurous gargle. But T. Rex had Marc Bolan with his angelic face, his pursed-lipped pouting, his precious Ts and Ss, sung from the front of the mouth. Noddy Holder was never Slade in the way that Marc Bolan was T. Rex. The three people who stood behind Bolan on *Top of the Pops*, in various stages of self-conscious stiffness, were not where one's interest lay. Whereas Slade was a group, a bunch of lads, rough-edged, raucous good-timers, their sound thicker and heavier than Bolan's spangly shards of guitar. I couldn't quite get on with Slade. It wasn't Holder I objected to. It was that other one, with the long straight hair and the goofy grin – Dave Hill. He looked like a nerk to me. Ditto the drummer, the one who just sat there chewing. And there was no sitting on the fence, so I opted for Bolan.

Clearly, much was encoded in this choice. Were you a team player, responding to the garrulous network that was Slade, or were you an individualist, smitten by Bolan's singularity? Did you like boys who looked like girls, or boys who looked like Victorian factory-owners? Girls on the whole preferred Bolan, so to be a boy who liked T. Rex was to be one of the girls. I was lucky enough to know Karen Jones who liked neither and was prepared to trade me the colour Bolan pin-up from her copy of *Jackie* for nothing more than four Black Jacks, which seemed to me a laughably good deal. It went on the back of my bedroom door along with the selection of images from my brothers' magazines and papers which formed my Bolan mural. In the end, the door was completely papered: some thirty Marc Bolans looking out at me in various states of pout and sulk and grin.

Was this about sex? I think, in part, it may have been less

sexy than that – and more male. I wasn't nearly as interested in sleeping with Marc Bolan as I was interested in pasting neatly clipped articles about him into my specially designated T. Rex scrapbook and making drawings of him in which I tried to get the shape of his guitar exactly right. I had no desire for him which throbbed as loudly as my desire to collect his records, keep them together in unblemished condition and label them thoroughly in biro – name of artist and song in top left-hand corner of sleeve, number of record in top right, large capital G at top centre, pair of mirroring, Baroque-style brackets on either side of the sleeve's central hole and, written round the rim of the hole in authoritative capitals, THIS RECORD BELONGS TO GILES SMITH. And what began with Bolan characterizes, I fear, a substantial portion of my affair with pop. There aren't many things so obviously in touch with passion and so frank in their emotionality as pop music; yet there's nothing like it for bringing out the librarian in me.

But, beyond this reflex, I was never aware of an urge to be together with Bolan in a pre-pubescent love tryst. The excitement that immediately followed his appearances on *Top of the Pops* – felt as a kind of nervous agitation, low in the stomach, right on the edge of unpleasant – and which could fuel half an hour or an hour of frenetic activity at the drawing pad or of repeated playings of the records, was excitement in which I disappeared completely, or hoped to. These were the spells in which I thought of myself not with Bolan but *as* Bolan, which, let's face it, would have complicated our union.

My commitment to Bolan had to weather extensive ridicule from my brothers – three of them, all well beyond the Bolan target audience, listening to Free, Led Zeppelin and the Rolling Stones and thinking themselves pretty clever with it. If anything, their mockery only confirmed me in my belief. The eldest, Nick, who was twenty at this time, went to the trouble of sending me letters from college taunting me about Bolan, frequently in the idiom of Geoffrey Willans's Molesworth books. 'Marc Bolan is a weed and a wet,' he wrote. 'I diskard him uterly.' 'Van Morrison,' I wrote back, 'is a hippie.'

Jeremy and Simon, meanwhile, who were in their mid-teens, developed an exaggerated and high-pitched version of Bolan's trademark yowl ('Ow!'), which they performed jeeringly whenever I entered the room. Their campaign of disdain intensified around the time of the release of 'Telegram Sam', which sounded almost exactly like 'Get It On'. 'All his songs are the same,' they crowed. 'He's useless.' They missed the point badly there. Innovation wasn't something I wanted nearly as much as I wanted consistency. I liked 'Get It On', so the more Bolan's other records sounded like it, the happier I was.

Given the amount of comic mileage my brothers got out of my Bolan obsession, it was, of course, in their interests to encourage me in it. And without my brothers I would never have found out about the 'Power Play' slot in the evenings on Radio Luxembourg, in which they played a new record every hour for a week. In the evenings, Radio Luxembourg was nine parts interference to two parts reception. Most of the countries of Europe seemed to be represented in its permanent background of crossed-line chatter. Occasionally the signal blew loud and ugly with distortion and then settled again. But I tilted my head towards my brother's transistor radio and listened, ahead of its release in Britain, to T. Rex's 'Jeepster' fading in and out of the Norwegian shipping forecast. And then I waited an hour and heard it again, this time obstructed by the Finnish time signal. It had one of Bolan's neat, chippy riffs. It had drums and clapping and stamping. Like all of the T. Rex singles, it was produced to sound close, immediate. Even through the chaotic white-noise of Radio Luxembourg, it spoke to me.

It's perhaps a little odd to say of a Marc Bolan song that it 'spoke' to me, given how little of what he said I actually understood. The words to 'Metal Guru' and 'Telegram Sam' made no paraphrasable sense whatsoever but that didn't stop me thinking they were powerfully communicative at the time. It didn't help, clarity-wise, that I was such an innocent. I misheard a line in 'Get It On' as: 'Well, your duty is sweet.' As Nick manfully explained, what Bolan was actually singing was: 'Well, you're dirty and sweet.' I now realize that Bolan was either utterly baffling or explicitly sexual and there was no middle ground. The chorus of 'Get It On' urged the girl who was 'dirty and sweet' to 'get it on, bang a gong, get it on'. 'Hot Love' sounded more like the title of an adult film than a pop song and incorporated some saucy exhalations of breath. 'Jeepster', which included the puzzling line 'Girl, I'm just a jeepster for your love', ended with the more explicit 'I'm gonna suck ya', followed by some coital panting, leading to a loud orgasmic gasp. For the pubescent girls who screamed at Bolan and grew hysterical in his presence, these words and primal calls must have seemed thrillingly promising. I didn't scream. I was oblivious and, in any case, too busy filing the records and clipping out the pictures.

By the time 'Jeepster' came out, I had my own record player. My parents, fed up that whenever they wanted to play their own records, they were always having to remove from the turntable either 'A Windmill in Old Amsterdam', my Tubby the Tuba EP, or that appalling pirate version of the *Jungle Book* soundtrack, had passed over to me a Murphy F4 which had originally belonged to my Aunt Eileen. Barely bigger than an LP, it featured a rudimentary plastic turntable set inside a small pink cardboard suitcase, complete with moulded handle and metal snap-fasteners. You set the needle down on the record manually. And quite frequently, you set the needle down on the mat beside the record by mistake, where it howled in protest.

This was a prototype portable machine, though clearly there was no intention that you should walk around with it while it was in operation. In any case, if you were a self-conscious nine-year-old, you wouldn't have been seen dead out and about with something that looked like Barbie's overnight bag. The simpler notion here (and what must have sold my aunt on the idea) was that once you were tired of playing your Ray Conniff and Perry Como records in the sitting room, you could simply whip the machine away into the bedroom and start all over again in there.

One crucial thing about the Murphy F4: it was – and I would be prepared to argue this vehemently before any jury of hi-fi specialists – supremely unjoggable. I'm not sure what the technical term is for 'joggability' though I feel sure there is one, and that it is probably something like 'platter destabilization ratio' or 'needle-to-groove interface parameter'. What's more, there are doubtless a hundred different factory tests for it, involving wind tunnels, vibrating steel surfaces and copies of Dire Straits' *Love Over Gold*. I had one test, and one test only and when I praise the Murphy F4 for its resilience, I simply mean that whenever I leapt from a standing position on the bed, bounced once on the floor and dropped to my knees in the manner perfected by Marc Bolan as seen on television (though he was using his drummer's podium at the time, rather than a bed, and was on a stage in some unspecified auditorium, rather than at home, and the floor was shiny rather than carpeted, enabling him to glide open-mouthed towards the camera on the knees of his flares) the vibrations on landing didn't automatically hump the needle into the paper label in the record's middle – a problem I would later have with the Ferguson, hurriedly passed on to me by Jeremy (who didn't explain this design fault at the time).

What I didn't realize about the Murphy F4 was that it wasn't giving me the whole picture. I discovered this when I took my copy of 'Jeepster' (plain sleeve, but with a full colour picture label on the B-side, featuring Bolan in a turquoise top) round to see my cousin Nigel. Nigel had recently shown me the first picture I had ever seen of a naked woman (this would have been a week or so after he gave me my first ever cigarette) and in the spirit of reciprocation, I thought it was only fair that I should share with him the new T. Rex single. Generally I found Nigel intimidatingly advanced, but music is a great leveller. Nigel might have had precocious access to porn mags and Embassy No. 6 but he was lining himself up to buy an album by Lynsey de Paul, so to some extent he needed all the help he could get.

Nigel thought we should play the single on the family radiogram, which was, in essence, a coffin on legs, situated against the wall in their sitting room. There was a deep thunk as Nigel turned the machine on and then we waited while valves the size of milk bottles slowly warmed. With me anxiously looking on in case he fingered the playing surface, Nigel rested the record on the flanges at the top of the miniature silver pole in the middle of the turntable, and clipped it there with the L-shaped bracket. Then he flicked the deck-level tog from OFF to REJECT. The record flapped down on to the turntable and we watched the big, bulbous arm, like a model helicopter on a stick, travel above the platter and put down on the single's rim. At which point we repaired to the leather-look sofa on the other side of the room and readied ourselves.

The record started – drums first, the stamping and clapping on the beat, then Bolan's riff. I was checking Nigel's face for a reaction when I noticed it: this second guitar coming out of the right-hand speaker, playing little runs and fills, quite independent of the guitar playing the riff, a detail that I had never heard when I played the record on my suitcase at home. Almost immediately I was off the sofa and over to the record player in a state of anxious confusion.

Because I *knew* about T. Rex: there were four in the band – Bolan on lead vocals and guitar, Mickey Finn on bongos and high voice, Steve Curry on bass and Bill Legend on drums. There was no other guitarist in the band, only Bolan. So what the hell was going on? Who was this other person fiddling about? I couldn't understand it. I had counted them all out; now I was counting them all back in again, and there was more of them. Almost ill with incomprehension, I dipped my head into the radiogram and inspected the needle for fluff.

Nigel was unimpressed by 'Jeepster' but, then, I had rather spoilt it for him, yanking the needle off after ten seconds like that, then putting it back on and yanking it back off and so on, before I finally gave up and let the thing run through while I slumped back in the sofa, wearied by my own perplexity.

It took Jeremy to explain, back at home. 'It's multi-track recording. It's not just the band, playing the song in a studio. They can add other bits afterwards.'

What he was saying, it seemed to me, was: the whole thing was a fake, a confection. I had thought 'Jeepster' represented, if not a mirror held up to nature, at least a microphone held up to T. Rex. But it was all much more complicated than that. I felt royally cheated. Next he'd be telling me the groups weren't actually playing when they appeared on *Top of the Pops*.

It wasn't this that stopped me looking for Marc Bolan in Colchester – though stop I did, eventually. The cumulative effect of the weekly disappointments, and of the Weeley incident in particular, must have worn me down. But, of course, it's when you're not actively looking that you're most likely to see . . .

On a misty autumn Saturday afternoon in 1975, when I was thirteen, I was playing football on the pitches at Wood's Leisure Centre where there's a sports hall which doubles as a small-time pop arena. And suddenly a long, sleek, black car pulled into the car park and a small crowd seemed to materialize instantly, out of nowhere, round its back window. And all the people in our football game streaked that way too – just abandoned the match and ran over. By jostling a bit, you could see the wound-down window, some lacquered hair, a hand with an enormous ring on it.

It was Alvin Stardust.

Chris Sutton (not the Chris Sutton who became for a while Britain's most expensive footballer, but another one), who was bolder than the rest of us, spoke to him.

He said something like, 'Hey, Alvin – like your records.'

And Alvin Stardust said something like, 'Thanks. Thanks a lot.'

Eventually, his car pulled away again – maybe he was just checking the place out – and everyone stood around laughing and congratulating Chris Sutton and saying, 'Amazing! Alvin Stardust in Colchester! Who'd have thought?'

I didn't say anything, though. I hated Alvin Stardust.

T. Rex again

Marc Bolan was killed in a car crash on Barnes Common in south-west London in September 1977. He was in the passenger seat of a purple Mini driven by his partner, Gloria Jones. The Mini left the road on a bend and hit a tree. Jones survived, Bolan died. He was twenty-nine.

My mother told me about his death at breakfast, just as three years later she would wake me with a cup of tea and the news that John Lennon had been murdered. I wish I could say that I flung myself to the kitchen lino, hauled myself back up the stairs to my bedroom, moaning noisily, and spent a week there, inconsolable in a ring of candles. But that's not how it was. I felt that chilly standstill which happens in your chest when you hear about a death. But I felt nothing more personal.

The point is, I was long over Bolan by 1977. I had bought 'The Groover' in 1973, but mostly for old times' sake. I didn't really like it. Worse, by the time he died, I was fifteen and, to some extent, in denial about my Bolan phase. For a year and half there I had behaved as if nothing else was important. And then in direct contradiction, I had moved on to Sweet and Mud and a host of others – taste an early casualty as a paper round caused my disposable income to burgeon. In 1976, brazenly faithless, I'd even take a mild interest in Peter Frampton, who was a kind of Bolan flashback, baby-faced, angel-haired. In other words, where Bolan was concerned, I had made the short journey from passion to indifference and had begun to indulge the heartless polygamy of the pop fan.

I thought about him more warmly much later. In the

1990s, some pop stars are granted a reincarnation. They come back advertising jeans. In 1991, whether he liked it or not, it was Marc Bolan's turn. '20th Century Boy' was heard in a Levi's commercial, one of the series using old pop records to lodge in your mind some striking, trouser-related visual scenario. How you feel about this depends largely on whether you are disquieted at all to hear the soundtrack for your past converted into the soundtrack for somebody else's sales pitch. But that year, for the first time, I visited the Bolan tree, the scene of the car crash, which T. Rex fans have appropriated as a kind of shrine.

This was no pilgrimage: I was living ten minutes up the road at the time and I went there to write a newspaper article. Throughout the year, the tree is festooned with tributes, but as the anniversary of Bolan's death approaches, these swell in number until the thing is a ribboned maypole, its branches wrapped with poems, flowers in bright paper, rosettes, drawings, photocopied pictures and record sleeves. The tree is situated where houses and street lights peter out into a network of roads crossing the common. The ground slopes steeply down a track on one side of the tree and the area is now pinned in by a crash carrier on the other, Bolan being by no means the only person to have made an unscheduled stop at this point.

It was drizzling that night and miserably autumnal but about twenty people were there, sitting in vigil, carrying on a muted conversation as the rain spattered in the trees and cars sluiced round the corner. Most of the gathering had been over to Golders Green crematorium during the day to pay their respects at Bolan's memorial plaque and then had come on to the tree. 'Solid Gold, Easy Action' was playing on a car stereo parked in the road below.

I was an imposter here, a lapsed Bolanite among these

keepers of the flame, these people whose fixation had held for twenty years after mine had fizzled out. But we had some things in common: 'Hot Love', 'Get It On', 'Jeepster', and an unease about the Levi's commercial. I squeezed on to the crash barrier next to the guy in prime position by the trunk. He was my age, had Bolan-length air and a strip of purple glitter under each eye and he stared mournfully at the neck of the electric guitar he was holding as he said: 'Marc didn't even *wear* jeans.'

Sitting in the rain at night by a tree under which someone was crushed to death in a Mini... well, this opens itself rather easily to the charge of morbidity. Thinking obsessively about anything is a kind of self-entombment, but the more glaringly so when the object of the obsession is itself entombed. Yet it struck me by the Bolan tree that the solemnity was mostly the weather's fault and that something straightforwardly cheerful was going on under those dripping branches: some people were remembering Bolan and a handful of records which had stirred, and continued to stir them. And if the Levi's commercial wasn't in the true spirit of Bolan as they saw it, then this gathering was.

There was some conversation about getting back to the true spirit of Bolan by going direct to Bolan's spirit. One of the company mentioned someone he knew who, following a near-fatal car accident of his own during which a T. Rex tape had been playing on the stereo, claimed to have communicated with Bolan in a Ouija board session. Somebody else raised an objection.

'The thing is, they bullshit you.'

'Who?' I said. 'Mediums?'

'No, spirits. They'll pretend to be the person you want to get in touch with – Bolan, Hendrix, whatever. They lie, just like we do. So who can you trust?'

Relic

The disadvantages of growing up with older brothers are many and varied. They share your bedroom and put pictures of scantily clad women on the wall right where you wanted to put a picture of Chelsea's Ron Harris. They offer you money to eat a spoonful of mustard and then don't pay up. One of them gets the front seat of the car every time. They're much bigger than you and don't really feel it when you hit them.

From a pop music point of view, though, it's a different story. Pop-wise, older brothers are a boon. They flood the house with records and you become the indirect beneficiary of their advanced spending power and more mature tastes. True, much of the music they listen to you hate precisely because they like it: I was twenty before I got over my eldest brother's infatuation with Van Morrison. And I can't say I've ever been grateful to any of them for putting me in touch with Jethro Tull's *Aqualung*.

But I got to hear *Ogden's Nut Gone Flake* by the Small Faces and *Surf's Up* by the Beach Boys and *Can't Buy A Thrill* by Steely Dan when I was, by rights, too young to be involved with music as good as that. And, thanks to older brothers, me and a handful of rock essentials genuinely go back: ('Sittin' On) The Dock Of The Bay' by Otis Redding in 1968 when I was six; 'Honky Tonk Woman' by the Rolling Stones in 1969 when I was seven; 'Whole Lotta Love' by Led Zeppelin in the same year.

Other advantages of older brothers include: hi-fi hand-me-downs (not just the Ferguson, but a whole range of discarded amps, dodgy decks and battered speakers); access to the *New Musical Express* and *Melody Maker* at a time when many of my friends were forced to glean their pop knowledge from *Look In*; and prototypes for filing systems (I picked up everything I know about record collection curatorship by watching my second brother with his sticky labels and fastidious handwriting). And, if you're really lucky, two of them will form a rock group and take you to see it.

That's how I came to be at Lexden Church Hall on a Saturday night in 1972 for the first public appearance of Relic. On lead guitar and backing vocals was Jeremy, soon to depart for teacher training college, with his hair down to his shoulders. On drums was Simon, with still more hair, whose greater interest was stripping the engines out of cars. You only needed to watch him drumming to know this. He was of the Keith Moon school, though 'school' may not be quite the word for what is clearly a form of musical truancy, founded on the principle that if it doesn't move, hit it with a stick until it does. On the front of his bass drum, in black stick-on letters, was his nickname: Sniff. People would say, 'Is the band called Sniff, then?' And he would have to say, 'No, it's called Relic.'

The other members were drawn from their friends, a large, hairy and, to me, bottomlessly charismatic gang of people named things like Nuts, Fitch and Spiney. Relic had taken shape in the course of several rowdy rehearsals in the front room at a house up the road from us. This was where Fred lived; Fred had volunteered early on to become Relic's roadie. It's a myth that roadies are people who want to be in bands but can't play anything. Some people just want to be roadies. When Relic rehearsed at Fred's, you could hear them three hundred yards away in our garden.

In the run-up to that inaugural performance, I was privileged to sit in on a Relic rehearsal, which took place at the house of their newly appointed singer. His family lived in a

sumptuous manor with a fully floored and brightly illumi-
nated attic – a facility which, just possibly, eased his passage
into the band. The top three qualifications to get you into a
band, irrespective of musical ability, are, in descending order
of importance:

1. Ownership of a van.
2. Ownership of a PA speaker system.
3. Access to practice facilities.

In the singer's attic, Relic were trying to learn 'All Right
Now' by Free. There were evident tensions. The rhythm
guitarist was devoting a lot of time to perfecting a forward
skip in his plimsolls, a move he reckoned looked great. Elsewhere in the band, the feeling was that this wasn't important
right now. Then again, only that morning the whole lot of
them had posed for publicity stills in the seats of a Cadillac
convertible belonging to the singer's father. And it's fair to
say, even with a week to go before the show, fewer man-hours
had been spent rehearsing than designing the band logo –
Relic, written in a flourishing Gothic Script.

Still, when they ran through the song, I was impressed.
Impressed by the noise, which was gargantuan; impressed
that the song was even vaguely recognizable as 'All Right
Now'; impressed by the way Simon slammed into the kit,
apparently determined to tunnel his way downstairs;
impressed by the way the singer flung himself around the attic
as if there were four thousand people looking on, rather than
just me and Fred the roadie, who was asleep.

After extracting certain guarantees about the hour of my
return, my parents decreed that I could attend Lexden
Church Hall for Relic's big night. They were supporting Plod.
Only in the early seventies could you have seen fit to call a

band something as grimly pedestrian as Plod. But Plod had a local following so my brothers were confident of a big crowd. People would turn up to see Plod.

Odd, this business of going out to 'see' a band. My parents, when they were younger, would probably have talked about going to hear a band or going to dance to one, and would not have recognized or understood the ritual that evolved with rock: clumps of people solemnly gathering to face the stage. Years later, I saw this taken to an extreme at a John Peel Roadshow at Essex University where almost the entire audience huddled at the foot of the dancehall podium. What they were watching so raptly was a disc jockey (albeit a famous and much-loved disc jockey) playing records. 'I don't know what you're looking at me for,' Peel remarked, half-way through. 'I don't actually do anything.' The audience laughed but, reared as gig-goers, they could only carry on staring.

I could hardly wait to stare at Relic. I was excited about it for a week in advance. I put on jeans and an amber football shirt specially. Simon had been busy at the hall for most of Saturday, what with the soundcheck and hanging up the bedsheet backdrop with 'Relic' painted on it. I fiddled at home neurotically until he collected me near showtime. He seemed nervous – slightly stiff-faced. I had pre-gig nerves, too. We travelled in silence, right up to the hall's side door.

Lexden Church Hall was a typical modern municipal amenity: orange and green curtains, a squeaky floor and a faint smell of hospitals. To encourage an atmosphere, most of the lights were off. I was put on some steps beside the stage, out of the way. My brother disappeared into the dressing room. People in their late teens and early twenties were beginning to drift in, offering up their wrists at the door to be tattooed with an inky date-stamp. A makeshift bar in one corner was serving beer and Pepsi in plastic cups. The DJ had his decks and boxes of records set up on a trestle table. Occasionally he would turn on a faint white strobe light, let it putter for a few seconds and then turn it off again. Finally the houselights went out altogether and I heard the DJ say, 'Please put your hands together and welcome . . . Relic!'

From the darkness of the stage came four bars of cod Charleston music – Relic's cheeky opening motto. Then the cumbersome curtains were withdrawn and a light came on, revealing Jeremy, stamping on a distortion pedal and churning out a monstrous riff, dimly discernible as the opening to 'Paranoid' by Black Sabbath.

BLAN, BLAN, BLAN, DIDDLE-DIDDLE-DIDDLE-DIDDLE
BLAN, BLAN, BLAN, DIDDLE-DIDDLE-DIDDLE-DIDDLE.

Then some more lights came on and the whole band piled in.

I had stood up when the curtains parted but was nearly forced to sit down again by a sickening combination of excitement and fear, which I was to re-experience not long after this at Ipswich stock car stadium, watching a friend of the family compete in a hot-rod race. Except the gig was more intense than that because even then it occurred to me that you risked public humiliation and personal injury far less driving a souped-up Ford at speed round a dirt-track than you did playing with Relic.

They crashed through 'Long Train Running' by the Doobie Brothers. They thundered into 'Locomotive Breath' by Jethro Tull. The evening offered more than a bit part for Fred the roadie. He scuttled on, two minutes in and every three minutes thereafter, bent over at the waist in approved roadie style, to carry out running repairs on the fatigued metal of Simon's drum kit, nobly ducking the bits of splintered drumstick and the hot cymbal shards as he worked.

No one had the confidence to move around during the songs, except the singer, who had confidence to spare. He wore a body-hugging scoop-necked T-shirt and a pair of white trousers as tight in the groin as they were loose at the ankles. He seemed to have learned by heart the *Bumper Book of Mike-stand Manoeuvres*. He lifted its circular weighted base off the floor and toted the stand like a barge pole, in the manner of Rod Stewart; he hopped across the boards, towing it behind him; he forced it down towards the stage in an aggressive tango; he howled into the microphone and then thrust it away to arm's length. Only the low ceiling prevented him from slinging the thing skywards.

During instrumental passages – guitar solos mostly – he maintained his place at centre stage, mouth open, nostrils flared, shaking his long blond hair, clapping in time, posturing madly. It was an utterly commanding performance – the performance of a man who knew exactly whose show it was. Accordingly, shortly after this gig, the band voted to replace him with someone much calmer, who came on in a nine-foot scarf and mostly stood at the mike smoking. They lost their rehearsal space but they must have figured it was worth it.

The on-stage lighting was coming from a set of black-painted, chipboard boxes, hammered together by Jeremy in our garage. A lackey was operating a primitive switchboard to match the lights to the music – all of them on and flashing like an ambulance during the fast ones and, during the slow one (there was only one slow one – 'Nights in White Satin'), all of them off except for a pair of dull green bulbs behind the drum kit.

At five-second intervals, I glanced down the hall to see what effect all this was having on the audience. It was having very little. The place was about a quarter full and most of the men, in various combinations of leather, denim and sheepskin, were leaning against the back wall with their thumbs in their belt loops. The handful of people dancing animatedly at the front were all, I noted, girlfriends of the band. But there were three or four other girls watching intently whom I didn't recognize. They looked on gooey-eyed at this frank display of white loon pants and cheap electric guitars.

Near the end of Relic's allotted twenty minutes, Simon closed 'Honky Tonk Women' with a magnificent final flourish. Sadly there was still a verse to go. Everybody else, catching the imperative force of that last, juddering drum figure, had come to a halt with him. There was a pause, probably only a couple of seconds long, but suddenly time felt heavy as lead. Relic exchanged bewildered looks. I felt as if I was about to throw up. But then, like the cavalry regrouping, they set off once more, ground their way back up to speed, beat a path through the final verse and ended again, Simon's flourish sounding a little more sheepish this time. After that, they were gone. And no encores.

In the brief interval between Relic's set and the arrival of Plod, the hall magically filled. Plod had more equipment, more lights, more make-up, more hair. But I only saw half their set, at which point one of my brothers came and shouted in my ear, 'I've got to take you home.'

I lay in bed that night with singed ears. With hindsight, it has occurred to me that Relic were really, by default, Colchester's first punk band, breathtakingly meritless. But I didn't think about that then. I thought about the noise, the lights, the leaping around. I thought about the gooey-eyed girls. I thought I could see a way forward.

Faces

My father, who hated pop music, would ask, 'Why does it have to be so loud?' Sometimes this was a rhetorical reprimand, but sometimes it was said with the straightforward curiosity of someone amazed. Because quiet was a project of his. He was after a quiet life. He would go around the house turning things down – the radio, the television, the record player – a pained expression on his face and then a look of exaggerated relief as he stood and exhaled and said, 'Now, *that's* better.' (The scheme extended to a time-absorbing determination to remove all extraneous interior noise from the family car – rattles, hums, lumpings – a fated struggle given its age. My requests for an in-car stereo were, needless to say, blanked.)

My father would also say other things about pop: that he didn't know what I heard in it; that it all sounded the same to him; that it was just noise. Well, maybe, but what a noise! Especially if you turned it right up. And some records just commanded you to be generous with the volume knob, like 'Pool Hall Richard' by the Faces in 1973, which doesn't so much start as trip up and then turn its stumble into a run. And when it was loud enough and the bedroom door was shut, I could run with it, over to the mirror, hands shaped around an imaginary guitar, thumb and forefinger of my right hand pressed together and twitching against my thigh while I mouthed lyrics at my reflection. In which I became a historically inaccurate figure. Because Rod Stewart, who was singing, didn't play guitar on these tracks. But that's how good the record was: I wanted to be doing both and if I could have mimed the drum part at the same time, I would have. (There's a crude piece of psychology which relates guitar-playing and simulated guitar-playing to masturbation, but I think we can crush this directly. Playing a guitar is nothing like masturbation. Playing a guitar is much more difficult.)

But sometimes you needed the noise for other reasons. You were busy qualifying as a teenager, putting in the hours, in your bedroom, on your back, on the bed, with a record on, stuffed rigid with unfathomable woe. These were your Samuel Beckett years. And sometimes pop would talk you out of it, but often pop would talk you down into it, which was where you wanted to be. At which point you would flip 'Pool Hall Richard' over and play the other side, which was 'I Wish It Would Rain'.

There is nothing like pop for getting you out of yourself; but the opposite and equal truth is, there is nothing like pop for centring you *in* yourself. Here's pop, this monumentally outgoing, life-affirming force, proof of the raging heart and the racing pulse. Odd, then, the solipsistic nature of so many of the pleasures you took in it: the bedroom hours (not lonely, to adapt Roddy Frame, but just alone), the solo dancing, the mirror miming, the listening through headphones in the dark, which is even now my favourite way to hear things, to sink into them, sealed off, so that there's no distraction. At which point, pop was not the soundtrack to your life, it *was* your life.

Why does it have to be so loud? Because when it's loud, the bass pumps through and the drums kick up and the guitars come skidding across the room and the whole thing hits you in the chest. Because when it's loud, you can't hear anything else, particularly the people who would ask you why it has to be so loud.

Scott Joplin

Fate did not smile kindly on my plans for global rock domi-
nation the day it made me a piano player. And my mother
did not smile kindly on those plans the day she gave away
my piano to a local psychiatric hospital, but more of that
later.

The agony of being a pianist is, it seems to me, easily
sourced: you aren't a guitarist. As it became clear, in my early
teenage years, that I was the former and not the latter, I
entered a period of desperate refutation, flinging myself at
anything that vaguely resembled a guitar – those near-string-
less ukuleles, an orange plastic Beatles toy guitar found lying
around and, when my brothers were out, their thrilling full-
size acoustics and electrics. And I pulled and plucked until my
fingers were sweaty and cramped but I could never wring
anything from these instruments above the most halting and
rudimentary level. The riff from 'Jeepster' played on one
ukelele string was an early triumph whose promise I never
fulfilled. Shortly after that, Jeremy showed me the three
chords which comprise Creedence Clearwater Revival's 'Bad
Moon Rising', of which, after months of gruelling application, I could turn out a pretty nifty version – if you didn't
mind waiting two minutes between each chord change while I
cajoled my fingers into position, sometimes using my right
hand to fold my left hand into shape.

The piano felt more possible and I should have been grateful that I at least had that. The piano is, in many ways, the
more satisfying instrument on which to be competent; it is
self-sufficient and adaptable and sociable. But none of these
advantages compensates for the instrument's one crucial

drawback from a pop perspective: your restricted ability to strike poses of a rock'n'roll nature while playing it.

In all my life, I have never stood before a mirror in a bedroom pretending to play a piano. Whereas I have made some sort of act mimetic of guitar-playing, however casually, in all of the rooms, in all of the houses in which I have ever lived. By the age of ten, I had saturated myself with images of Bolan and his Flying V, bunching himself up and twisting his hips behind its body, trotting and sliding and grooving. Gilbert O'Sullivan, slope-shouldered at a grand piano in his pullover, didn't offer quite the same buzz.

A friend confides in me that he spent a lot of the private moments of his youth furtively pretending to be Ray Manzarek of the Doors. He would play Doors records and waggle his fingers along an imaginary horizontal plane. Sometimes he would use the edge of the bed. I would maintain this was a fairly isolated outbreak of keyboard wishfulness. At concerts, you will rarely see keyboard players celebrated with the abandon that greets guitarists: during keyboard solos, there is, in the audience, no unison holding aloft of hands and waggling of fingers. We have no settled idea about what it would be to be an air keyboard-player.

As I reached twelve and thirteen and it became clear that the piano was the only instrument on which I would ever hold my own, I looked in vain for role models. But keyboard players seemed to be people like Tony Banks from Genesis, perhaps the least expressive man in rock, whose idea of a crowd-pleasing freak-out is to nod gently to himself. Ray Charles and Stevie Wonder look great, swaying and weaving round the microphone the way they do, but partly their responses are 'blindisms', reflexes of the visually impaired, and to impersonate these is to risk the charge of bad taste. I watched Elton John get himself up in daft specs and elaborate frocks and prance about on the lid – but it didn't seem to make him very happy. I just thought, If he'd been a guitarist, he wouldn't have had to try nearly so hard.

Acknowledging this tragic hole at the centre of the pianist's life, during the 1970s one of the instrument manufacturers developed a keyboard that you could wear, guitar-style, around your neck on a strap, forcing you to pat at the keys as you might pat at your pockets, but enabling you to cut loose from your static position and shake your thing with the rest of the band. It was particularly popular with members of Earth, Wind & Fire, less so with me, who couldn't have afforded one anyway. This triumph of technical engineering didn't make you look like a guitarist; it made you look like a keyboard player with a bad case of career-envy.

Not for the keyboard player any of that leaning back-to-back with the bassist in a display of leering chumminess. None of that dropping a shoulder and stepping away from the microphone stand to peel off a quick lick or a rippling run. You're just stuck there, like someone serving at a check-out. I noted that Rick Wakeman chose to compensate by mounting a defiant display of synthesizer armoury, setting himself at the centre of several tottering stacks of keyboards, many of them redundant to his purposes as a performer but just there as a threat – the musical version of a military march-past. Today's slimline technology, in which one keyboard can do the work of ten, deprives you of even that satisfaction – unless you're Wakeman, who continues to pack a stage to the rafters with old keyboards, for old times' sake.

As a pianist, I saw how you could at least work the sensitive balladeer angle, the Billy Joel option. You, the slightly brutal loner, inexpressive except for those moments late at night when you settle at the keyboard and pour it all out of yourself. And she drifts towards the piano, wine glass in hand, thrilled and impressed.

'Hey, what's that you're playing?'

'Oh, this little thing? Oh, you know, just something I'm kind of . . . fooling around with.'

I would settle for that now, at thirty-two, making the best of a bad deal. As a teenager, this held no appeal whatsoever.

Clearly, the best thing to do behind keyboards is behave like Vince Clark of Depeche Mode and then Yazoo and then Erasure, or like Chris Lowe of Pet Shop Boys. These days, keyboards are so advanced that you can generate the noise of an entire orchestra at the drop of a finger, and one of the splendid things about Clark's and Lowe's solution to the problem of being a keyboard player – they remain for the most part facially expressionless and physically static – is its honesty about the extent to which the machinery is doing the work. Lowe knows that a sizeable amount of what he does is the job of a computer operative. He is quite prepared to acknowledge that from time to time he is genuinely bored. If only he had been there to lead the way in the 1970s.

On the piano we had at home, you struggled to generate the noise of a piano. It would probably have been turned down for the bar-room scenes in a cheap Western. The instrument had belonged to my grandfather, who, old and stooped, still went to it frequently when he visited, although only ever to play one tune, 'In An English Country Garden', whistling the melody to supplement the notes his fingers slipped past. Strangely, he always played it standing up, like Little Richard. Only not.

Unpleasantly florid, and perhaps designed for an Edwardian Liberace who hadn't quite got the nerve to go all the way, the piano had a pair of brass candle-holders bolted to the front, although the cups that had held the candles were long gone. When you depressed the loud pedal, there was a deep clunk inside, like someone changing gear on a traction engine. The biggest disadvantage was that the frame was one of the old-fashioned wooden ones which were not made to hold up well under the pressures of the modern 1970s home environment. Basically, a piano tuner would call every six months or so, put the instrument into startlingly melodious condition and leave. Then the central heating would come on and four minutes later the thing sounded like a Hawaiian guitar.

When I was seven, my parents decreed that I would be taught piano by an elderly lady called Mrs Galley, who did home visits rather in the manner of a district nurse. I have often wondered how sensational I might have turned out to be had the time of my weekly Thursday afternoon lesson not coincided exactly with the start of *Scooby-Doo* on TV. This made me a ratty, pent-up pupil and not just because of the thorough excellence of *Scooby-Doo*, but also because the cost of missing it was social ostracism; in the playground the next day, people would be saying, 'Wasn't it great when Shaggy bit Velma?' and how would I know? I was busy bad-temperedly screwing up a simplified version of Bach's 'Ode to Joy' at the time.

I don't suppose these lessons were much of a treat for Mrs Galley either, although I don't necessarily link their taxing nature to her death, midway through Grade 2. She was, I insist, elderly. Still, her dying didn't help matters with regard to my accomplishment at the keyboard. But it did mean that I had a period of some years subsequently in which I was free to roam unfettered at the keyboard, instruct myself according to my instincts, generate my own playing style. I could hear myself giving interviews in the future in which I would casually allude to something Paul McCartney once said (or 'Paul'

– or even 'Macca' – as I hoped to be calling him by then) about how he had always shied away from classical learning, even later on when it was offered to him, for fear that suddenly knowing some of the rules would somehow stop up what he had been doing all these years in almost complete ignorance of them. 'Yeah,' I would say. 'I can relate to Macca there.'

Left to my own devices, I developed two tentative forms of boogie-woogie. One was mid-tempo and went jud d'jud d'jud d'jud. Then there was a faster one which went judda-judda-judda-judda. Also I contrived a two-fingered version of the theme from the television series *Robinson Crusoe*, one of the great melancholic TV themes: the series was dubbed from, I think, the original French, but a strangeness seemed to have overcome the entire soundtrack, including the title music, making it muted, slightly woozy and saddened. I also worked out, by ear, a version of Scott Joplin's 'The Entertainer', in which I could be fairly accused of selling out to popular pressure. In the mid-1970s, everyone who played the piano played Scott Joplin's 'The Entertainer'. Most people, though, had access to the sheet music, whereas I had to feel my way in the dark. Still, it was a storming little version I produced, even if it was a bit shy of the black notes and didn't involve me once changing key in the left hand where, having found that big sprung leap which powers the tune along – boom ching, boom ching – I held it in the same place for fear of losing it.

Mostly, though, I played the one which went jud d'jud d'jud d'jud, followed by the one which went judda-judda-judda-judda. My mother said, controversially, 'Why don't you learn something you can play all the way through?'

I suspect she had once had a vision of me with perfectly parted hair and impeccable manners, perhaps in a velvet tuxedo, descending from my room in the late afternoon to entertain her friends with dextrous little pieces of Mozart. But this vision had faded. Now she saw the piano as an ugly encumbrance, taking up space in a room she quite wanted to 'do something with'. She was also thoroughly fed up with the theme from *Robinson Crusoe*. 'Why can't you play something *nice*?' was another refrain.

I was to have one more shot at becoming a 'proper' musician. It happened when I was seventeen, at the point where I had all but exhausted the appeal of my repertoire and could see no way forward: marooned for ever with the theme from *Robinson Crusoe*. I booked in with Mrs Forbes, a tutor recommended to me by my sister-in-law, and started attending lessons, in the overheated front room of her semi-detached house off Drury Road. Mrs Forbes was younger than Mrs Galley, but only just. She had dyed black hair, strictly controlled by pins and clips, and she wore white cotton blouses with ruffs at the neck and wrists. On her doorstep I would pass a pupil coming out, a five-year-old girl with a pony-tail. Perhaps because she had found her rhythm in the previous hour and now couldn't shake it off, Mrs Forbes spoke to me as if I, too, was a five-year-old girl with a pony-tail, rather than a seventeen-year-old with a raging appetite for an albums deal.

She tried me on Satie's 'Trois Gymnopédies' – which was to the late 1970s what Scott Joplin's 'The Entertainer' was to the mid-1970s and which has now been debased by its use in television advertisements for deodorant and facial scrubs. I trapped my fingers in it, horribly. In about our fourth session, in order to lighten the atmosphere, I played her a piece that I had recently made up ('. . . just something I'm kind of fooling around with . . .'). I thought she might enjoy it, being rather close in mood to the music we had been working on. In truth, the piece was probably more Eric Sykes than Erik Satie. When I finished, she said, brightly: 'Well, we're quite the little composer, aren't we?'

I lasted one term and still couldn't read music and still consoled myself with the thought that neither could Paul McCartney.

It would have been around then that the piano tuner, a cheery man with a moustache who bounced in as if fresh from a successful cabaret season, called on what I thought was going to be another of his routine visits. But after five minutes alone with the piano, he emerged from the room wearing a grave expression unusual for him. He said he had some bad news. There was no point in beating about the bush: he was going to give it to us straight. It was about the frame: things looked bad down there. Getting the piano to concert pitch would have involved tautening the strings so radically that the frame would have been bent into a straining C-shape, cocked like an animal-trap, ready to explode in lethal fragments across the sitting room. You wouldn't want to be sitting in front of it, playing jud d'jud d'jud d'jud when that happened. He could tune it roughly, within limits – make it comfortable. But basically it was inoperable and there was nothing we could do now except settle down and wait for the end.

Except there was one thing we could do, if we were my mother: we could get straight on the phone to a local residential centre for the mentally handicapped and ask them if a clapped-out upright would be any good to them. A few days later they sent a van.

Bad enough to be a pianist. But for something like three years I was a pianist without a piano. I lost ground.

10cc

It's broadly understood that pop groups are not meant to be like relatives or football teams. You don't stand by them through thick and thin. Mostly you stand by them through thick on the understanding that during thin it's perfectly OK for you to go off and buy records by someone else. This is the fabulous democracy of pop: it stands or falls on the popular vote. I would have to say in my own case, though, that my career as a record buyer has been distinguished by strange lingering attachments to bands long past their sell-by date and bouts of what I can only describe as loyalty purchasing.

Take 10cc, for example. In his third year at teacher-training college in London, my brother Jeremy became Social Secretary and his absolute triumph was to book 10cc for the end-of-term party. This was in June 1974 when 'Wall Street Shuffle' was in the charts and just before the band became huge. It was the last college gig 10cc ever played. I was twelve and disqualified from attending by my parents. But one of my brother's girlfriends made sure to get me autographs – Lol Creme, Graham Gouldman, Kevin Godley and Paul Burgess (the spare drummer) but not Eric Stewart, which was the one I really wanted.

By way of compensation, in 1975 when 10cc came to Ipswich Gaumont, my brothers took me. It was the first rock show I ever saw. (The first one I went to unsupervised was the Tom Robinson Band gig at Essex University, 1978, supported by Stiff Little Fingers.) I remember how Eric Stewart walked out of the wings with his guitar very slowly, when the rest of the band were already in position, which I thought was really cool. And they opened with 'Silly Love' and finished with 'I'm

Not in Love' and my ears rang for an entire day afterwards.

This must have been when I started, in a sense, 'supporting' 10cc. At school shortly after this, there was some tedious swimming gala and all those not involved were meant to be watching. But I was with some friends round behind the changing cubicles, listening to the Tuesday lunchtime chart announcement on Radio 1. And when it became apparent that 10cc's 'I'm Not in Love' had gone to No. 1, I fisted the air in triumph.

'*Yesssss*!'

The point is, there was no real reason to go any further than this with 10cc. The first two albums were fun – irritating in places, and more than a little smart-arse, but what the hell – the second two were patchy, and when Godley and Creme left, the band lost everything they had ever had in the way of wit. But, in some terrible way, I was trapped. I kept buying the albums: *Deceptive Bends, Bloody Tourists, Live and Let Live* (the double live album) . . .

I remember reading Julie Burchill in the *NME*, very late on in 10cc's career, as late as 1979 maybe, saying, out of the blue, that she quite liked Eric Stewart's voice and feeling a huge surge of relief and gratitude towards her that she should come out and admit this. (She may have been taking the piss, of course.) But I stored her praise away, ready to bring it out and vamp it up slightly in case of attack: 'Well, Burchill's with me on this one, actually . . .'

I never did use it because in the end I gave up even pretending that my relationship with 10cc was defensible on grounds of merit. Why bother? Returning to school after a lunch hour with a copy of the *Look Hear* album (1980!), I was forced to produce it, sadly, from the bag by someone who wanted to have a look at the sleeve. It was terrible, and so was the album – not one decent song on there – but I was in too deep.

And a year later I bought *10* (their tenth album and mine too) as well and I'm pretty sure I never even got round to playing side two.

I'm at a loss to explain this, except to say that 10cc were the first band I saw live and I guess you never forget your first time. And maybe they are only the most vivid among many instances in my collection of record buys that have nothing to do with music, or at least music is a distant, barely remembered part of the motivation.

Pony

By the time Jeremy returned from teacher-training college, it was all over for Relic. But out of the ashes of Relic came Pony.

Pony was Jeremy on guitar and lead vocals, Simon on drums and Jeremy 'Fitch' Mead on bass. And, later, me on keyboards. They had cooked up the name in a pub. Staring desperately across the bar, one of them had caught sight of a bottle of Pony, 'the little drink with the big kick', to use the old advertising slogan. It could have been worse, I suppose: we could have been called Babycham. Or Gents.

Then again, at least Babycham or Gents would have had no unfortunate Cockney rhyming-slang resonance. No one much uses Cockney rhyming-slang in Colchester and I remained ignorant of the alternative meaning of the word 'pony' until some six years later during a stay in hospital. I was two beds down the ward from a cheery middle-aged Londoner, who bounced to his feet one evening, clapped his hands together in a business-like way and announced, as he headed for the bathroom, 'Just time for a pony before *The Professionals*.' Took me a couple of minutes, but I got there: pony and trap – crap. This little semantic detail may explain why, at the peak of our career, though we could secure bookings as far east as Chelmsford, Pony were unable to break into the Metropolitan region.

When I joined – aged fifteen, for a gig on Silver Jubilee Day, 1977 – the band came interestingly close to being an all-family affair, like the Osmonds, say, or the Jacksons. Jeremy was often on at Nick to join and complete the family set.

He was, after all, a guitarist and as able a musician as any of us. But Nick was never interested in performing and in any case, was about to get married. He kept his distance. 'You could call yourselves the Smiths,' said my mother one mealtime, and we jeered derisively. As if anyone was ever going to be successful with a dumb name like the Smiths.

The Silver Jubilee Day gig took place in Boxford High Street. We performed from the trailer of a lorry, covered over with tarpaulin, parked opposite the pub. The band paid to hire me a bottom-of-the-range electric piano from a shop in Colchester. It didn't sound much like a piano; it sounded more like a musical box or some ghastly Austrian clock. I hadn't learned many of the numbers at this time, so I was presented with the quandary of what to do during songs in which you're not playing. It occurred to me that you could clap in time and hop enthusiastically from foot to foot, exhorting, with hand gestures and winks, the audience to dance. I didn't have the nerve for that. Or you could lose yourself in some dance of your own to the band's music, eyes closed, head shaking. I didn't have the nerve for that either. I opted for sitting down on the stage, directly behind the keyboard and out of sight of the audience. Then I would stand up when it was time to play. From the street it must have looked as if I was on a piece of hydraulic flooring. We gave them 'Caroline' and 'I Knew The Bride (When She Used To Rock'n'Roll)' and 'Let's Stick Together'. The Silver Jubilee was where punk found a centre for its anti-institutional seething. I spent it on the back of a lorry in a village playing 'Hi Ho Silver Lining'.

Jeremy decided we should go commercial. There was money to be made from providing music for dinner dances and club socials, and there was no money in playing anarchic cover versions of 'Paranoid' in deserted youth clubs. We rehearsed a set of foot-tappers for all ages. 'Jailhouse Rock'. 'One Of These Nights'. 'Annie's Song'.

A friend took a photo of us, lined up along the side of Jeremy's Transit van, and sent it off to Walkerprint, the publicity-photograph people, who printed up copies with a white border round them and the word PONY in neat Letraset along the bottom.

We took out a small ad in the 'Entertainers' section of the Classifieds in the *Essex County Standard*. It read:

> **BOOK "PONY"** Colchester's
> most reasonably priced,
> versatile pop group.

We were listed along with Mr Magic Man from Frinton ('Children's Parties, delightfully different, jolly hour's entertainment'), Dick's Disco ('revived 45s and country and western, plus chart sounds') and 'NELLY QUACK ventrilo duck also puppet shows, home/hall, brochures – Twinstead 449'.

Jeremy bought four matching nylon shirts – light blue with navy blue collars and cuffs – from some discount boutique in the town centre. We stencilled the name of the band on the sides of the van and on the rear door. We were one of the only bands in Colchester who had our name on our van. Simon still hadn't removed the black stickers on his bass drum reading 'Sniff'. He refused to. Now people would say, 'Is the band called Sniff, then?' And he would have to say, 'No, it's called Pony.' So we introduced a giant cut-out hardboard pony, suspended above the stage, or propped up at the back, or however space would allow. It cost Jeremy about a fortnight of intensive labour with a hacksaw in the garage.

And the gigs flooded in. Clacton Town Football Club,

Sainsbury's in Colchester, the Grenadier Guards Association, the Colchester Police Community Unit, the Halstead Motor Cycle Club and other brightly lit halls with stackable chairs and stackable tables where some local wag would want to take the microphone for 'True Love Ways' straight after the raffle. We were out most Saturdays, and some weekends we were out on Friday too. And soon there was enough money in the kitty to buy me my own electric piano, a Crumar Compac. And we were charging £50 and pocketing £10 each after expenses.

We played 'Una Paloma Blanca'. Also, with me heavily featured at the keyboard, 'The Birdie Song', at which point the floor would be thick with dancers in lines or circles, doing prearranged routines that differed from club to club – flapping their arms, slapping their thighs, tweaking each other's noses, etc. – as if every town in Essex had evolved its own peculiar way to birdie on down.

We were a human juke-box. 'Under The Moon Of Love', 'Write Myself A Letter', 'There Goes My Everything'. Also, 'Happy Birthday To You', 'The Hokey-Cokey', 'Knees Up Mother Brown' and the National Anthem. During 'Nights In White Satin', Simon, who was bored a lot of the time, would thrash hell out of the single snare beat just before the solo. Shaping up, he would take the stick back way behind his shoulder until it was poised like a loofah, somewhere near the small of his back. And then he would bring the thing down in his furious fist, so you would hear the bass guitar's gentle trip down the scale and then . . .

CRACK!

Sometimes you would see couples' shoulders leap up around their ears in surprise.

'Goo'night,' Jeremy would say at the end. 'And if you're driving . . . don't forget your car.'

On New Year's Eve Jeremy would lead everyone in the countdown to midnight. Then there would be a balloon drop or a streamer shower and people would be jumping into each other's arms, whisking each other around, kissing and shouting. Up on the stage there would be this redundant minute or so before we launched into 'Auld Lang Syne' or some spivved-up version of the Can-Can, a minute in which there was nothing to do but look out at this mayhem and wonder whether in the band was really the best place to be after all.

Fallout

Rick (guitar/vocals) and David (bass) came up and said they'd finally got permission for the end-of-term gig – their band Fallout, during lunch-hour, in the school hall, anyone who wanted could get in to watch, admission free – and Doug from Codpiece was probably going to get up and do something and maybe, what with me being in Pony and all that, I might want to come on for a couple of numbers. It would have to be on guitar, mind, they added hurriedly, because keyboards wouldn't, sort of, fit in. (Go on, say it, I thought, *because keyboards are for ponces*.)

I nodded calmly, looked down at the playground, sucked thoughtfully on a cheek. I was thinking: Supergroups, eh? Well, doubtless there's going to be a lot of this kind of thing out there in the future, when the career finally takes off, so why be churlish and diffident now? 'Sure,' I said, slowly. 'Sure.'

Inside my stomach, meanwhile, a line of cheerleaders was raising its pom-poms high, high in the air and shaking them madly for joy. A gig! In front of the entire school! On guitar! Changed for ever in the eyes of my beholders – for this was what seemed to me to be at stake here; this was the chance pop was now smilingly extending to me; with one bound, a rethink of the story so far.

It is not given to all of us to be rebels, much as we would like, and at school I was always too cautious to be properly disruptive. I wasn't the one who left the gas on all through chemistry. It wasn't me who popped out during morning break to phone for a taxi in the name of our history master, so that the school secretary had to come trotting along the corridor to fetch him, midway through a double period. I wish I could say it had been me, I really do. But I didn't have it in me. I lacked the initiative.

But what about this for an opportunity? If I could only stand, even briefly, on the school stage (in other words, right at the centre of the school's institutional life, on its very hearth), legs apart, knees bent, tongue rudely protruding, and launch just one screaming howl of feedback and distortion the length of the oak-panelled, we-think-of-ourselves-as-rather-refined hall, well, I would have to come out of that partly remade, wouldn't I? I could already picture the bunching around me afterwards, the backslaps as I tried to wrestle down my smiles of pleasure: 'We had you down for a bit of a stiff, Smith. But you were ready to rock all along. Good work.'

Some years after this, Elmore Leonard wrote a novel in which a character wears a T-shirt with the slogan: 'You've probably mistaken me for someone who gives a shit.' It was my avid hope that up there, on stage with Fallout, cannoning power chords off the board inscribed 'Oxbridge Successes 1947–55', I would metaphorically speaking, be wearing that shirt.

Fallout (influences: Hendrix, Zeppelin, Thin Lizzy, anything that managed to combine distorted guitars with calming, hippie perspectives) was pretty much Rick's band. Rick was in the year above. He had long hair, hunched shoulders and a big loping walk. He wore a formless black corduroy jacket beneath which he rotated a small wardrobe of brownish polo-neck jumpers – shagged, primordial, some of them almost certainly unfinished. He also had a perpetually stoned grin, chiefly because he was perpetually stoned, and he drove to school in a shabby grey Cortina Estate, with tapes of Hendrix, Zeppelin, etc. howling from its crippled speakers.

Sometimes, if I timed my exit right, I got a lift home.

To accept a lift from Rick was to subject your ears to a rigorous sonic challenge. Nowadays, the noise you associate with other people's car stereos, heard at traffic lights or as they pass down the street, is a chassis-shuddering boom. Advances in acoustic technology mean it's possible to generate a big, rich noise using a small, cheap speaker. (Hence those dinky mini-systems for home use, with their virtually invisible wall-mounted speakers. Once upon a time you would have needed a pair of wooden cabinets the size of dustbins to make that kind of a racket.) But during the 1970s it was apparently impossible to get an in-car stereo that could manage bass frequencies unless you were prepared to spend as much again as the car cost having it armour-plated and lined with fur. Inside Rick's Cortina, the music had to force itself over the noise of the engine by sheer treble power, eliminating conversation, causing loose bolts to fizz in their mountings, the dashboard to judder dizzingly, the carpeting to rise up slightly and the air within to become dangerously static, until you stepped from the car at your destination and stood in shock on the pavement, deafened, spike-haired and waving stupidly.

At the wheel, though, Rick always looked entirely undisturbed by the noise. Indeed, he would normally be swaying to some slight, unheard rhythm at the heart of it. Rick's closest ally was his band partner David, and they were stylistically of a kind. Both were great users of patchouli, the perfumed oil that makes you smell like a joint. And both were firm believers in the astonishing affective powers of Tiger Balm, that greasy ointment which comes in tiny tins and glows warmly on application to the skin, a kind of hippie Vick.

Thus perfumed and greased, their idea of the best time

possible was to take a Tupperware tub of hand-picked magic mushrooms to a screening of *Woodstock* at Essex University's film club (where it showed most weeks, in repertory with *Easy Rider*). Their idea of the second best time possible was to drive out to the shoreline at East Mersea – 'away from the public glare', as the author of the *Rock Gazetteer* puts it – smoke themselves into a stupor, lurch unsteadily on to the beach and fly kites. In some respects, the original 1960s hippie was nowhere near as true to type as the mid-1970s derivative model.

The combined effect of these various balms, oils, resins and fungi tended to lend David and Rick a distance, as it were, a slightly partial purchase on the world, which certainly worried those charged with their education. But from where I was, in the year below and inside a school uniform, they seemed thrillingly remote. If I could just be seen playing with them – and, what's more, playing electric guitar with them – even if only briefly, if only as a guest, a temporary import, an obvious outsider, something would rub off.

Rehearsals for my appearance amounted to a less than exhaustive two. The first was a preliminary session in the music room, after school, Rick's bold, flame-orange guitar providing a cocky contrast with the tambourines, the xylophones and beaters and other junior orchestral debris. I had borrowed my brother's deep red Gibson Les Paul (or at least, it was a copy of a Gibson Les Paul, made by a company called Avon, who were not, I think, related to the cosmetics giant, though I could be wrong). Tears of gratitude flood my eyes, even now, at the thought that I had the kind of older brother who would loan me his electric guitar. Guitarists don't lightly pass their guitars into other hands. They think of them as pets, only more human. Of course, the loan had been painstakingly negotiated and narrowly agreed on a number of stringent conditions which amounted to it being fine for me to borrow the thing, as long as I didn't actually touch it. But, even so, I was moved then and I still am.

David had forgotten to bring his bass to school that day and the drummer hadn't been able to bring his kit along and, anyway, he had to get his bus at five fifteen. But they both sat in anyway, looking on enthusiastically while Rick and I used the time to sort out my two guest numbers – Thin Lizzy's 'Rosalie' (chosen for maximum power chord potential) and Dylan's 'All Along The Watchtower' (chosen for its virtually idiot-proof chord sequence).

'Yeah! Rocking!' said Rick.

The second rehearsal, this one full scale, took place in the loft of a barn situated on a farm in the countryside just outside town. It belonged to some friends of the drummer's family who, with considerable magnanimity and no respect whatsoever for the country code, handed it over to us for a Saturday afternoon. But, even here, what had seemed in anticipation a luxurious abundance of time rapidly dwindled to nothing. First, all the bulky paraphernalia – amplifiers, drums, guitar cases – had to be hoisted into the loft up a set of steps which, though almost certainly the width of a late Victorian farmer carrying a hoe, was not designed with the Marshall 4×12 speaker cabinet in mind. There was about half an hour of muffled grunting, in a scene I was going to see replayed so often in the next years, before and in the aftermath of gigs – thin, stoned figures grappling unmanageable objects.

Ah, the aimless confusion of rock'n'roll in rehearsal. I've never forgiven Prince for a scene in his movie *Purple Rain* where the character he is playing arrives late for a rehearsal with his band, scoots up on to the stage, apologizes crisply, slips his guitar strap over his neck and off they all go, into perfectly mixed, effortlessly disciplined pop heaven. And this is Prince, of all people: a man who has spent nearly all his life in rehearsal studios, who must know more than any human alive about the ear-aching tedium of raising a band. Shame on him for this falsification. The truth is, most band practices are so painful that it's a miracle any band bothers to take it further than the rehearsal room.

At the start of a practice, there's no useful boardroom etiquette, briskly applied: nobody raps confidently on the table and says: 'Right, let's get down to business.' Instead, there is an obligatory opening period, lasting anything from ten minutes to two and a half hours, known in the trade as 'noodling around'. Some of this, to be fair, is taken up with the necessary business of taming recalcitrant electronics. There's a lot of coughing into microphones ('One two, chk! One two, chk!'), a lot of gales of feedback and spasms of static.

From the guitarist's amplifier: *Waaaaarrrmm.*

From the singer's PA: *Nyeeeeeeee. Seeeynk . . .*

But all the rest is basic, straight down the line, 100 per cent, 24-carat pissing about. A guitarist finds it constitutionally impossible to have a guitar round his neck and not be playing it. A drummer is the same when there are sticks in his hands. The bass player has to perform, not less than fifteen times, that ponderous figure from Fleetwood Mac's 'The Chain' (the music which opens the BBC's Grand Prix coverage). And so it goes on, everyone somehow transfixed in their own little world, doing their own purgatorial thing.

It's no surprise that most of the bands that make it have a sizeable authority figure right at the heart of them, a power freak or an egomaniac, someone big enough to wrestle with this chaos of self-indulgence, to rise above the racket shouting, 'Orright, orright, orright. Let's do "Funny Farm" ', or some such. Fallout, alas, were seriously short of a figurehead. Several potheads, yes, but no figurehead.

Still, after all the conventional arsing around, we finally fell into one of the allotted numbers. It was Thin Lizzy's 'Rosalie', that great, hulking, metal monster . . . in Thin Lizzy's hands, at any rate.

Me, David and Mike the drummer went: BLANNNG.

Rick went: KLANNG, WIDDLE, WIDDLE, WIDDLE.

The rest of us went: BLANNNG again.

And then we all set off together, or thereabouts: BLANNNG, KLANNG, WIDDLE, WIDDLE, WIDDLE, BLANNNG, etc.

I think the question surfaced in my mind even then: how could such dedicatedly peaceful people create such a horrendous racket? Imagine a tractor dragging a plough over concrete while being repeatedly buzzed by a helicopter. I stood at the side, up to my ankles in straw, endeavouring to force my fingers into the shapes that Rick had shown me and falling entire half-verses behind – though in truth, this barely mattered for, as a unit, we had bludgeoned our way into a space beyond time, in which the concepts of 'early' and 'late' no longer applied.

In the brief seconds in which I dared take my eyes off my terrorized hands, I caught sight of Rick through the dust now being shaken by vibration out of the rafters above us and falling like snow. He appeared bafflingly calm at the centre of this apocalyptic storm, leaning into the microphone to sing, his eyes closed, an expression of amazing serenity on his face, what you could see of it between the strands of hair. You'd got to hand it to him: he looked the part. For all I know, he sounded it too, but I couldn't hear him because of the noise.

After two and a half minutes, there was a muffled pop as

the barn's ancient electrics gave out and the loft plunged into darkness and silence, but for the dry rattle of the drums which continued for at least another minute (the time it took the drummer to realize that something was afoot).

'Whoa!' said Rick.

There followed a brief conference during which Rick decided, with glazed glee, that we would just have to busk it on the day. Then we humped all the equipment down the steps again and went home.

Acquiring the right to mount a pop concert in the school hall had proved harder than getting planning permission for a cocaine dispensary on the playground. Many of the senior staff members only had to hear the words 'pop music' to fear for the souls of their pupils. Rightly so, in the case of Fallout plus Very Special Guests. Not that I imagine anything we could have done would have inspired moral depravity or an outbreak of bestial behaviour in the third form: you've got to practise a lot harder than we did before you can guarantee that effect.

But almost certainly, two or three hundred children, exposed to Fallout (irradiated, if you like), would have decided there and then that they never wanted to listen to music of any kind ever again. I think this would have weighed on our consciences.

In the end, it didn't come to that. Two days before show-time, Mr Balch, who was an English master, died of cancer, suddenly, shockingly. During the morning assembly, the headmaster formally announced the death to the whole school, and right at the end of a few words in tribute, added: 'Tomorrow's concert in the hall is, of course, cancelled.'

My mother charitably took our side when I told her about it at home that night. 'How ridiculous to cancel it,' she said, genuinely irritated. 'As if Mr Balch would have wanted that.'

But my mother hadn't heard Fallout. And Mr Balch certainly wouldn't have wanted it. Even dead.

Andrew Ridgeley

It needs underlining: in 1977 no rock band had ever played live in Colchester Grammar School's hall – or in the head-master's study, or in the staffroom, or anywhere else on the premises for that matter, since live rock was not considered educational. It needs underlining because that's not the way things are now.

In March 1990, Minsthorpe High School in Pontefract booked the House of Love for a Monday night concert. Not the school bottletop orchestra, not even some neighbourhood folkie with an acoustic guitar and a local history slideshow, but the House of Love, a noisy, Velvet Underground-based, bona fide, albums-out-and-everything rock act on the Fontana label. What is going on at that school? Are the teachers utterly without responsibility? Don't the parents have any-thing to say about this? (Answer to the last question: no. Most of them were probably there, in fact, moshing down the front, crowd-surfing, stage-diving on to the heads of their offspring with lemonade spraying from their plastic beakers.)

In the 1970s this would have been inconceivable. Pop music didn't even bother turning up on the first day of term; it knew it was automatically expelled, absolutely out of bounds. It resigned itself to hanging around outside the school with its hands in its pockets, waiting for the end of the day when we would run out and join it. Perhaps the occasional trendy English master would devote a lesson to unpacking the lyric of the Beatles' 'Eleanor Rigby' or Pink Floyd's 'Arnold Layne', but you knew it was chiefly a public-relations job, a crude, vote-winning strategy and that, at all other times, the windows would be crowded with garlic and crucifixes against any possible pop-related intrusion.

Finally, though, education has said to pop, 'Come on in, have a cup of tea.' Right now, there are GCSE music students programming synthesizers and building up sophisticated 4-track demo tapes – in school time! As work! The two have gone from resistance to collaboration, and their battle is now all but forgotten.

Consider a teaching pack prepared in 1989 by the education department of the British Film Institute, for use in classrooms, tying in with the GCSE course in Media Studies. Its topic is the career of Wham!, 1982–86. I am sure it is not unique in its scope or its intent, though it is almost certainly the only publication of an educational nature that contains a foreword by Andrew Ridgeley. 'What you learn from this pack', the tanned former Wham! sidekick calmly promises, 'may stand you in good stead should you choose to go into the music industry.'

The teaching material includes a wedge of worksheets and project cards headed 'Product', 'Promotion', 'Consumption', intended to explain the way the music business works and to encourage some sort of critical capacity by close analysis of records, chart performances, videos and so forth. Essay suggestions include:

> Watch the beginning of 'Club Tropicana'. Look at the chart above and continue the list of denotation/connotative shots up until the first shot of George Michael.

Also:

> From your graph and research, describe in your own words the progress of 'Wake Me Up Before You Go Go' through the charts.

I was taught by people who genuinely believed that pop music wouldn't survive as far as the millennium, let alone make it through to the curriculum. But look at it now: in business courses and career studies and instrumental workshops. Rock has gone to college. Maybe it's only jealousy that makes me feel there's something rather chilly about this. Maybe it's because I wish I was there now, charging around the corridors with my synth and my lyric sheets.

'What you got this afternoon?'

'Double Hip Hop.'

'*Bor*ing!'

But it does seem to me that a group like Fallout was specifically about forces that school could not contain (and not all of them to do with smell). And I can't help feeling that when George Michael crops up in an exam question something has come full circle and stopped with a shudder.

Rose Royce

'If you're going to kiss this girl,' I tell myself, 'you've got less than two choruses in which to do it.' I'm on the floor at the Embassy Suite on Schools Disco night (Wednesdays), in a rugby shirt, probably, and jeans, one of a room full of highly glandular teenagers, many of the male ones wearing Brut. And, behind the decks, DJ Gary Soul (possibly not his real name) has put on 'Wishing On A Star' by Rose Royce. And because her friend has egged us on, I and my putative partner are among those moving slowly but going nowhere under the dim lights and I have my hand in the small of her rather thrillingly hot back.

The thing you have to watch about 'Wishing On A Star', though, is it starts out spare and dreamy but gets a bit tempest-tossed at the end. If you're already kissing at that point, you're OK: you can up the pressure a little and sway on through. If you aren't, you're lost.

And why else would you be dancing to 'Wishing On A Star', if not in order to end up with your lips glued to someone else's? That was what the slow ones were for. Otherwise, if you danced to pop, you danced alone, without contact, cutting extraordinary shapes of your own devising, or modelled on those of John Travolta. And I only had to watch my parents at weddings, gamely hoofing it with the young ones for their one token number, to see the generational divide. My mother obviously found 'disco dancing' fun in a parodic way but my father, who could happily whizz through a foxtrot or a waltz, was lost, just completely lost without another body to work with, couldn't see what this solo wriggling had to do with dance or music or anything.

Nowadays, I'm inclined to see my father's point. I won't dance. Don't ask me. I used to. I used to think I was pretty nifty on my toes. I knew Paul who did a lot of the discos at the parties we all went to and he would play Steely Dan's 'Kid Charlemagne' *just for me* and, because of the way that song is a mesh of details and flips about even as it lopes forward, there were all these fabulous twitchy bits that you could respond to with your elbows and your knees. In the end, though, sense prevailed, which is why I evolved a strict no-dancing policy. Not that I don't find it heartening that pop can pass an electrical charge through people, jerk them into life. It's just that I have a deep-seated conviction that white English middle-class males should be banned from dance-floors, this stipulation enforced by the rigorous use of fines and, if necessary, cattle prods. Have you ever watched white English middle-class males dancing? All that bobbing and flapping, all that chewing of bottom lips, all that tragically stiff pelvic work? I rest my case.

Dancing *with* people, of course, would be exempt. And down there on the Embassy Suite floor, with time running out, I managed to lever my chin off her right shoulder, bring my head in a cautious arc round the outside of her hair, simultaneously tilting my face through about 60 degrees, left to right, and briefly checking her expression for receptivity, before locking on for the final engage phase. And thus docked and mouthing mechanically, we made it to the close. And I just had to thank God it was 'Wishing On A Star' and not 'Freebird' by Lynyrd Skynyrd, which *changes pace* at the end, goes from being a smoocher to a fast one, leaving you one of two choices: either to jump apart and look foolish by attempting to see out the rest of the song solo, or to remain in the clinch but increase the pace of your body movements to something like the speed of the song, thereby enduring the very real possibility of getting your tongue bitten off.

How people ever got to kiss each other before the invention of the record player I have no idea.

Stevie Wonder

In *Rhythm and the Blues*, the autobiography he wrote with David Ritz, the great Atlantic record producer Jerry Wexler talks of his teenage years, the 1930s in New York, when he would cruise the Bronx, Queens and Brooklyn and dig for musical jewels in the boxes of secondhand records in old furniture stores tucked under the elevated sections of the subway line. At night he would hang out at music clubs and jazz joints in Harlem, a white man in a black world, but getting by OK by playing it cool. 'I moved to the tempo of the streets,' Wexler says, 'the rhythms of jazz.'

That's all very well in New York. In Colchester, moving to the tempo of the streets was more problematic. What exactly *was* the tempo of Straight Road, of Sanders Drive, of Wordsworth Avenue? Would you hear rhythms there, or lawnmowers? Would you know what to listen for in any case? Shrub End, anyone?

You couldn't feel the rhythms of jazz as you walked the streets, but that didn't mean you couldn't sit in your friends' bedrooms and hear the rhythms of soul. Sometime in the summer of 1976, my friend Simon played me *Innervisions*, a Stevie Wonder album so gorgeously tuneful it's virtually unfair: 'Golden Lady', 'Don't You Worry 'Bout A Thing', 'Misstra Know-it-All', 'Higher Ground' . . . The album was already about three years old but that didn't stop a handful of us from taking it up and running with it for a while as a kind of cause. When groups of friends form allegiances to records, the decisions made between you about what constitutes a good one, a record you are going to stand by and play to death, aren't necessarily to do with prevailing fashion or a general mood. All it needs is someone with the confidence to get behind something.

That autumn, Wonder released *Songs In The Key Of Life* and I convinced my mother to buy it on vinyl for me for Christmas – a double album in a gatefold sleeve with a thick, glossy lyric booklet and four additional tracks on a giveaway 7-inch EP. Thirteen years later, I convinced her to buy me the whole lot again on CD. I had heard nothing in between that I liked nearly as much or anything which seemed quite so immune to the effects of repetition. It is tempting sometimes to believe that pop records are at their most exciting the first few times you hear them and then gradually lose their flavour ever after: that they wrestle you to the floor on your first date and from then on the two of you are forever attempting, rather self-consciously, to rekindle that initial spark. Relationships with singles are frequently torrid in this way. But *Songs In The Key Of Life* seemed to want to know me on a different footing altogether. There are many things I have had the time to go off since 1976 – Supertramp, the Rolling Stones, *Top of the Pops*, Radio 1, Robert de Niro films, cricket, various girls – but *Songs In The Key Of Life* remains a constant.

I worked backwards and bought the crucial earlier albums – *Innervisions*, obviously, and *Talking Book* and *Fulfillingness' First Finale* and *Music Of My Mind*. At this time a store in Colchester stocked an array of imported and massively discounted Portuguese versions, whose sleeves left a lot to be desired. Apparently printed on an old donkey-drawn hand press, they were like looking at the original through frosted glass or an especially bad migraine. As for the vinyl itself, it hadn't been pressed so much as rubbed lightly against a decent full-price copy. It was all the needle could do to find a groove to sit in. But at £2.99, and given the sounds that eventually emerged, who was arguing? As Noël Coward would have said, if he'd only shopped at Parrot Records, 'Extraordinary how cheap potent music is.'

I liked the way Stevie Wonder could set up and lock down a rhythm. It seemed to me that if you didn't respond to the clipped keyboard over the striding drums in the introduction to 'Superstition', the chances were you had died. But mostly it was his voice that drew me along, the new angles it finds just when you thought the melody was fixed, the tangents he can spring away on. At the end of 'You And I' on *Talking Book*, in a passage I referred back to again and again, he sings the chorus an octave higher than where you first heard it, then shifts through another key change upwards and then, just when you think he can have no breath left, he holds a long note in the highest part of his range while the piano chords storm down beneath him to the final resolve. I didn't see how pop could get much more intense than that. I still don't. (Neither do I know a better piece of track-sequencing than the placement, directly after 'You and I', of 'Tuesday Heart-break', which starts with a wheezy sax and a woozy clavinet leaning together briefly and then skips off as the drums slip in – a cool flannel after the steambath of the previous track.)

And not since Marc Bolan had I felt so strongly that a voice on a record had come into the room specifically to address *me*. Whatever he sang seemed instantly applicable. Any crush he happened to talk about was the one I happened to have. Any yearning he was doing said it all about my own yearning – or inspired me to yearn if I hadn't already thought of it. Because although occasionally one might talk about the songs that 'bring it all back', referring to some emotional period in one's past for which records formed a conveniently apt parallel, sometimes the records were the reason you had those moods in the first place or the reason they took the shape they did. For most people, the drama of adolescence cuts one of two ways: either you are made frazzled and explosive by the sheer quantity of feelings you have that you don't understand, or you worry trenchantly about your zombiefied incapacity to feel anything at all. I fell squarely into the second of these categories and I don't think it would be much of an exaggeration to say that, during this awkward and uncommunicative phase, most of my feelings were Stevie Wonder's idea.

I did the fan-like things for a while. I thought hard about what Stevie Wonder's days might be like when he wasn't performing. I envied him a life concentrated so purely in music. I sat at the piano and put my hands on the keys the way that he does (with his right hand he uses only the four fingers and trails his thumb along the edge of the keyboard below the keys). Occasionally I tried playing with my eyes shut to see if it made any difference. I thought about writing to the Stevie Wonder Universal Family, at the address in America printed on some of the album sleeves, though I never did. And I went to the Wembley Arena in 1980 and saw him on the Hotter Than July tour and wept silently when he was led on at the start.

Since *Hotter Than July*, there has been a string of long gaps broken by only intermittently satisfying albums. I suspect I would have been one of the few people in 1985 who bothered to hang around in a record shop, waiting for the morning postal delivery on the day of release of the mostly disappointing *In Square Circle* album. Still, if you're in it for the duration, you learn to handle the anticipation and the let-downs, while at the same time developing a fairly strong stomach for fanciful philosophy. Stevie Wonder is politically radical, a powerful black activist, and yet some of his ideas about universal brotherhood read like a charter for Disneyland and many of the rest are plain baffling. And yet there must be something in his claims about music breaking all known barriers between the peoples of the world if, musically speaking, he can bring together my mother and me.

In 1984, in one of her rare 7-inch vinyl purchases (I'm fairly sure it was the first single she had invested in since 'Knock Three Times' by Dawn in 1971), my mother bought 'I Just Called To Say I Love You'. It was a hopeful but frustrating moment because, although I can't bring myself to dismiss completely anything that Stevie's hand is on, I like nothing he has done less than this ballad, with its pat key-changes and its karaoke backing track. So here we were, my mother and I, astonishingly, on the same ground – and yet miles apart, with me tempted to wonder if I could somehow talk her back from there to 'Uptight (Everything's All Right)' – a record up around the top limits of happy – and set the two of us on a new plain of understanding. Impossible, as it turned out. 'You can feel it all over,' Stevie Wonder sings on 'Sir Duke', his brassy Ellington tribute. But my mother says that, for the most part, she can't. Still, I know *I* can.

Pink Floyd

It could all have gone wrong at this early stage. I could have ended up a Pink Floyd enthusiast. It happened to a lot of people I knew and they weren't necessarily to blame. I understand because I came damn close. But I got away with it.

I was dimly aware that Pink Floyd had been another kind of group altogether back in the 1960s; that there had been a figure in the band called Syd Barrett who was clearly some kind of off-the-cuff genius and who wrote trippy, psychedelic and yet strangely insightful little pop songs. Unfortunately, drugs or success or the uncontrollable loopings of his own imagination, or some volatile combination of the three, had driven him mad and he'd gone to live with his mum in Cambridge. But I'd missed all that, and since then Pink Floyd had turned into sulky, earnest, self-conscious, pompous rock stars, prone to large-scale, surreal public events, like floating a giant inflatable pig above Battersea Power Station. You could see why they went down well with sixth-formers. Leaving aside the publicity stunts with air-filled animals, you're looking at a fairly accurate personality profile for me and most of my closest friends, *circa* 1978.

Pink Floyd played progressive rock. (And continue to play it, despite a serious rending of the group's social fabric which has led Roger Waters to stomp off on his own. Waters was, some would argue, the band's lynchpin – though don't get into this with serious Floyd fans unless you've got at least a week to spare.) This is to say, they are not renowned for snappy, chart-busting singles, but are instead spoken of, in reverent tones, as 'an albums band', a distinction which, during the seventies, one rather generously bestowed on any group that couldn't come up with a decent chorus. Most progressive rock bands contain a classically trained keyboard player who will explain during interviews that the organ figure in 'Asylum Of The Sane' is, in fact, based on a piece by Bach. You don't call them songs, you call them 'tracks', and a track isn't really pulling its weight if it comes in under seven minutes. Progressive rock is pop with big ideas.

Retrospectively it's easy to see what an ill-founded notion this was: after all, one of the best ideas pop music ever had was not to have too many ideas. But back there in the early throes of adolescence, when we were pimply with unfocused rage and wielding ungainly concepts of our own, Pink Floyd shone like a beacon of good sense. They wrote surly epics about how money was screwing things up, about how Americans were screwing things up, about how authority and television screwed you (and things) up. And at precisely this time, we'd get together at each other's houses and bore on about the evil which is money/America/authority and the pernicious effects of television (which all of us were qualified to pronounce upon, given the gigantic quantities of it we happily watched).

The key text was, of course, *The Dark Side Of The Moon*, the one with the prism on the sleeve. One critic called it 'a moody paean to bleakness which has so outdistanced the competition that most thinking people believe it may never be equalled'. (He didn't say what most unthinking people thought.) Certainly, few records have been so relentlessly popular: 25 million copies sold; in the British albums chart for 301 weeks; in the American albums chart for more than twice that. My brother Simon bought it when it first came out in March 1973 and, for what seemed like fourteen years (though in reality it was probably more like two months), he played it as if it was the only record he owned. He steeped himself in it, scrutinized it exactingly, as if hell-bent on tilting this talismanic object through every conceivable angle. I once wandered into his bedroom to find him hunched determinedly over his record player and a cassette machine containing a tape of the album. He was running the tape recording and then manually dropping the needle onto the record, attempting to get the two versions to play simultaneously but with one just slightly behind the other, in order to create a strange echo effect. He said he was trying to discover how *The Dark Side Of The Moon* would sound if it was being played in a field. I nodded encouragingly and left. It was that kind of album.

But my own time with the *Dark Side* came later, and like many educative experiences during this period, my friend Jim was involved. For me, and the handful of others who contrived to get near him, Jim had taken on the status of legend. Awesomely advanced, he was experimenting with hallucinogens when the rest of us still thought cola-flavoured Spangles were pretty risky. Someone so far ahead of their time was inevitably going to be a loner. One summer holiday, without notice, Jim took himself off to Europe by train. Others would get round to InterRailing in years to come – would set off with overstuffed backpacks and return a month later to talk excitedly about meeting Australians at Florence station and eating bread and cheese in train corridors. (It never seemed to occur to anyone InterRailing to get off the train, unless it was to wait for another train.) But Jim went to Amsterdam and Bruges and hung out and took drugs and got into all sorts of character-forming adventures, which he never quite related to us because, as he rightly assumed, we weren't cool enough. When he returned, his hair was on his shoulders and he had affected a pair of round glasses so that he looked like John Lennon. This earned him mysterious relationships with wild-looking girls with extremely long hair and tattered dresses. We were impressed.

Of course, it was to Jim's advantage that he had parents of a virtually Swedish liberality. My own mother and father were unhappy about me travelling on Colchester Corporation buses much after ten thirty, let alone taking night trains across Denmark. By contrast, Jim's parents – Marion and Bob as they encouraged us to call them – had enlightened views on hairstyles, pornography and smoking. They were the kind of people who imagined they had as much to learn from their children as their children had to learn from them. We speculated, secretly, that they probably wandered around naked a lot. Jim didn't have a bedroom, he had a two-room apartment with its own separate entrance on the ground floor of the family house. While some of us had to fight hard for pinboard rights, Jim was allowed to draw on the walls – which he did, fluidly in wax crayons, lathering the surfaces with lurid variations on Munch's *The Scream*, loud atomic explosions, bits of nuclear aftermath, and sundry impressions of wild-looking girls with extremely long hair and tattered dresses, until the place looked like a tattoo parlour in a mineshaft. God, we were impressed.

It was in this disturbing den that we gathered that night, as we would whenever Jim would allow it, maybe four or five of us, slowly replacing the room's oxygen with our own collective scent of musty duffel coat and old trainer. And maybe as the result of some trenchant discussion or other about the fate of the planet, or perhaps in order to inspire one, Jim suggested we listen to *The Dark Side Of The Moon*, all the way through, in absolute silence and in the dark, the better to soak up its portents and bathe in its mind-boggling oddity. So we listened to 'Breathe' with Dave Gilmour's hollow tones, to

'On The Run' with its spooky synthesizers, to 'The Great Gig In The Sky', where the female voice comes in, the noise of someone screaming for the fate of us all at the end of time.

Each of us sat there in the black-out, overawed. Even at the end of side one, as somebody groped their way to the hi-fi and flipped the record, there was silence – just the fizz of a match as Jim pensively lit another of the cigarettes his parents had probably popped out to the newsagent to get for him. On, then, through side two, through 'Money', its rhythm built around the clank of coins and the ratchet of a till, on into the floating 'Us And Them', which softly proclaims the unity of all people, rich and poor, black and white, thinking and unthinking, through 'Brain Damage', swelling now imperiously towards the close, and on then to the final, the anthemic 'Eclipse', the music dying around us in the slow agony of the final fade-out. At which point, as the needle rose again from the record, Stephen Goodridge took it upon himself to release a rounded, vibrant and fully conceived fart.

About three hours later, we finished laughing and went home. All in all, it wasn't really on to break wind during Pink Floyd albums. That wasn't what they were for. So this moment contained the thrill of heresy. But it also brought with it the feeling that a benign and magnificent good sense had entered the room. If you are lucky, there are these occasions in your life when the unsayable gets said (although perhaps 'said' is the wrong word here). And if you're not lucky, you're left in 1994 celebrating the twenty-first anniversary of *Dark Side Of The Moon* by buying the CD re-release, further investigating Roger Waters's solo albums, maybe queuing up for thirty-quid tickets to see the Floyd at Earl's Court. We were just the fortunate ones. I would wager good money that no one who was in that room that night has bothered to listen to *Dark Side Of The Moon* again.

Incidentally, I don't hear from Jim any more, but I understand he's now an accountant.

Bob Dylan

A friend has just made me up a Neil Young compilation on a C60: 'Powderfinger', 'Cortez The Killer', 'Only Love Can Break Your Heart', 'Albuquerque' and a number of others. As he's explained it to me, it's a taster, a starter pack, a Neil Young tape with training wheels in place. Once I've ridden around on this for a while, he'll move me on to something more wobbly and harder to manage. And if I do OK there, we can move on to a Neil Young tape with gears and then I'll be free to venture off on my own.

I'm looking forward to it because I know absolutely nothing about Neil Young. Actually, that's not true. I can sing this:

> Hey hey, my my,
> Rock'n'roll will never die

Also this:

> I've been to Hollywood
> I've been to Redwood [? I've *seen* a Redwood, maybe?]
> Der der der der-der der der heart of gold
> Der der der *der* der
> Der der der der
> . . . der der der der der der heart of go-wold
> And I'm gettin' old

But that's it: that's my total knowledge of the music and lyrics of Neil Young, an artist from the late 1960s who, it is widely reported, is continuing to prove his worth into the nineties, issuing albums as exciting as any he's done. (He's one of the few, if this is the case.) As for me, I own nothing that he has released. I'm fairly confident I own no records on which he even appears as a guest. I have heard none of his music except in as much as it has floated into my ears from the radio or the television, whence all but the lines quoted above have floated out again. Somehow, it never quite happened between me and Neil.

I can only think the roots of our failure are somewhere in my early years at secondary school, not long after 'Heart Of Gold' was a hit in 1972. (I looked up the date.) Someone – and I'm pretty sure it wasn't me – decreed that Young's voice was comically trembly. I have a dim recollection of a competition in the school showers to bounce off the tiled walls absurdly contorted impressions of him singing 'Heart Of Gold'. And this must have established in my mind a picture of Young as a figure of fun with more than a hint of naffness about him, an impression I have managed to hold on to for some twenty years.

Neil Young is by no means the only seminal, unmissable, late-twentieth-century musical icon about whom I remain in a state of pure ignorance. Bob Dylan is another. I have never listened to a Bob Dylan album. I don't own any. I have been in rooms where other people were playing him, but none of it seemed to stick. Here's an awkward thought: I have spent more time listening to Whitney Houston than to Bob Dylan. I have bought one Whitney Houston album (*I'm Your Baby Tonight*) and the 12-inch of 'How Will I Know?', whereas I have never spent any money at all on the work of perhaps the finest lyric poet of his generation. And I can see how reason and judgement laugh in my face here, that, under all manner of objective analyses, it is Dylan who is the heavyweight cultural figure, not Whitney Houston. Unfortunately, where I am concerned, buying pop records begins where objective analysis ends – assuming objective analysis ever began.

My skipping Dylan is not the result of anything you could call deliberative, critical thought. It has its basis in a couple of childhood memories which I have turned into reference points and never updated. I associate Dylan with my eldest brother Nick, whose early tastes I actively resisted on account of the extent to which he ridiculed me for mine. There was also a formative incident in which Simon played to death a copy of 'Watching The River Flow': just played it again and again and again in an experiment, I think, to test the limits of his own endurance. He would have been about fifteen, I would have been about nine, and my endurance snapped before his. People often say Shakespeare was ruined for them at school; Bob Dylan was ruined for me at home.

So that's Neil Young and Bob Dylan; and then there's David Bowie. He's sixth in the *Guinness Book of British Hit Singles* 'Most Weeks on Chart' list, but no thanks to me who has never bought anything with his name on. He's made something in the region of twenty-five albums and I've never listened to any of them. He's changed his image virtually on a monthly basis, and have I cared? Did I so much as cast him a glance? No, I did not, which was timid, critically questionable and downright ungrateful of me. And my reason? *He was liked by someone at school whom I didn't like very much.* That was it. That was enough to set me off on a path leading away from Bowie, one which has never looped back round to him, though one C60 compilation tape is probably all it would take.

My acts of neglect flourished in the early 1970s and they were allowed to do so, I think, by the speed at which things happened then. Every time you bought a single, the world appeared to change shape and the shape it had held before was something you could quite happily forget. You had the sense that, as you moved forward, the past was rolling up tightly behind you like a carpet and the speed of that forward momentum forced upon you the need to specialize in all sorts of arbitrary ways. Neil Young? Daft voice. David Bowie? Crap fans. And there never seemed to be a shortage of other people to occupy you in their place, so prejudice was a luxury you felt you could afford.

I am less gung-ho these days because the pickings seem to me leaner and I have to be cautious about casually discarding things, unless I'm going to end up with absolutely nothing new to listen to. But in any case, that sense of being sucked along by pop, torching the bridges as you go, is absent from my life. Sometimes I shuffle forwards (that Snoop Doggy Dog album – that sounded like nothing I'd ever heard), but far more frequently I am treading water and sometimes I am completely in reverse. I have to resign myself to the knowledge that my world will not change shape with the release of the new Suede single, though I am aware that there are those, younger than me, for whom it will. But I wonder if even they have the impression that pop is bowling them along, rather than gently circling like an aeroplane in a holding pattern. Today's teens listen to Hendrix. They have none of the contempt I had then, and felt obliged to have, for 'old stuff'.

That goes for all of us, though, and this is the up-side. In the 1990s, as a pop fan in my thirties, I am freer than ever to listen without prejudice. This is a heartening development and it has partly to do with getting older myself (I don't find myself in communal showers with my friends so often these days and I don't feel the pressure to make sure my tastes tally with those of the pack). But it has also to do with pop's growing up and acquiring a past. You can look back across pop much as you might look back across classical music or back across the Broadway song, and take your pleasures there without continually having to worry about who likes it and whether it's new. So – me and Neil Young. Why not?

XTC

When punk rock hit the provinces, the provinces weren't quite ready. Anarchy in the UK, maybe, but not really in Colchester.

Sure, in the fifth form, Peter Sellers (not the comedian and film star, but another one) promptly erected a giant, three-inch Mohican, shaving the sides of his head entirely the better to send this raging crest into relief. But you can gauge the solitary nature of his display from the fact that the local paper phoned the headmaster to ask if they could send someone round to photograph it. The head, sensing the possibility of unwelcome PR ('School Is Crazed Punks Haven', or some such), forced him to lop it off. What hope for the revolution when the powers that be so easily took back the reins?

We got the reverberations of punk, the tremors, the secondary shocks, rather than the full-fledged, snot-tossing, real thing. But that doesn't mean we weren't moved and changed – phlegm-flecked in our own way. We read about it first in despatches in the *NME* – excitedly, slightly disbelieving sometimes, sensing that something was coming, perhaps even a little fearful of the inevitable disruption and the uncertainties that lay beyond that. (Pressing questions that I was keen to table early on included: what were the implications for our Supertramp albums and our duffel coats? How were 10cc going to come out of this? And would anybody object if I passed on the nose-chain option?) And eventually, it wasn't punk but New Wave, its bastard offspring, which got a hold.

Through 1977, the physical manifestations of the change

were subtle but crucial. Trousers were tightening by the minute, especially at the ankle end: most of us now special-ized, at evenings and weekends, in black cotton constructions which required you to fold your foot in half to get it through the leg-hole. Blazer collars were up. Badges were small: the gaudy, wing-mirror sized proclamations of old ('All You Need Is Love', 'Smile!') had shrunk to curt buttons – Clash, Pistols, Adverts, Gen X.

There was a King's Road punk fashion for patching up trashed jeans with old pub bar towels and this had filtered down in a small way to a friend of mine who took to walking around with SKOL printed across his buttocks. But the intended anarchy of this, its overt wretchedness, was somewhat diminished because the jeans were always crisply laundered and ironed in detail by his mother.

This, though, is one of the inherent drawbacks about being middle class: your gestures of rejection and dissent get tragi-cally compromised along the way. My girlfriend has told me that in 1978, aged fourteen and wearing a second-hand dinner jacket and stilettos, she attended a Boomtown Rats concert at the Hammersmith Odeon with a schoolfriend, both of them wearing badges which read: 'We Are The People Our Parents Warned Us About'. What the badges didn't go on to say was, they were also the people whose parents had just dropped them off at the door.

So it was with the solitary safety pin I took to wearing from time to time on the lapel of my school blazer. I think even then I was aware that, as acts of negation and defiance go, this was fairly low on controversy. As I self-consciously clipped the pin under its catch, I did not imagine that I could hear the Establishment cracking amid gasps of outrage and horror. I realized that, to be playing the punk game by the rules, I should really have been stabbing the thing, without anaesthetic, through the bridge of my nose – and preferably outside Buckingham Palace. I had to do something, though, and this was the best I could manage – a small gesture of solidarity with those, safety-pinned to the hilt and gobbing on my behalf, in the front line.

We bought some of the things the *NME* told us about at Parrot Records, the intimidatingly small, faintly damp-smelling shop up a narrow side street in the town centre. Its only window was plastered over with record sleeves so inside the place had an authentic, low-lit rock club gloom. The plastic covers in the browser bins were greasy to the touch. And so were many of the people shopping there. Parrot was itself a sign of the times, an independent store devoted largely to independent music and to the new alternatives. And you couldn't get much more alternative than Nigel, the bloke who served behind the counter.

Tall, thin, spike-haired Nigel was usually to be found entertaining himself by auditioning, at brutal volume on the shop's ridiculously large sound system, the latest box of rabid arrivals. He favoured anything punishingly tuneless, short and with the word 'fuck' in the title. The pleasure he took in these records was uninhibited by his duties as a shop assistant. He remains to this day the only person I have ever seen pogoing while on the phone. In his more reflective moments, though, he would lean with his arms across the counter, hands locked, waiting for customers on whom to practise his legendary rudeness.

We spoke of Nigel's rudeness in tones of awe, mingled with jealousy and sprinkled with a fat handful of fear. No one was safe, though Nigel preyed mostly on those people – misguided music lovers, hapless aunts and their nieces' birthday lists – who had accidentally entered Parrot assuming this was an ordinary record shop, selling nice, ordinary things. But it wasn't. It was a horrible record shop selling terrifying things. And it was staffed by Nigel.

Someone would inquire, perfectly innocently, 'Excuse me, where will I find Lionel Richie?'

And Nigel would sniff and say, 'Probably at home in LA, asleep.'

Once a soldier entered the shop and walked confidently to the counter. 'Got anything by George Benson?'

Nigel replied, 'Nah, we don't stock that soul crap.'

For a few chilly seconds, the two of them stared at each other. And then the soldier turned and left. There was nothing in his training to prepare him for a confrontation with Nigel.

It would have been February 1978, a lunch-hour. The country had only recently struggled free of the deathly grip of Paul McCartney's 'Mull Of Kintyre' (so much for punk's purgative fires) and we were hanging around as usual, conspicuous in our purple blazers, flicking idly through the clammy plastic sleeves, hoping to catch Nigel savaging a customer or playing something disgusting. I didn't realize it, but, without any physical contact, Nigel was about to change me for ever.

We heard the needle clomp into the run-in groove, a couple of ticks and specks, some preliminary platter rumble. And then, after an abrupt introductory splatter on the snare drum, in came the bass, pounding hard, slightly ragged at the edges with distortion. So far, so Nigel. But the bass took its four-note riff round the circuit and then dived for cover as the guitar piled in, chopping at a chord which was cacophonous, hard, ear-splitting and yet strangely melodic, as if the song had started out in tunefulness but couldn't quite remember how to get back there. The singer's words were virtually indecipherable at first shot, sung through a contorted throat and apparently out of a gurning mouth. Less than three minutes later it all built to a frantic jabbering and stopped dead.

There's barely a pause before track two, just the slightest break as if in compliance with some kind of vinyl shortage – or as if the band have got this song and they just can't wait for you to hear it. This track is weirder still: pieces of guitar, chipped out at random, more contorted gibbering for vocals (though from another voice this time), mad, scrawny keyboards, and yet, as before, somewhere at the heart of this chaos, a hook, a lure, some memory of tunefulness half heard.

And then track three, and by now I'm not even pretending to look at the sleeves, but just standing with my back to them, listening. Track three is slower, though still driven by an itchy fury, cleaving to a discordant guitar, as if notes from different songs have been crunched together in a thin, tinny slab. The voice from track one is back, sounding more exuberant still, heading towards the song's peak.

And then, with a stamp and a punch, the chorus – a barely musicalized shout, a whoop of glee, a rude wake-up call:

> This is pop, yeah yeah!
> This is pop, yeah yeah!
> This is pop, yeah!
> THIS IS!

Before it had finished, I had approached the counter, pointed at the speakers and – oblivious even to the threat of Nigel's abuse – had said: 'I'd like to buy *this*, please.'

I slipped the sleeve from the brown paper Parrot bag before I left the shop. The album was *White Music* by XTC, track one, 'Radios in Motion'; track two 'Cross Wires', track three

'This is Pop'. No glam gatefold: just a piece of thin, matt cardboard. No inner sleeve: just a plain black liner bag. No lyric sheet: just a few notes on the back in scratchy handwriting. Reared on more sumptuous kinds of packaging, I couldn't help but feel a tinge of deprivation. But I would come to study for hours the bare information on this sleeve – staring at the pictures of the singer and songwriter Andy Partridge, at the white trousers with black traffic arrows he's wearing on the front and at the partly unravelled black and red jumper he's wearing on the rear – and the regret would pass. Fibre at last, after all those cream cakes; a bit of grit, after all that decadence.

In the end, XTC turned out not to be a punk band at all. They were laughably tame by hard-core punk standards – not snarling bondage-wearers with curled lips and metal teeth but a mischievous small-town (Swindon) pop group, one of the cluster who hitched a piggy-back ride on punk, capitalized on that moment when a stunned record business lost control, panicked and threw the doors wide open. In went Elvis Costello, and Paul Weller of the Jam, and Hugh Cornwell of the Strangers, and Sting of the Police, and Andy Partridge of XTC – British pop songwriting's last big boom.

It wasn't much more than a blast of static, but *White Music* seemed to change the air I walked around in. To love it was to see the virtues of the short over the long, the spiky over the lush, the quick over the dead. By rights I should have gone back to Parrot Records very shortly after this, knelt before the counter and intoned: 'For this epiphany, Nigel, much thanks.' But he would have headbutted me.

The Buzzcocks

1978, and bliss was it in that dawn to be alive, what with Elvis Costello, all lippy dismay, singing 'I Don't Want To Go To Chelsea' with the Attractions boiling behind him, and what with Squeeze, a high voice and a low voice and a squally guitar, pumping their way through 'Take Me I'm Yours'.

And the Only Ones sang 'Another Girl, Another Planet', which came at you weirdly, the voice dragging lazily against the beat, like Lou Reed on *Transformer* in 1973. And the Motors sang 'Airport', with its swoony key change into the first verse, its daft backing vocals ('Did-did-did-did') and that piano solo, which I spent hours trying to master, though it's harder than it sounds, but I did a good impression of that desolate background scream you hear ('airport!') as the song heads for its fade.

And Blondie released 'Hanging On The Telephone', which had the best opening of any pop song *ever* – two beeps from the phone, one line of vocal and pow. And the Buzzcocks sang 'Ever Fallen In Love (With Someone You Shouldn't've)', and I had, so when all the instruments piled in at once and the spiralling guitar figure set off like a rocket, with the drums trying to follow it, I was there too, mouthing Pete Shelley's every precious, sibilant 's' (the precursor of Neil Tennant in this) right through to the beaten up and breathless note at the end.

And the Undertones played 'Teenage Kicks', which had the brilliant idea that you didn't need to play a guitar solo, you only needed to strum the chords harder; and the drummer didn't need to play any rolls or fancy rubbish, but could just occasionally switch over to the ride cymbal and beat the hell out of that; and if you didn't use any reverb you'd produce a record that just smacked people in the face, direct, with the back of its hand, though where you were going to find another plangent wobble like Feargal Sharkey's, nobody knew.

And the Jam made 'Down In The Tube Station At Midnight', with its skittering hi-hat, the chipping and digging of the bass and the guitar splintering all over the place. And Paul Weller sang, 'I've a little money and a takeaway curry' and no one had sung that kind of line before. In the best shots of the Jam on stage at this time, Weller and Bruce Foxton are both airborne, miles off the ground. Well, of *course* they are.

Before punk rock (or, to be strictly accurate, before post-punk rock), so much of the music I had listened to had been in denial about its origins. Chiefly, people sang in American accents and wrote lyrics about the earth and mankind and stars and space – anywhere, frankly, other than the street where they lived. And suddenly wherever you turned your ear, there was music about somewhere you came from, somewhere life was crap or boring or funny, or all of those things and more.

Dean Friedman

On the other hand . . .

1978, and bloody murder was it in that dawn to be alive, what with Justin Hayward whispering insipidly about how it was 'Forever Autumn', and John Travolta and Olivia Newton-John clowning their way through 'Summer Nights' from the movie *Grease*, a song which was catchy in the way that certain skin irritations are catchy.

And what with 'Lucky Stars' by Dean Friedman, duetting with some woman whose name I can never remember, on what must be the corniest record ever released, a late-night lovers' tiff dramatized, in which Friedman makes the bold reconciliatory claim that, though he may not be all that bright, he does at least know how to hold her tight, though frankly, by the end of the song, you doubt that too.

And what with 'Rasputin' by Boney M, 'Mexican Girl' by Smokie, and 'Again and Again' by Status Quo . . .

In 1994, when people complain that the charts are full of crap, they forget one crucial thing: that even when they were brilliant, the charts were full of crap. Crap is what the charts are made to be full of.

Rickie Lee Jones

I once went to a Barry White concert at Wembley Arena – the Walrus of Love out there on the stage, mopping himself down with a series of blanket-scale hankies and sexing it up from the bottom of his fathom-deep voice – and I suddenly noticed, off to the side on one of the upper levels, a young couple stretching their arms out towards him. And in the arms of the man was a baby. You don't often see babies offered up to the stage at Wembley Arena and I could only assume that this was an infant conceived to the Barry White sound and its parents had returned to pay tribute to the man for his inspiration.

Personally, even despite this evidence to the contrary, I'm not sure how well music and sex mix, and I've wondered about this since the beginning. She was my first proper relationship and it took us a while to get together because when I met her she was in the process of leaving someone else: not a school-age nerd, but someone, it weakened me around the stomach to learn, six years older than me with a job and a house. But of all the things she told me about him, one detail more than any other comforted me and stiffened my resolve: he had taken her to see Judy Tzuke. All the way to the Ipswich Gaumont to see boring old Judy Tzuke! I was home free.

And all our talk had finally led to where we were now: at my house, with my parents conveniently absent for the evening, in my bedroom, in the dark with just a light coming through the door from the landing, and with, at her suggestion, the first Rickie Lee Jones album on the turntable.

I had been reluctant to have music on in the background at

all, the notion of 'background music' being anathema as far as I am concerned. If music is on I tend to listen to it, and the quieter it is the more I strain after it. (The inevitable result of this is a kind of absorption unacceptable in many social situations and one that has regularly got me into trouble leading to accusations of sulkiness in restaurants and charges of silence bordering on downright rudeness during dinner parties when I've simply been enjoying the Isley Brothers, or whoever.) Clearly, in the sensitive circumstance I'm describing, a lapse of concentration like that could have proven deadly.

Another reason that I didn't particularly wish to musicalize my sexual awakening was that one of my most irritating habits when music is on is an involuntary propensity to beat time on the nearest convenient surface. Now, while an unforeseen outbreak of this might represent an acceptable and maybe even welcome variation in an established sexual relationship, it's not something one would want to risk first time out.

So these things were going through my mind in the dark there. I was also wondering whether I really wanted, for ever more, to associate this momentous rite of passage with the first Rickie Lee Jones record, the one with 'Chuck E's In Love' on. I mean, it was one of my favourite albums: even if things went well, wouldn't this be to contain its relevance to me somehow? And, worse still, what if the whole event was a disaster? What if I couldn't manage it at all and, say, the beautiful, frail strands of 'Company' spoke to me for ever more of flaccidity and shame? In the end, I had to get out of bed and take the thing off. Some people worry about doing it with the lights on. Call it beginner's nerves, but I found I couldn't do it with the sound up.

It may be that where sex is concerned, pop works better as

anticipatory fuel. A girl I know got her boyfriend to drive sixty miles to be with her in the middle of the night in the middle of the week and in lousy weather by the simple but brilliant expedient of playing Phyllis Nelson's 'Move Closer' to him *down the phone*. Even at a distance, through a tinny handset, the track's sultry tug worked like a magnet. That, it seems to me, is the way to play it.

The Orphans of Babylon

The first recording session with Geoff Lawrence (guitar/ vocals) took place in my bedroom in the spring of 1981. We were scheduled to lay down some of the songs Geoff had written and performed as an acclaimed acoustic solo artist around Colchester's pubs and clubs. We would go 'live' to my brother's reel-to-reel, with me adding in some synthesized strings to develop the material, bring it along a stage. As we discussed the project before-hand, it became clear that we saw ourselves as, potentially and in the very near future, a kind of British Hall & Oates.

Unfortunately, every time I depressed the record button Geoff kept laughing, so instead we turned into the Orphans of Babylon.

What were the Orphans of Babylon? After all this time I am still at a loss to explain. Comedy duo? Joke band? Well, yes, in that we played it for laughs, though we grew to take the whole business terribly seriously. Satirists? Art terrorists? Not really: the Orphans had nothing much to do with art or terrorism and we didn't really have the focused grudge that satire requires. A pile of old tosh? Yes, definitely that. But, at the same time, there was something grand about the Orphans, something indefinable yet majestic, something thoroughly rock'n'roll.

When that first session finally broke down for good, we left the tape running and started throwing songs at it off-the-cuff, absurd little snatches of tune spontaneously generated, berserk bits of keyboard and guitar, with Geoff dreaming up, on the spot, screeds of nonsense verse until tears of helpless mirth were running down our shiny faces. (You had to be there, really.)

Afterwards, we agreed that this was the most fun that either of us had ever had in anybody's bedroom. We christened ourselves the Orphans of Babylon after a truly terrible track on Bebop Deluxe's *Modern Music* album and agreed to meet whenever possible to record what we now referred to as 'albums'. We named the songs on them, designed elaborate cassette sleeves for them, gave them titles: *Frank Sneezes*, *Lie Down And Brown*, *Lemon Shipyard*. At our most experimental, we took some instruments and a ghetto-blaster out to a field on the edge of a wood, for that *al fresco* feel. The farmer who owned the field made it across to us after about twenty minutes.

'What the hell d'you boys think you're doin'?'

'Er, we're just, er, recording a few songs,' said Geoff, sheepishly.

This was later to become the famous *Interrupted By A Farmer* album.

Geoff worked as a nurse at a psychiatric hospital (the one my mother claimed to have sent my piano to, though Geoff said he'd never set eyes on it there) and I think it would be fair to say that he picked up ideas, attitudes and expressions in the course of his work which, if you didn't know him well, could make his own claim on a position within the community seem tenuous. His talent for spontaneous melodic and lyric invention was, it strikes me, genius and, if called upon to back up that judgement, I would point no further than his work: 'Milk Teeth' off the *Tin Full of Toffees* album; 'I Love You, Colonel' on *Selected Kippers*; 'Burning Fires of Hell' from *Bap* ('Love cold as icicles/ Love slow as bicycles'); and 'Wine, Women and Wine' and 'No Way To Stop Them (Once They've Started)' off

Natureveldt Shoe. (Bracketed song titles were a particular obsession.)

It was the end of the year before we dared fashion this material into something resembling a live show, and even then only for a laugh at a Christmas party. We dressed up for the occasion in some old silver lamé, ridiculous stacked shoes and an entire packet of face-paints. We looked like Ziggy-period David Bowie crossed with Ronald McDonald, and even in an atmosphere of convivial tolerance befitting the season, our twenty-minute set on tacky keyboard and fuzz guitar was greeted with horrified amazement. Except by the other musicians in the audience, who seemed to enjoy us enormously, perhaps because we dramatized their darkest fears of waking to find yourself on a stage, in absurd clothing, with inadequate songs and inadequate equipment. Soon we were quite regularly in business as an opening act, a warm-up routine, other local bands quickly realizing that, after our scratchy incomprehensibility, pretty well anything with drums and bass in it sounded exultantly professional and exciting.

On stage, Geoff was nervous but unembarrassable, a horse stung by a wasp, charging and stamping around in the space available to him. (It is the lot of the support act to perform in whatever space is left unoccupied by the equipment of the main band; this is normally a thin strip along the front of the stage so that, as the songwriter Boo Hewerdine once memorably put it, 'you end up looking like an Egyptian frieze'.) As for me, I found my mind turning a lot to Ron Mael, the moustachioed, Brylcreemed keyboard player in the duo Sparks, who had one unaltering facial expression which seemed at once to have nothing to do with what he was playing and to want nothing to do with the antics of his brother Russ, the singer, who flounced about in a more archetypally camp rock'n'roll manner. I seemed to have this expression by default while playing with the Orphans of Babylon – a kind of perturbed earnestness, informed by genuine anxieties about what Geoff might do next. I was the Ernie Wise to his Salvador Dalì.

And because there is no pop act of any kind or scale anywhere who does not believe in the possibility of a professional future, before long we began to think in terms of record deals – as incredible as it may seem and though to do so was to fly in the face of the available evidence. In a vain attempt to make ourselves easier to swallow, we began to perform a version of the *Dr Who* theme and a ludicrously sped-up rendition of the Righteous Brothers' 'You've Lost That Lovin' Feelin''. These little 'popular' touches didn't take us any closer to radio exposure.

I know this because John Peel, the broadcaster and all-round hero, told me in person. Not in so many words (he would never have taken it upon himself to be so openly discouraging), but with one telling and suggestive gesture in a darkened car park at Essex University. This was following our appearance in the university dance hall – a career highpoint – as the performance interlude during a *John Peel Roadshow*. (I still have the tape and have played it to within an inch of its life: not our set, which was the usual stack of old nonsense, but the part at the beginning where the record fades out – 'What is Life?' by Black Uhuru – and John Peel introduces us: 'Right, boys and girls, it's time for some live music. They're lurking in the wings, wearing extraordinary costumes, ready to delight you tonight, would you welcome please, the *Orphans Of Babylon*! Thunderous applause!'

That 'thunderous applause' was generous of him. What we got was a short burst of unreasonably hysterical screaming from our friends at the front. But just to hear our name spoken in those familiar tones seemed like a thrilling endorsement.)

At the end of the evening, because he was a man of famously eclectic tastes (and because it was what you did if you were in a band), I bashfully approached Peel with a copy of one of our tapes.

'Can I give you this? I don't know whether . . . perhaps . . . Anyway!'

'Let me show you something,' he said, and he took me out to where his car was parked and opened the boot.

It was filled to the brim with demo tapes – innumerable cassettes, hours and hours of unsolicited listening, most of it, presumably, shockingly awful. He explained that this was about three months' worth, that they were *en route* to his home where he would see what he could do about working his way through them. He said that, obviously, where this quantity of tapes was concerned, his methods were bound to be a little random. And he told me the story about Terry & Gerry, a rather wonderful skiffle duo from Birmingham who Peel had championed early on. He said he originally pulled their tape out of the pile because he had an aunt and uncle called Terry and Gerry and the coincidence was too much to let it slip. And with that, he slid the Orphans in with the rest of them and clicked the boot shut. (I was thinking: An Aunty Orphan, an Uncle Babylon?)

I realize now that what he was saying, in the nicest possible way, was: Give up, surrender now, before someone gets badly hurt. And, like a fool, I ignored him.

But that's how it was in the Orphans of Babylon – crazy, reckless, devil-take-the-hindmost . . . in a word, stupid. And it had been like that ever since the day when, as the seriousness of our purpose hardened, we decided it was time to go and see Dave Woods.

Dave Woods was the rock critic on the *Essex County Standard*, the local weekly. He had a sizeable picture by-line: 'Rock,' it said, 'Dave Woods'. Not surprisingly, policing the Colchester rock scene wasn't a full-time job for Dave. Rather, it was just one of his many duties as a news reporter and probably, in truth, not the one he was wildest about. It meant that in any week he might have to give up his Tuesday evening to go to St Mary's Arts Centre on heavy-metal night and see Aardvark supported by Plumber's Fist; and then, because local papers, unlike bullying, arrogant national papers, try to cultivate a kindly, nurturing tone, he had to find something encouraging to say about it afterwards.

It also meant he was ceaselessly harried in the streets and pubs by local musicians hoping to tempt him into writing a major promotional feature ahead of a key local gig at the Affair Club. With scant regard for his privacy or the sacredness of his spare time, people would thrust upon him, as if he was John Peel, cassettes recorded at practices in sitting rooms and bedrooms, saying, 'It's just a rough mix, of course, Dave', or 'The sound quality isn't that special, but you'll get the drift.'

The way it worked out, Dave was, by default, Colchester's biggest rock powerbroker. You wanted to get your name about, you had to go and see Dave. Dave had the whole pop publicity thing in his pocket.

It must be said, there were risks attendant on the kind of exposure offered by the *Essex County Standard*. The recognition, the pestering in the streets, the pressure of becoming a local 'face' overnight – none of these was at stake. But there was, instead, the chance of embarrassment, the grim likelihood of coming out of this venture ashen-faced with entirely the wrong result.

It was mostly a question of tone and detail, a clash between what the paper wanted out of its pop report and what you, the aspiring star, wanted. You could see that it made sound journalistic sense to work people's ages into these pieces: 'Colin, 24 . . .'. Even proper professional pop stars had to endure that in a profile. Slightly more belittling, slightly more at odds with your touchy sense of self in this matter, was the insistence (the first rule of local journalism being to stress the local angle) on printing an address: 'Colin, 24, who lives at 46 Allthorpe Drive . . .' This didn't seem quite commensurate with superstar status – or even imminent superstar status. It looked uncool. They didn't go in for that at the *NME*.

But these were minor detractions compared with the very real possibility that the paper would see fit to print your occupation – an entirely well-meaning act on the paper's part, just another device to help the readers get a grip. But the unfortunate consequence, from the aspiring musician's point of view, was the implication that when you weren't tooling around with some daft pop group or other, you had a *proper* job. 'Colin, 24, who works in the bedding department at Williams and Griffin's . . .'

What you wanted the piece to convey was your all-involving pop identity, that you were Colin from the Tadpoles, or whatever, and the reader had better watch out. But the piece might just as well have read: 'Sad part-time singer Colin kids himself he has a future in the sad part-time band he sings with part-time.' Headline: 'HOPELESS CAUSE OF PART-TIME COLIN'.

But how else were we to make a splash locally, shift the career up a gear? So, a handful of gigs into the Orphans' performing history, and with one or two particularly spicy support slots coming up, Geoff and I decided it was time to visit Dave. We called at the paper's office in the middle of one weekday afternoon and were surprised to be invited up to see him in the clacking newsroom. Dave did an amazing impression of someone who was pleased to see us, found us seats, pulled a notebook from the busy clutter of his desk and spun back to face us, mock-interestedly, with his back to his typewriter.

'So,' he said, 'what are your influences?'

'Oh, you know,' I said, 'XTC, Todd Rundgren, Stevie Wonder . . .' trying to make it sound as if these artists formed some kind of natural continuum, when, for all the sense it made to string them together, I could just as well have been snatching words out of the air: 'Oh, you know – tractor, alarm bell, bracelet . . .'

'But we don't sound like any of them,' added Geoff, accurately but confusingly.

'It's a sort of comedy thing, Dave,' I said, and then launched into some pointless, windy paragraph about pop pastiche, about how each of the songs was a parody in miniature of a conventional pop music style, the whole show functioning as a satire on rock's self-absorption. 'You know, humour but with an edge.' None of which I believed for a second, although I would still be prepared to argue that it sounded better than saying, 'Well, basically, Dave, we just get up there and arse around.'

At this point, Geoff planted a quote which both of us were keen to see used: 'I'm expanding in all sorts of interesting directions,' he said.

Dave nodded patiently and took the odd note and tried bravely to maintain something resembling a keen and supportive facial expression. We handed him a black and white photograph of the two of us, taken at the bus stop outside my house (wise of us, I think, to take our own image along rather than trust to the *Standard*'s tastes because photographers on local papers always want to take musicians *holding their instruments*, which looks terrible; not that the *Standard* would have gone to the trouble of organizing a portrait of us anyway). We also passed over a sort of press release we had cobbled together about the upcoming gigs and a copy of our tape.

'The sound quality's not that great,' I assured him, 'but you'll get the drift.'

And then, quite abruptly, I thought, Dave whipped the jacket from the back of his chair and said he had to be off right now (some major marrow story breaking on the allotments over at Shrub End, evidently).

'Thanks for coming in,' he said, smiling again as he steered us towards the stairs. 'I'll see what I can do.'

Walking back up the hill, Geoff and I were completely confident that we'd blown it.

And we were wrong. That Friday, I leafed through the paper almost casually, so much had I given up hope. But there it was on page six, half-way down, next to the Entertainments guide: ORPHANS ON THE ROAD TO LAUGHTER, 200 words plus picture. Maybe some big piece on the family folk-act Farley's Rusk had fallen out at the last minute – who knows? But what did it matter? We were there and we were jubilant. Better still, there was no sub-clause mentioning Geoff's job, nothing about me going to university and no reference to either of our addresses.

And best of all, there, verbatim, was Geoff's quote: ' "I'm expanding in all sorts of interesting directions," says Geoff, 20.' (Sadly, though, it had not, as we had fervently hoped, been taken out for use in the picture caption: 'Geoff Lawrence: expanding in all sorts of interesting directions'.)

Still, Dave Woods had done us proud. The Orphans of Babylon were go.

Three Times A Day

When I was in my late teens, everybody I knew in Colchester was in a band. That's because I wasn't interested in knowing anybody who wasn't in a band. Except girls. The majority of the girls I knew were not in bands. Clearly, there were years of cultural stereotyping ensuring that this was the case; pop music was so boys-y, so laddish. Though I would also say that the girls I knew who wanted to be in bands *were* in bands. The majority of the girls I knew actually didn't want to be in bands.

But all the girls I knew liked listening to bands. That's because I wasn't interested in knowing any girl who *didn't* like listening to bands. Neither was I interested in knowing any girl who didn't like talking about *being* in bands. Or who didn't mind listening while the people who *were* in bands talked about being in bands. Because people who are in bands don't talk about anything else. That's what's really boring about people who are in bands.

Geoff and I, the Orphans of Babylon – we bored for Britain on the subject of bands. And so did everyone else. We all sat in pubs and the topic of conversation was bands. Never politics, or art, or books: just bands.

This was a good time to be in Colchester in a band. There were the Reasonable Strollers – noisy, angular and strange. And there was Three Times A Day, fronted by Nel, who had a bush of spiked-up hair, wore silver trousers and what looked like a clump of seaweed for a top. His name was Peter Nice, but nobody called him that. Everybody called him Nel. He had been in a band called the Toys and they had appeared, just once, on Saturday morning television. My mother was working in a department store at the time and she had seen Nel's mother, who worked there too, hop through to the TV department to catch it. Everyone thought the Toys were going to make it. But their single stalled somewhere down in the 70s and that was that.

Still, Three Times A Day were good. They released an EP: 'I Crave To Be A Hermaphrodite' and 'X Ray' on side one, the epical 'Storm' on side two. Eventually we got to know Nel and he started to come out with us to the pub and talk about bands. Bands, bands, bands.

The Orphans of Babylon soon had a tape out too. Just locally. It was recorded by a friend called Dave, who wasn't in a band, though his wife was, and he was a studio engineer so he talked about bands all the time. He got us into a 24-track studio in Chelmsford for a day when the owner was away. We finished it off on a reel-to-reel in Dave's sitting room. We called it *Pinch Me, I Think I'm in Kent* (Geoff's title). It included our best numbers so far: 'Separatists', 'Tree-mouse', 'Milk Teeth (Are Good Until You Lose Them)' and the snooker-inspired 'Helluva Break By Ray Reardon', which went:

> That was a helluva break by Ray Reardon
> That was a helluva break by old Ray
> That was a helluva break by Ray Reardon
> Green, yellow and blue.

Lots of our friends bought it – lots of our friends who were in bands. Of course, it was just a local band's tape, not like a real album. But there was no question that you judged the one by the standards of the other. You didn't expect a tape by Three Times A Day to rank, in terms of sound quality, along-side your copy of Steely Dan's *Aja*. You know it had been recorded round at Chris's where there were old sofa cushions nailed to the walls for soundproofing. You didn't expect it to be album length either – five or six tracks was ample.

It was clear that there were, for us, two distinct musical worlds: the professional one, where people did deals and released albums and went on tours; and the world of local bands. And we dreamed of getting to the place where the one magically glided into the other.

Quincy Jones

I have traded liberally in fantasy futures. I have imagined myself in high-profile roles for which I was obviously unsuited, dreamed of far-fetched lives. These dreams pause and amuse for a while and then pass. Except for the pop music one. The pop one sticks. It's there and, no matter how I shake it, it will not budge.

Why won't the real world intervene? What is its reluctance to go nuclear and finish this off, once and for all? With my other lost causes, reality just got straight in there, no messing about. My plans to become an astronaut, for instance, carefully nurtured since Neil Armstrong took his first lunar step in July 1969, terminated at the end of 1972, when NASA pulled the plug on the Apollo space programme after Apollo 17. (Assuming a smooth career parabola and a glitch-free training programme, I had reckoned to be in the running for the crew on Apollo 36.)

Something less arbitrary, but equally devastating, shattered my conviction that I would one day play for Chelsea FC. I remember clearly the initiation of this dream. It began with me bursting angrily on to the primary school playground after ignominious failure in a fourth-form mental arithmetic test, and thinking, Sod the lot of you – I'll be a footballer. (And I proved my point just six minutes into that break-time, picking up the ball well inside my own half of the playground, skipping and jinking though the challenges of seven or eight breathless defenders and several hundred other kids who weren't involved in the game at all, ramming the thing between the piled-up jumpers and celebrating, Brazil-style, over by the railings, through which, I firmly believed, it was only a matter of time before Chelsea's scouts would be proffering their rolled-up registration forms.)

But I remember exactly where that dream stopped, too. It was the moment, only two years later, when, after a hopelessly ineffectual performance with the school side, away at St Helena, I was substituted at half-time. After this crunching tackle from the real world, I had to face facts. Either you've got it or you haven't. I hadn't.

In any case, with football dreams, if a lack of skill doesn't get you, age will. This is not how it goes for ageing musicians. We don't think it's all over at all. We think it's just hotting up. In fact, we think the big moment, always imminent, has never been *more* imminent (degrees of imminence being the crucial unit of measurement when you are a would-be pop star seeking your break). Life has not rapped us on the shins in an attempt to bring us to our senses. Or it may have done, but we haven't noticed.

How old you were must have counted for something once, when pop was almost exclusively made by teenagers for teenagers (with some older people in the background, counting the money). Presumably, if you were an aspiring musician getting nowhere in the early 1960s, your nineteenth birthday would have come round with a grim tolling of the bell. You would have realized that, at some point during the next twelve months, unless things really picked up for you in that Tuesday-night residency down at the Greasy Quiff, you would have to resign yourself to becoming an estate agent. McCartney gave himself until he was twenty to make it because after that, he thought, he would be too old and it would be back to the drawing board, career-wise. (He was indeed just shy of his twentieth birthday when the Beatles signed with EMI in June 1962.)

But now this simple process of selection and wastage is lost to us. Who, in the music business, bothers to lie about how old they are any more? Fresh-eyed youthfulness is beside the point in a context in which oldies like the Rolling Stones keep swinging back with faces chewed up like dogs' rubber balls. And just as the rock-star sell-by date has gone back and back, so has the career start-by date. As I have grown older, I have not felt myself drawing closer to the horizon: on the contrary, I have watched the horizon recede tantalizingly before me – with, it must be said, considerable relief but also some distortions of perspective.

What admiration I have for the singer-songwriter Tori Amos, for instance, has mostly to do with her being around the same age as me and that she was in her late twenties when she finally made it and became, in my eyes, a brilliant torch of hope. I would have liked to have taken her aside and said, 'Way to go, Tori! Can't say I like your début album very much, but it's a major strike for us late-starters.'

Similarly, I was moved by the success of her male counterpart, Marc Cohn, not because I was particularly drawn to 'Walking In Memphis', the song that cracked it for him (smart lyrics, but a rather obvious-sounding thing, taken whole), but because I knew that he had turned thirty when this success came his way in 1991 which I found deeply consoling in relation to my own failure thus far. Also, he gave me a new benchmark for late-starting – a mark that Sting, twenty-seven before the Police got properly under way, supplied me with for some years, until my own twenty-seventh birthday came and went without any noticeable hit singles on my part.

What is the pop equivalent of my half-time substitution? This is a realm, it seems, where you can't be ruled out on the grounds of an absence of skill. People who are not fans of pop music will tell you that artistry has very little to do with it, at least as far as the performer is concerned. The real work, they will claim, is done by producers and haberdashers and hairdressers: it's a studio confection at every level, a matter of camera angles, a tweak of the knob, a trick of the light, the ultimate victory of style over content. This is a bitter and pessimistic view, but you can't say it hasn't been true in some cases – I think of Milli Vanilli (the singing duo who had to hand back their Grammy Award when it turned out they had mimed the whole thing) and Bryan Ferry. And, as a pop hopeful, you don't have to buy entirely into this argument to take succour from it. If the music industry can fix it for Milli Vanilli, then why not for everybody?

There's another feeling about pop music, related to this one, which again upholds the aspiring star in his or her self-belief: the apparent ease of it. Pop deals – a lot of it, nearly all of the best of it – in simplicities: big emotions, basic thoughts, straight-ahead tunes. How much skill do you need? What can it possibly take?

Frequently, of course, the ease is deceptive. 'Every Breath You Take' by the Police is perhaps the best song Sting has ever written. It's built on one of the oldest, simplest rotating chord patterns in the book. It contains a one-note piano solo. One note! Look at those lyrics: 'take'/'make'/'break' . . . rhyming dictionary doggerel, by Sting's own admission. You think this is easy, though? Well, sit down and write one if you can.

Or what about 'I Will Always Love You', that Whitney Houston single from the movie *The Bodyguard*? True, this song is mostly an excuse for Houston to have hysterics every time the chorus comes around (it's one of those bet-you-can't-hold-your-breath-as-long-as-I-can specials, like the blue-faced end chorus of Bill Withers' 'Lovely Day'), but somewhere beneath all that is a song written by the country singer Dolly Parton.

Picture her now, toiling over those lyrics. She's thinking, How can I best convey that the performer of this song feels that they will always love their beloved? There is a brief pause. 'Goddit!' she shouts, and writes: 'I will always love you.' No metaphor, no simile, no crafted line, no twist. Money for old rope! And yet, it was Dolly Parton who couldn't be bothered to think of a metaphor, not you. (And it's Dolly Parton, not you, who is currently salting down those royalties.)

This is the pop conundrum: either you've got it or you haven't; but what is it? In the absence of an answer, hope is free to carry on springing. Perhaps you have been overlooked for years: then you console yourself that you are misunderstood, that it's only a matter of time. (Nobody thought Pulp were any good for eleven years and then – bam! – into the Top Ten.) Or maybe you're so bad it's good, like Gary Glitter.

Of course, there are recognized sources of critical response. Record companies, for instance, with their rejection letters – although these are, in my experience, just a rumour. Over the years, I have positively rained down on record companies appalling tapes of half-baked material and have never seen such a thing. Still from time to time you can't help but notice, or so you would think, their silence. You would imagine that years and years of no response would become, in its own way, richly eloquent, peculiarly final-sounding. If you were routinely ignored for the best part of a decade by someone with whom you were in love, you would probably construe this as meaning, 'I'm sorry, but you're not quite what I'm looking for right now.' Yet, somehow, where pop bands come from, this great refreshing wind of rationality never blows. On we go and on.

Every week, the *NME* performs a valuable service free of charge. It sends young, courageous and by no means over-paid writers to get their feet dirty right down at the roots, in the little clubs, the primordial swamps where rock first crawls from the slime and tries to stand upright. These writers – or those who survive with their limbs and their sanity – come back and, where necessary, do the decent thing and file reviews which, if read between the lines (and sometimes if read *in* the lines), say, 'Oi. You're crap. Forget it.'

And are people in bands grateful? On the contrary: they blame the press for its 'cynicism' and they blame the record industry for its 'cowardice', its 'reluctance to accept the challenge of the new' or some such. I once spoke to an aspiring pop musician whose long-fought-for support slot at the Fulham Greyhound in London had been casually, and justifiably, savaged in an *NME* review. 'Well, that's just the view of one journalist, isn't it?' he said, when, no, actually, it was the view of the entire world – excluding the members of the band and their close family, and even the close family had their doubts. It is nothing short of heroic the way a would-be pop star will continue, undeterred, in the face of universal indifference and – more amazing still – active opposition. The pop dream is indestructible by mere fact. It is like an alarm clock in a cartoon, which continues to ring long after its vital components have been pulped with a baseball bat.

True, the fantasies may modify themselves with time. My own have become a touch more genteel – more adult, I guess. I managed a long time ago to kick posing in front of the wardrobe mirror. And it has been at least fourteen years since I pretended that a tennis racquet was a guitar (except in bored moments during games of tennis, which, on the grounds of being open, public and clearly satirical displays, don't count). The fantasies still rage, but they take less florid forms.

It can come from nowhere. I can be in the Gents in a pub, at the basin, washing my hands. And the noise will drift in from the bar – a track off the juke-box, Prefab Sprout's 'Cars And Girls', say. At which point, something inspires me to draw slightly closer to the mirror above the taps and begin to mouth the words at my reflection. And, in an instant, I am Paddy McAloon and this is my song. Right then, of course, someone else bangs through the door and I have to freeze, with my jaw set in an extraordinary rictus, and pretend to be examining my teeth.

Here's another. No actions involved in this one – it's in a straightforward daydream format. I can drift into it at almost any point, but tend to do so particularly when driving. Virtually any kind of song will do as a catalyst for it, but I'm made especially vulnerable if the soundtrack happens to be something from the poppy end of black American R&B, early 1990s-style, with its pretty tunes, thick harmonies, its rhythms derived from swingbeat – Toni Braxton or El Debarge or Brian McKnight or Ralph Tresvant or someone like that. And, as the writer of the song and also in my capacity as co-producer, I am in the studio with LA & Babyface or Jam & Lewis, a welcome and chummy interloper on these production partnerships, sitting at the mixing desk with them during playback, rocking in my seat.

(The source for this image is a television documentary on the life of the producer Quincy Jones, called, I think, 'We Love You, Quincy' – not the astonishing biographical movie, *Listen Up*, which came out in 1990, but a slightly soppy French-Canadian tribute affair, which I stumbled on inadvertently on Anglia TV in the middle of the night in about 1985.

It included footage of Quincy and his engineer in a studio mixing 'Yah Mo B There' for James Ingram. Both of them, totally absorbed, are rocking in time to the rhythm track, which has that fabulous little catch in it – that one snagged drum machine 'clap' noise, which is 50 per cent of the song's appeal – and occasionally either Quincy or the engineer leans into the incomprehensible sea of buttons and sliders on the mixing desk to make some imperceptible but doubtless utterly crucial adjustment. And, watching this, I just thought: What a fantastic life! Imagine doing a job where you spend your day rocking backwards and forwards at your desk, with music flooding through you.)

So I'm at the desk with Babyface or LA or Jimmy or Terry, and occasionally I suggest a little nudge on the backing vocals to lift the chorus slightly, and maybe a touch less top on that tambourine – what do you reckon, Jimmy? No? OK, fine – and we're pursed-lipped but cool, exchanging nods of satisfaction. Chiefly, though, I'm rocking to and fro at the desk, like Quincy Jones. Producer fantasies! Now there's a sign of age.

It's not the daydream itself that troubles me: it's my residual conviction, based upon no grounds whatsoever (no production projects in the pipeline – no production projects *ever* – no songs out there with the publishers, no intention to write any such songs), that *one day it will come true*.

It's during the dark, guilty moments of self-scrutiny after these worrying indulgences that I am tempted to argue for the reintroduction of National Service – just for me. That would sort me out.

Nik Kershaw

I don't want to sound like I'm crowing or anything, but we knew him before the 'c' fell off. We knew him when he was just plain Nick. Later, as Nik, he would release a handful of hit singles – 'Wouldn't It Be Good', 'I Won't Let The Sun Go Down On Me', 'The Riddle', all of them vapid, naggingly catchy pop songs made with crunchy synthesizers. He would become a real pop star and have thousands of pubescent girls screaming at him in public and plastering their bedroom walls with his pouty image. But, as I've told a lot of people since, it wasn't like that for Nick back in the early days, when he used to play those pubs gigs in Colchester and Ipswich. It wasn't like that when *I* knew him.

I had better come clean right here and set out precisely the extent of my friendship with Nick Kershaw before 1984 when he became, just briefly, a national pin-up. It boiled down to maybe three or four short conversational exchanges, all of them in pubs at the end of evenings on which Kershaw had provided the live musical entertainment, and each of them taking roughly this form:

Me: 'Nice gig tonight, Nick.'

Him: 'Oh, er, thanks.'

Me: 'Well, er, see you next time.'

Him: 'Sure, yeah, see you, then.'

In addition, I would beg the jury to take into consideration a slightly more substantial (but still brief and embarrassing) visit to his house along with my friend Geoff. But that's it.

The thing is, the slightness of our acquaintance was something I rather played down following Kershaw's first hit single. And after his second and third, to listen to me going on about the hell Nik and I used to raise, back in those early Colchester days, you would have assumed we were related by marriage. Or married. I would claim in my defence that I was by no means the only person who tampered with the evidence in this regard. In fact, shortly after Kershaw's first appearance on *Top of the Pops*, most of the people I knew were claiming to figure prominently in his past and vouching for their own presence at all kinds of mysterious parties and undocumented jam sessions. Just as pretty well everyone from Liverpool, aged between forty-five and fifty-five, will tell you about the night in 1961 when they bought Paul McCartney a Coke down at the Cavern, so a sizeable slice of the population of Colchester has its Nik Kershaw tales, nearly all of them home-grown.

(Once, on a camping holiday in France, I met a rather mournful Liverpudlian with an acoustic guitar and we spent a broody evening sitting outside my tent, with him strumming a few quiet, plangent chords and running through little fragments of songs from the sixties. And he told me all about buying McCartney a Coke in the Cavern and I told him all about me and Nik Kershaw. It was, on reflection, the most factually ridiculous conversation I have ever had.)

Now, a lot of people (especially those not drawn to the music of the man one of the less charitable music papers immediately nicknamed 'the pop elf') might suggest it would have been wiser to deny all connections with this diminutive, nasal-voiced, temporary teen idol, rather than painstakingly manufacture a relationship with him. McCartney is one thing. But *Nik Kershaw*? The baby-faced composer of 'Human Racing'?

But it is not given to all of us to be choosy in this matter. Of course, I regard it as typical that the one sizeable pop star who brushed past my shoulder on his way to the firmament

ended up being bracketed, not with substantial, timeless figures like Leonard Cohen or Van Morrison, but with Howard
Jones, another serious-faced yet hugely naff mid-eighties hot-
shot. (Both of them favoured mohair for that kinetic-but-
cuddly look.) You wouldn't think there were many situations
in which one could drop the name Nik Kershaw and hope to
get a result. But that doesn't seem to have stopped me trying.
Such is the allure of fame when it passes you close by. I
should add that the Kershaw we knew, before MCA Records
got hold of him and started marketing him as a schoolgirl's
gonk, was actually – dare I say it? – quite cool. Some of us
stood by him.

Partly his example served as an encouragement: it was
proof that stardom did come even to those grubbing around
Colchester's pubs with a cheap amplifier. But there was something else about his success that was intensely frustrating. I
wanted to dine out on my association and couldn't quite
reconcile myself to the fact that my raw material didn't even
constitute a starter. We all know from countless interviews
given by whingeing pop stars (including Nik Kershaw), that
fame brings unforeseen pressures and it is difficult to bear; I'd
like to make it clear that the fame of someone you almost but
didn't quite know is pretty hard to swallow, too.

Nick Kershaw used to play guitar in a band called Fusion.
It must have taken them minutes to come up with that name.
Still, it was the only disappointing thing about them. Fusion
played cover versions of other people's songs in pubs and
clubs all over Essex – like a million other acts, except Fusion
could play the difficult bits. Not for them a confused, nine-
minute version of 'Johnny B. Goode' and a drunken stab at
Free's 'All Right Now'. Fusion breezed their way through a
repertoire selected with, what seemed at the time, impeccable
taste and nerve: 'Green Earring' by Steely Dan; 'Jolly Coppers

On Parade' by Randy Newman; 'Cos We've Ended As Lovers', a little-known but fabulously poignant ballad that Stevie Wonder wrote for Syreeta Wright to sing; even Weather Report's 'Birdland', that absurdly convoluted jazz-funk instrumental which we all hated really, but which Fusion, to our enduring awe, had note-for-note.

They didn't play much of their own material but we weren't about to demand originals when the fakes were so well observed. To be fair, the band later scraped some money together and put out an album of new compositions, *Till I Hear From You*, which came in a cheap cardboard sleeve displaying a grainy photograph of somebody pretending to be dead in a phone box. The record was released on blue vinyl, and the whole package would be one of the most tasteless items in my collection, if I hadn't lent it to someone and never received it back. Needless to say, there was nothing on it as good as 'Jolly Coppers On Parade' though it did contain a dirge credited to N. Kershaw – the dreaded 'Human Racing' – which, in almost identical form, provided Kershaw with a hit single in 1984.

The members of Fusion were dispersed across a fifty-mile radius: the keyboard player was from Braintree, the drummer from Southend, the bassist from Colchester. Kershaw himself lived about twenty miles north of Colchester, in a village off the road to Cambridge. This was an odd and inconvenient arrangement for a working band but there was a simple explanation: if you were as talented as each of them was, you would have to drive around a bit before you found anyone worth playing with.

Kershaw, in particular, was a frighteningly dextrous musician, a blindingly fast and bafflingly inventive guitar soloist – although it now seems irrelevant to say so, after what became of him. There have been many conversations in which I have tried to make myself heard above the laughter and justify him – and, more particularly, my interest in him – by referring to his diligent interest in the jazz guitarist Allan Holdsworth. But, perhaps, inevitably, this line of argument meets with suspicion from those who know him only as a man who once appeared in *Smash Hits* on the back of a horse wearing a kind of woolly armour. (If he'd only known the derision he was going to bring down on me with that single photo-shoot: why couldn't he have just stood by a wall in a pair of jeans and a T-shirt, like everybody else?)

But in those glorious, innocent days before fame stole him away from us, we could watch and listen to Kershaw with impunity. And we did. Our appetite for Fusion knew no limits. Sunday lunchtimes we would watch them in the Colne Lodge (Colchester's premium young person's gathering spot, populated almost exclusively by underage drinkers, adept at making a half of lager shandy stretch across three hours). Sunday evenings four or five of us would drive to the White Horse in Ipswich and watch them all over again. We travelled to Southend and Tollesbury. We went to Rayleigh. Nobody goes to Rayleigh for a night out. Not even people in Rayleigh go to Rayleigh for a night out.

We loved Fusion but we never imagined that the stretch limo of fame was going to reverse its shiny boot on to their drive. It must be said, record-industry executives were hardly tearing across the country in a rush to sign anyone who could execute an inch-perfect Jeff Beck instrumental. Also, it was the keyboard player's misfortune not only to play and sing like Stevie Wonder, but also to be blind – and as he once mournfully remarked, 'Who needs a honky Stevie Wonder?'

And we didn't have screaming girls and unreasonable wealth in mind for Nick Kershaw. He had discouraging, science-student hair and wore unbuttoned waistcoats of doubtful origin (Mr Byrite? Kool'N'Kasual? Children in Need?). Worse, he affected unwisely coloured ties with fat knots, casually slackened to mid-chest level. And yet Geoff and I had evolved for this figure the kind of crush girls get for gym mistresses. He was commandingly good, so he tapped into that power that musicians have, which has nothing to do with television, or wealth, or with any sense of what these people might mean beyond the room they are in. You see them perform and you wish you knew them. But that command is forbidding, too, so you hover shyly on the way out.

'Nice gig tonight, Nick.'

'Oh, er, thanks.'

'Well, er, see you next time.'

At that gig in Rayleigh, we bootlegged the show, perching a ghetto-blaster on our table and sitting in silence for the entire evening so the machine wouldn't pick up our voices. And afterwards we walked out past the stage with the recorder still running, so it would catch Kershaw saying 'Goodnight' to us. In fact, what he said as we approached was, 'Hey, your red light's still on.' Outside, we knelt in the car park and screamed with embarrassment. (I still have the tapes: they contain a prototype version of 'Wideboy', later a hit off Kershaw's second album, as well as the aforementioned 'spoken-word' passage. If the market for Kershaw rarities ever catches fire, I shall be buying myself an airline.)

Geoff and I even developed and honed a detailed impression of Kershaw taking a solo. If you want to try it, it involves setting your right foot neatly over your left, bending at the knees slightly, sucking in both cheeks and woggling your pursed lips according to the dynamics of the music. After several months spent trying to conceive how we could enlarge on our skimpy acquaintance, Geoff ventured up to Kershaw and, in a brilliantly conceived variation on the regular 'Nice gig tonight, Nick', asked him if he taught guitar. Kershaw said he didn't, but he would be happy to spend an hour some afternoon showing off a few tricks and tips. Just like that, Geoff was in.

It says a lot about Geoff's big-heartedness that he volunteered to share this adventure with me, knowing how much it would mean. Obviously, I couldn't sit in on the session, but the plan was that I would accompany Geoff on the twenty-mile drive into the middle of nowhere where Kershaw lived, and then I would make myself scarce while the two of them jammed and bonded. Geoff would explain to Kershaw that he had a friend with him, a keen photographer who was using this opportunity to take some pictures of the countryside. And at the end of the hour I would turn up at the house where, who knows, the kettle might be on, and I too might get to share some quality time with Nick.

We were pleased with this explanation of my presence which we felt had the smack of authenticity about it, although, in truth, I probably remain the only person in this century to have gone on photo-safari in Great Yeldham. After an hour spent staring redundantly across flat, fallow fields, I knocked at the door of Kershaw's small, white bungalow. Geoff opened it (he was nearer the door, apparently) and I stepped in and hovered just over the threshold. Kershaw was seated in the middle of the room with a guitar.

'Hello,' he said.

'Hello,' I said.

He seemed really nice, but the kettle wasn't on and there wasn't a lot to say.

'Goodbye,' said Geoff.

Evidently, the guitar session had gone OK: Kershaw had graciously shown Geoff some chord shapes and some fingerings and had played him a couple of tracks featuring Allan

Holdsworth. But at no point had he and Nick exchanged high fives, talked about old girlfriends, vowed to form a band together, or even swapped phone numbers, which was the point of the whole exercise. In the car on the way back, both of us were muted, busy pondering a spectacularly large hole in our enchantment. (Although, of course, to listen to Geoff crank on about it now, anyone would think that, while I was stomping pointlessly up and down muddy lanes looking at my watch every five minutes, he and Kershaw were busy co-writing what later became Kershaw's first two albums.)

Not long after this, Fusion split up. I suppose there's a limit to the number of times you want to play 'Birdland' in front of broke minors. They vanished from our lives abruptly, as local bands tend to. There was nothing about it in the press – they just stopped turning up. Eventually, the keyboard player re-emerged as a solo pub act with a snazzy drum machine and a sequencer, a kind of high-class home organist. The bassist cropped up in other people's bands. The drummer, everyone said, was busy with session work. As for Kershaw, we knew nothing. And then, after nearly a year, I sighted him.

It was in Colchester's shopping precinct, outside Lasky's electrical store and at the back of Marks & Spencer's. And this was not the Nick Kershaw I had known (or rather, not known). First there was the hair – all spiky and bright blond as if a small bomb containing bleach had gone off on his head, the *de rigueur* 1980s pop-star plumage. And then there were the clothes. No more wearisome waistcoats, no more duff ties. He was wearing a tiny black jacket with some complicated fastenings, and black drainpipe jeans which bottomed out in a pair of pointy boots. There were only two possible explanations: either a major record company had signed him up and had got its people to make him over, ready for stardom; or Kershaw had retrained as a hairdresser and was now working in a shiny-floored unisex salon in Chelmsford – Sophisticut, maybe, or Hair Today. Naturally, I assumed the latter and shook my head ruefully all the way home on the bus.

And, of course, I was wrong. The haircut and the grimly fashionable threads were courtesy of MCA, who were right at that moment priming Kershaw, ready to detonate him and his new hair in the teen market. There was a faltering start: 'I Won't Let the Sun Go Down' was released in late 1983 in a cheap sleeve which seemed to have been slung together in a lunch-hour by someone with a thick black pencil and a photocopier. I recall seeing, with some incredulity, the sleeve mounted in the window of a small record shop in Leytonstone and wondering if the whole thing was about to take off, and finally deciding, no, of course it wasn't.

But then 'Wouldn't It Be Good' came out and suddenly he was on *Top of the Pops* for the first time. I watched with a friend who had come round specially. The room positively thrummed with our nervousness, our proximity to this momentous event and our feeling of tragic non-involvement in it all. We leant close to the screen as the camera swung from whichever Radio 1 DJ was presenting that week, across the backs of the squawking audience and picked out Kershaw, alone amid the fake chrome piping and the flashy lights.

It shook us that he had no guitar round his neck. (*Top of the Pops* was completely mimed at this time.) Instead, he was wearing a white boiler suit and a pair of fingerless gloves and clutching his bunched fists up to his chest like someone working out with a set of hand-held dumb-bells. At the same time, he would bring up a knee in the manner recommended by aerobics videos. Who had taught him to do this? It was certainly never a feature of his performances at the Goose

and Firkin in Tollesbury. Staggered, we realized he was also
wearing a snood – a tube of netting, of the kind you sometimes see protecting strawberries, bunched around his neck.
(It became a trademark of sorts.) He looked terrified, at least
to us seasoned Kershaw-watchers, but he bopped and
clenched and wilfully concentrated his gaze on the floor,
and as the song faded and the camera drew back, there was
the usual hilarious applause. We went to the pub afterwards
and drank in silence, alone with our thoughts.

Later we learned how MCA had asked him to remove his
wedding ring for the show, so as not to dissuade girls from
having designs on him. Kershaw had refused (though he
either didn't mind or was powerless to prevent the company
lowering his age by four years, from twenty-eight to twenty-
four in its publicity material). We had lots of earnest conversations about this disgraceful and cynical manipulation of
someone's image, about how this typified the relentless men-
dacity of the music industry. Meanwhile, I was buying everything Kershaw's record company released. Out of loyalty, you
understand. Because of what we had. Because we went back.
I bought all three albums, obviously, but the singles, too. I
bought 'I Won't Let The Sun Go Down On Me' when it first
came out, and then again when it was re-released (for the
different cover). I had 'Human Racing' in a 7-inch double-
pack with a gatefold sleeve (I needed the additional live
tracks, naturally).

Most of these items were passed to me over the counter
of Cambridge Our-Price, where I had developed a special
dismissive smirk-and-shrug manoeuvre, intended to convey
that I was buying this stuff for my sister. Relatively recently, a
friend who was crouched at my shelves, casually flicking
a forefinger along the spines of my albums, suddenly froze
and then gently turned to face me, holding like some sporting

trophy the 12-inch re-mix of Nik Kershaw's 'Drum Talk'. His face grew bright with slowly evolving glee, as if he had just discovered that I still slept with a teddy bear.

There was a nationwide tour and, yes, I went. I caught him at Bristol's Colston Hall and sat sheepishly in the circle, possibly the only male there, pretty well the only person over thirteen, and certainly the only one not screaming. The transformation was bizarre and gripping – from someone who, after a show, used to coil his own guitar leads to someone who had to be hurried by minders from the building into a waiting van (thus not seeing me, hovering pathetically on the wet pavement, up to my waist in brats with autograph books and hoping to catch his eye).

His fame was short-lived, as fast fame so often is. But even as it raged, Kershaw was giving interviews about his discontent, his uneasiness in the role of pop puppet, his desire to be regarded as a songwriter, a man of integrity, a guitarist. You hear this a lot from pop puppets and it always sounds ungrateful. Still, Kershaw's was a poignant predicament. He had wanted to be Joni Mitchell and he had ended up being Woody out of the Bay City Rollers. *Radio Musicola*, his third album, was deliberately pitched over the heads of the teenies, who, in any case, had already moved on to A-Ha. It flopped. I was one of the only people who bought it. Soon after, Nik Kershaw hung up his snood.

We still thought about him a lot. We hoped he was OK. There were rumours of him living in a large house in the Essex countryside, stories of him working in LA as a producer. Occasionally he pitched up on records by other people – with Tony Banks, the keyboard player from Genesis, with Elton John. MCA flattered him with a greatest hits compilation in 1993. (I bought that, too, even though I'd already got everything on it.) And he wrote 'The One And Only', a big hit single for the blonde heart-throb Chesney Hawkes. I think he's probably all right.

I saw Nik Kershaw not so long ago. On a weekend away I found myself standing directly behind him in the queue for a table in a restaurant in Lyme Regis. It was one of those places furnished to look like a sitting-room (flowered carpet, horse brasses, paper napkins folded into fans) called something like Harriet's Pantry or The Fisherman's Nook. In other words, it wasn't very LA. But there was Kershaw in a party of four, handing his coat to the waitress. I froze and abruptly began communicating with my girlfriend in a series of disguised nods, exaggerated winks and little flicks of the elbow. Eventually we were directed to a table, where I explained in an absurd whisper that that small bloke over there in the expensive-looking leisurewear was Nik Kershaw, 'You know, the pop star.'

'What?' she said. 'You mean your old friend, the guy you used to hang around with?'

I started to look uncomfortable. She put down the menu and swivelled right round in her seat to get a look.

'Well, why don't you say hello?'

'Er . . .' I was improvising wildly. 'He probably doesn't want to be disturbed . . .'

'But, surely,' she said, 'he'll remember you.'

'Well, er, you know. It was a long time ago.'

She looked at me very hard and then returned to the menu.

I spent the entire meal eavesdropping. (The couple with him seemed to be his brother and sister-in-law, and Kershaw and his wife were talking about looking at properties in the area.) The Kershaw party got up to leave before we did and I toyed with offering him a sentence on the way out. But I said nothing, partly because I could already see the blank look with which he would greet my manufactured smile of greeting and partly because, well, what would I have said? 'Nik, you won't remember me, but before you were famous I used to follow you around in a faintly sinister manner.' He probably would have called the police.

I still wonder, though: now that the pop-star business is over, does his wife (Sherry, unless I'm much mistaken) call him 'Nick' or 'Nik'?

Randy Crawford

I was getting ready to go away to university, stuffing everything I owned – books, clothes, mugs, but more importantly,
hi-fi, albums and singles – into old grocery boxes and stack-
ing these downstairs, ahead of the load-up and the car journey. My father appeared in the kitchen door occasionally,
eyeing with mounting disbelief the high-rise cardboard
shanty town I had created on the hall carpet. He was apparently growing fearful for the suspension on his Austin 1800
and at the same time, I would hazard, he was developing a
mild, instinctual annoyance at the sight of all this pop music.
On what must have been roughly my seventeenth heart-
bursting trip down the stairs, he cleared his throat and asked,
with just a hint of irritation, 'Why don't you leave some of
the records behind?'

Slick with sweat, I was awkwardly lowering to the floor a
box the size of a cow, wedged tight with old singles. I froze
with it and looked up at him incredulously through straining,
watery eyes.

'You're never going to have time to play them all.'

I didn't know what to say. I mean, yes, of course, he was
right: it had never even entered my mind, as I cautiously
boxed these 150 or so albums, guarding as best I could
against scuffing, slippage, warping and the possibility of
random abuses in transit, that I would listen to all of them as
soon as I got the other end. Preposterous suggestion.
Assuming an average playing time of forty-five minutes per
album, and allowing for eight hours' sleep each night, it
would have taken me very nearly a week of chain record-play
to work my way once through the pile, from ABBA to XTC.

A whole morning and a good part of one afternoon of that would have been spent listening to 10cc. And though I didn't know much about university, I had gathered from the advanced literature I had received – the various college guides and student handbooks, gesturing warmly to a world of enlivening ritual and busy sociability – that I was going to be way too occupied for such a mindlessly self-absorbed project.

As it happened, most terms, I was so radically under-employed and room-bound I could have auditioned the entire contents of one of the larger branches of Our-Price. But, in principle, my father was absolutely correct. Of those 150 albums, carted laboriously to university (and back again at the end of each term because I wouldn't agree to store them there during vacations), I calculate that I played with any regularity, in the whole of my time as an undergraduate, six. They were: *Talking Book* by Stevie Wonder, *Innervisions* by Stevie Wonder, *Fulfillingness' First Finale* by Stevie Wonder, *Drums and Wires* by XTC, *Black Sea* by XTC and *Songs In The Key Of Life* by Stevie Wonder.

So why didn't I have the foresight to save myself some effort, forget the boxes and just take those six? Well, for one thing, that kind of foresight is impossible. True, I hadn't felt compelled to play *Drastic Plastic* by Bebop Deluxe for nearly four years – or, to put it another way, since the week after I bought it. But how could I guarantee that I would *never* want to hear it again? After all, that track on side one, 'Surreal Estate', had some weird synthesized gloops and strangenesses in it, not to mention a rather fetching rhythmical sway and, in fact, writing about it now kind of makes me want to slip downstairs and put it on, if only for a quick burst, just to remember how disappointing it was.

For another thing, it seemed to me that I needed the bulk of the collection on hand to make sense of any individual decisions I made within it. When I went to the shelf and took down, say, *Innervisions*, I was just as importantly electing *not* to play *Jailbreak* by Thin Lizzy or *Venus And Mars* by Wings or any of those albums that had seemed like a good idea at the time, but whose appeal had dwindled with age or the dawning of good sense. I was able to prize the wheat in part because of its contrast with this enormous, patiently accrued pile of old chaff.

'Why don't you leave some of the records behind?'

What did my father mean by badgering me with this rigorous good sense, this sunny logic? It wasn't as if he was a man without dominant obsessions of his own. I wondered whether this might not be the time to raise with him, for instance, his detailed interest in castles. I only wished briefly to burden the Austin 1800 with my fad, whereas he, on holidays and at weekends, cheerfully burdened the entire family with his. His plans for a day out invariably centred on some craggy medieval outhouse, currently home to a rook, or on some hole in a wall somewhere. (When you're a child and your father announces brightly, 'Right! We're off to see a castle', your mind promptly fills with images of towers, drawbridges, moats. Later you learn to adjust your expectations.)

Unfortunately, my father's hobby didn't end there, among the rubble. It went, literally, deeper. He wasn't just interested in visible ramparts; he was interested in *places where castles used to be* – earthworks, mounds, dimly discernible troughs, outlines of ex-keeps, former stone floors now merely dips. Invariably these places were well off the regular tourist trail and frequently inaccessible by car, or even horse. We would park some miles from where my father, after much furrow-browed cross-referencing between obscure maps and obscurer books, had scented a significant slope. And then we would yomp off *en famille*, Father keenly shouldering forward, the rest of us strung out behind, moving with the numbed limbs of those condemned to spend inordinate amounts of their free time slogging over a hump to look at a ridge.

My father (who, I think, must have been quietly planning a book) made notes on his observations and kept them in an impossibly complex card-index system. You would think that, when it came to other people's interests, someone persuaded to document non-existent buildings would have learned to reason not the need. But apparently not if pop music was involved.

So we looked at each other in silence, me hunched double over a box and him in the doorway, abstractedly tapping his fingertips together, until his suggestion died in the air between us.

'Well, hmmm. Maybe not,' he said quietly, and disappeared.

The irony was that I *was* leaving at least *some* records behind. Only the night before, I had enacted the Great Record Collection Purge of 1981, dealing my collection a blow the like of which it had never felt before and has never felt since. It happened while I was packing the albums into the boxes, fussing like a fool, trying to bunch them tightly so they would stand upright rather than slump and sag against the end of the box, where the combined weight of the leaning albums might bend the sleeve of the one on the outside, which I would have regarded as a disaster.

Additionally, I was having to make a series of crucial adjustments to ensure that any album visible above the cardboard at either end of the box was not one I needed to be ashamed of if anyone caught sight of it at any point on the journey. A scenario I could envisage too clearly featured me, a lonely and friendless new arrival on the college stairs, lugging a box of albums up the functional bareness of my new room and having to stand back against the wall to allow the passage of some other students descending, already in a noisy, chummy gang. One of them would be looking directly at the box in my arms as he came down and would flip my shoulder with the back of his hand on the way past and say, 'Hey! Jermaine Jackson! *Nice* one!' and the sound of their mocking laughter would resonate in the stairwell long after they had disappeared.

Guarding against this awful prospect involved fairly simple decisions at each point and seemed more than worthwhile. For instance, the sleeve of Talking Heads 77, if pressed into service as an endpiece, wouldn't, it seemed to me, give out the wrong signals, whereas I deemed it better to bury internally my copy of *The Eagles, Their Greatest Hits 1971–1975*, not because I didn't think it was a rather fine album in places, but because I wouldn't necessarily want the first thing you knew about me to be that I did.

But as the packing of the collection began to take on the form of an impromptu review of its contents, and as I looked with a gulp and a queasy quickening in the stomach, on yet another utterly crap or desperately juvenile or just badly winded pile of old pop (Gallagher and Lyle's *Love On The Airwaves*, for God's sake), it dawned on me that there were one or two things here I could do without.

Because this was university: a new horizon, a fresh start. I would be beginning from scratch with people who didn't need to know that I was the kind of person who owned ten albums (ten!) by 10cc; people to whom, if one or two albums should 'accidentally' get 'lost' somewhere, I would never have to explain limply that I had bought Randy Crawford's *Secret Combination* not because of the hit single 'Rainy

Night In Georgia', which I always thought was a bit of a wash-out, because I mistook the saccharine lure of her intense and continuous vibrato for the expression of soul, but chiefly because of the guitar solo in the middle of 'You Might Need Somebody' and particularly for the sudden ripple of notes it finds to unfurl across the gap half-way through.

And more urgently, with *Secret Combination* magically 'disappeared', Pinochet style, there would be no danger of my ever having to explain the pathetic, melancholic, doe-eyed relationship I had struck up with its cover: not so much the front cover, although the camera's startlingly tight focus in the pupil of Crawford's right eye and the one stray braid of hair performing a scribbly halo above her head were heart-breaking in their own way, but more especially the portrait on the back where she has her hand laid flat across her fore-head, and is laughing this fabulous, smiley laugh, like you've just cracked a great joke and she can't *believe* how much fun you are to be around.

How liberating – or so I thought – to be able to check in some of this personal baggage, tear up the ticket and never see it again.

So I stopped packing and instead began examining the collection in earnest with a view to snipping a few things out, reshaping it and, in the process, reshaping myself, whittling out a few unwanted bits of the past, fashioning something modern and streamlined. There, kneeling on the bedroom floor, I drew a long breath and purged.

And when I had finished purging, when the violence was done and the room calm, thirteen records lay severed from the pack. Thirteen! I smiled wryly to myself. Unlucky for them.

In time, I created some space at the bottom of my ward-robe and committed these albums to the dark. Which is where they remained until recently when I started thinking about them again and returned home to retrieve them for the sake of this book. I had long since removed nearly everything else of mine from that wardrobe and it was full of my mother's clothing and bric-à–brac overspills from other rooms. But parting the curtain provided by a hanging dress and shifting aside what seemed to be a completely unused wine-cooler, I exposed them, preserved in the condition in which they had been left, these relics of the purge.

The thirteen were:

Status Quo: *Hello* (1973) and *Rockin' All Over the World* (1977)

I think this is self-explanatory. Yes, I could have taken these albums to university with me, but I could also have spent the whole of the first year walking about in a T-shirt displaying the message 'Nerd'. Following the Live Aid concert of 1985, which Status Quo opened, there was a nanosecond in which you could just about have passed off possession of at least the second of these albums as somehow charity-related. In 1981, though, the Quo were simply sad old bores, who had entered a strangely mellow phase. Having one of their early albums would have been bad enough; having a mid-period one, complete with the track 'Rockers Rollin'', which was imaginatively restricted, even by the Quo's own impeccable standards of artistic stasis ... well, this just wasn't done.

Why did I have them? They were, of course, mementoes of those nights at the Embassy Suite, sonic souvenirs of Coca-Cola and Brut. These were the things that came to mind on the night of the purge, which is why, pushing aside a pair of split plimsolls and jacket which had slid off its hanger, I tucked both these albums as far back into the wardrobe as they would go.

Heart: *Dreamboat Annie* (1976)

In 1985, after a long break and a personnel change, Heart returned as an all-American FM radio, soft-rock act and had a hit with a melodramatic anthem for the aspirational called 'These Dreams'. When they released *Dreamboat Annie*, however, they were a part-American, part-Canadian Fleetwood Mac: two chicks with long hair and flouncy dresses, two blokes with long hair and bare chests. The song 'Crazy On You', played repeatedly on the pirate station Radio Caroline, had enjoyed a vogue among my peers in the middle years at school, largely because it seemed to speak to us about the fetid crushes we were all developing at a rate of approximately three per day. If I was going to allow people to see me with this, though, I might just as well go the whole hog and take along my old Charlie Brown books and the unevenly glazed pottery ashtray I made in the fourth form.

Supertramp: *Crime Of The Century* (1974), *Crisis? What Crisis?* (1975) and *Breakfast In America* (1979)

As I would like to make clear, post-punk, Supertramp were a complete no-go area – no matter how fond you were of the piano break in 'School', no matter how suckered you might have been by the vocal ad libs at the end of 'The Logical Song' ('la la la logical', etc). So in one swift move, I canned their entire top-level career, bar one album. You may wonder why I didn't also dump *Even In The Quietest Moments*, which fell between *Crisis? What Crisis?* and *Breakfast in America*. The answer is: only because I didn't have it.

Electric Light Orchestra: *A New World Record* (1976)

Abandoned on the grounds, again, that it would command about as much respect among my new peers as a Garfield pyjama case and matching slippers. 'Goodbye, Jeff Lynne,' I muttered, 'and good luck.'

Wild Cherry: *Wild Cherry* (1976)

It's lesson one: never buy an album on the strength of a single. And it's amazing how I've failed to learn this, despite wasting good money on *Wild Cherry* by Wild Cherry. The single in this instance was 'Play That Funky Music, White Boy' – which one came to realize was self-serving and politically suspect, but which also featured a vocalist, Robert Parissi, who sounded like he had been gargling staples. Somewhere during the making of this album, Parissi ran out of staples and ended up just gargling. And I ended up wasting £2.99.

It is true that plenty of other irredeemably bad albums escaped the Purge of '81, but what seems to have swung it the other way for *Wild Cherry* by Wild Cherry was the album's sleeve, an item of such abject tastelessness that perfectly acceptable household objects began to look cheap and nasty in its vicinity. The cover image is a giant close-up of a woman's lips, given about sixteen coats of red lipstick and then one final top-coat of clear polyurethane to render them shinier than a brand new post-box. She is seen sliding a particularly glutinous cocktail cherry between her teeth. It's just a hunch, but possibly this was meant to be some sort of sexual reference. Anyway, it was out on its ear.

John Lennon: *Imagine* (1971)

Now, I was on good form when I shelved this one. Remember, this is the autumn of 1981: it's less than a year since Lennon was murdered in New York. The television has hardly stopped repeating that blowsy film of him singing 'Imagine' while wandering in a white suit through white-painted, furniture-free rooms. The rush of otherwise intelligent people determined to account for him, in death, as not just a surly rocker with a lippy wit, but as a philosopher and sage, was still at full flood. And the *Imagine* album, containing the poisonous, anti-McCartney song 'How Do You Sleep?' and with Lennon all misty-eyed and clouded out on the cover, was widely held to be talismanic, nakedly revealing, the real thing.

Me? I reread the statement on the rear of the sleeve – 'imagine the clouds dripping. dig a hole in your garden to put them in. yoko '63' – and binned it.

Rupert Holmes: *Partners in Crime* (1979)

This one virtually flipped off the shelf of its own accord and walked to the wardrobe with its hands up. Perhaps you remember Holmes's big hit, 'Escape (the Piña Colada Song)', or perhaps you have suppressed the memory. 'Escape' is about a man who is bored with his woman and so furtively advertises for another in the personal columns, listing his preferences (making out in the dunes, getting caught in the rain, Piña Colada – Piña Colada!) and a woman replies, saying she loves that stuff, and they fix a date and, guess what? It's his wife. To think I fell for this corn. Even Rupert himself doesn't look convinced by it on the sleeve, neurotically fondling his bottle-thick glasses. (Imagine Leo Sayer sapped of all self-belief.) And look at that tragically recent date. I couldn't even plead innocence on this one.

On the night of the purge, Rupert Holmes got to learn a lesson about fame: one minute you're at the top of the American singles chart, the next you're at the foot of somebody's cupboard.

Crown Imperial: The Royal Choral Society and the London Philharmonic Orchestra conducted by Sir Arthur Bliss and Andrew Davis perform music from the Last Night of the Proms.

Believe me, please, when I say I got this record for Christmas when I was ten. It must have been the year my parents noticed me enjoying the television broadcast from the Albert Hall and slipped me this in a doomed attempt to wean me off T. Rex and encourage in me an interest in classical music. As far as that Proms experience went, it's just possible I was more impressed by the streamers and the laddish behaviour than by the formidable coloratura of the woodwind. Now, this record simply screamed ignorance. I imagined, correctly, that at university I would meet people who genuinely understood classical music and who knew better than to respect albums on the Classics for Pleasure label.

And that's not to mention the possible royalist, fascist, militarist, jingoist overtones, all threatening to get very ugly indeed. This record had nothing going for me. It was closeted accordingly.

Genesis: *A Trick of the Tail* (1976) and *And Then There Were Three* (1978)

In as much as I had any sense of what a stereotypical male student might be, I had him figured for a Genesis fan. (I also reckoned there was a high possibility he would have that Athena poster of the woman tennis player showing her bum.) So I pulled these two in a pre-emptive strike. Fickle of me, when you consider how avidly I had argued in the sixth form – and against the prevailing intellectual grain, I should say – that the band's decision to down-size from blown-up eleven-minute, pseudo-classical epics to condensed, three- or four-minute pop songs was the best move they ever made. Now it was time to distance myself from these arguments altogether. (And, in any case, there's only so many times you can listen to 'Squonk'.)

As it turned out, 10cc and Randy Crawford escaped. They made the cut. And so did *Jailbreak* and *Venus And Mars*. And I think this is because I realized, even as the purge raged, that there is, in the end, a limit to the extent to which you can rewrite your past, unless you are a Stalin or trying to get into politics. It's like trying to claim you are the sum of your edited highlights, when maybe you ought to be saying: 'Yep, look, *How Dare You* by 10cc, there it is. It was me, I did it, I went out and bought it and I played it a lot, and I still don't really know why, but I want you to know that I take that on board about myself and I'm sorry, more sorry than I can communicate without physical gestures borrowed from other times and cultures. I am simply hoping to go on from here, make something with this and out of this, rather than compressing or twisting myself in its denial.'

So they are still with me, the thirteen. It doesn't surprise me that I didn't attempt to sell or exchange them. Their combined resale value, then as now, would have been ten pence (excluding the Lennon album, for which, given the posthumous clamour, I reckon I could have held out for at least twenty-five). Also, the transaction was potentially embarrassing, involving a public demonstration before the exchange-store assistant (and maybe with onlooking customers) that you once called these items your own.

But neither did it occur to me – or not to the extent that I acted on it – to take more drastic measures, to melt these betraying items down, or sack them up and dump them in a river. No. What I chose to do was to squirrel them away where I knew I could always return to them. And that tells its own story. They say, with respect to the law, you can run but you can't hide. With respect to my old records, I could hide, but I couldn't run. Now, as then, I have to live with it: there is a part of me which is for ever Rupert Holmes.

The Orphans of Babylon, take 2

The summer of 1982: a big break for the Orphans. An old schoolfriend, now the social secretary at Exeter University, gets us on to the bill for the end-of-term ball, supporting the Boomtown Rats. Or, at least, playing in a room adjacent to the main hall directly after the Rats have finished their set (estimated time 1.30 a.m.).

During the day of the gig, while the stages are being set up, we hang around in the hall trying to look casual about Bob Geldof being there. This is Geldof post-Boomtown glory days and pre-Band Aid but we're still thrilled to be alongside him and we take it in turns to go out on to the steps and walk past him while he's lying there in the sun, unshaven, reading the *Daily Star*.

Later we catch the start of the Rats' set and are impressed to see that Geldof hasn't bothered to change before going on: he's in the clothes he's been wearing all day. Then we go off to prepare for our own show.

Our opening is timed perfectly. Just as we go on stage, the crowd from the main hall floods the room on its way out from the Rats' show. We give them 'Teaching People To Fly (Ain't Easy)'. And everybody, but *everybody*, leaves. They all zoom out at the far end, to the comedy room, the casino room, the bar, anywhere.

Afterwards, we agree that you couldn't have cleared that room faster if you had used a water cannon.

Sade

Sometimes it's easy to buy records, but most of the time it's intimidating and degrading. The browsing business, that's fine. I can cope with browsing. Or at least I can cope until someone comes and stands right beside me just as I've started flicking guiltily through the section devoted to A Flock of Seagulls. What's difficult is knowing that, at some point, I'm going to have to take something to the counter. Because at the counter I'm going to have to hand a sleeve or a CD case over to a record-shop assistant, and with certain purchases I might just as well be passing them an instant data read-out on my personality, paying particular attention to its weaknesses and its least-focused desires.

At Christmas 1984, Geoff and I both managed to get holiday work at Parrot Records in Colchester, helping out with the seasonal rush. By this time, Parrot had closed down the poky shop where we used to spend lunch-hours and had moved over into the centre of town, into a larger store with aspirations to look as shiny and accessible as an Our-Price. And rude Nigel? Nigel was long gone. A management ruling insisted that the only records played in the shop were the top-selling chart albums, to create an atmosphere in which the broadest range of shoppers would feel comfortable. Any record with 'fuck' in it, or even a discord, had to wait until after five-thirty, when the doors were locked and you were sweeping the floor and wondering whether you'd make the five-fifty bus home.

That Christmas, a few rather serious-looking people came in to choose from the extremely limited range of items in the shop's plastic tray of Compact Discs. (Fools! we thought. It'll never catch on.) But mostly people were buying the big ones – the first Sade album (*Diamond Life*), *Now That's What I Call Music 3*, *Can't Slow Down* by Lionel Richie, *Legend* by Bob Marley and the Wailers. We emptied shelf after shelf of those.

And it was really busy in the shop, most of the time, so it was hard not to resent anyone who said, 'I wonder if you could help me . . .' Because this inevitably meant getting out the catalogue while the queue built up and looking up the title or the artist on an *old record*, which probably wasn't in stock, for some sap who didn't manage to buy it the first time. Much easier to reach behind you for the Sade album. And another Sade album after that. And another Sade album after that. And another Sade album after that.

I took a camera in one day and got a picture of Geoff behind the record shelves at the back of the counter. He is holding up the sleeve of Deep Purple's *24 Carat Purple* and has scrunched up his face as if attempting to pass a kidney stone. Some customer has brought this sleeve to the counter and is now waiting for Geoff to fill it, oblivious to the fact that the shop assistant is currently round the back, posing for a richly contemptuous photograph.

Knowing that that kind of thing goes on, how could I not be nervous about record shops? How could anyone not be?

The Cocteau Twins

A pop trivia question for you: what do Martin Fry, the singer with the Sheffield group ABC, and I have in common?

I'll have to hurry you.

Give up?

The answer is: both of us went down with the same type of cancer! And within months of each other, too! Martin contracted Hodgkin's disease three albums into his career, between *How To Be A Zillionaire* and *Alphabet City*. I got it in my second year at university and before I'd had any albums out at all. (Though I had all of Martin's.)

I'd like to be able to ascribe my developing a potentially fatal illness at this point to the creative chaos, the sheer weight of zaniness in the life I was leading – the pressure of all those Orphans of Babylon gigs, the inevitable overspill of the wild nights of rock'n'roll and chicks till dawn. Unfortunately Hodgkin's disease is less glamorous. If you're going to get it, you get it. During the glandular mayhem of early adulthood, your lymph glands throw a series of wild parties, before settling down for a quiet life. And in people like me and Martin Fry, the party goes on too long and gets nasty and the police have to be called.

It's a cancer but it doesn't exactly blow a fanfare on its arrival. I went down with something which felt just like flu, except when it passed it left half a golf ball under my arm. Only mildly concerned, I showed it to a GP who said, with heart-stopping cheerfulness, 'I think you'd better see a *proper* doctor.' And then there was a biopsy and a lot of worrying and I had to go back a week later for the results, sitting on my own in a day room, in a ward on the ninth floor of a

Cambridge hospital, a cup of hospital tea in my lap, waiting for the specialist to come round. And just knowing he'd got something big to say from the way he asked his students to wait outside the door.

I had to have my spleen removed. 'You don't need it,' the surgeon assured me. Your spleen is the size of your fist. I wondered how something as economically built as a human body could do without something the size of your fist. After all, you wouldn't happily agree to lose a body-part the size of your fist if the body-part in question was your fist. The doctor said I would be able to play the trumpet afterwards. Which was good news, because I wasn't able to before.

'Do you smoke?' he asked.

'No,' I lied, because my father was sitting beside me and he didn't know. Later, I crept back on my own and told the doctor I had lied about the smoking.

He said the disease didn't have anything to do with smoking anyway. So I carried on smoking. 'Maybe cut back to cigars just before the operation,' he advised me, cheerfully.

Tests conducted at the same time as the operation showed the disease had not spread. I had it in one place. I was reliably informed that you want it in one place, or less. Then you can go at it with radiotherapy. I had that for a month. It wasn't a problem. It was just like having an X-ray every day. At the start of the third week, you're feeling a bit knackered, but you're carried along by the fact that the lump is already visibly smaller, shrinking daily. A doddle.

Only they missed a bit. They didn't irradiate a sufficiently large area, so a year later the lump grew back and this time it had to be attacked with some fully fledged, properly nuclear chemotherapy: six months of bi-weekly injections and eighteen tablets every day, with vomiting, painful fluid retention, permanent out-to-lunchness, mild hair-fallout and almost complete loss of taste – my Lou Reed phase. And, after that little lot, Hodgkin finally fucked off.

In the middle of all this I was listening to *Treasure*, an album by the Cocteau Twins. The Cocteau Twins were reliably mournful – muted, chiming guitars, underwater bass, just-out-of-sick-bed rhythms. I don't know where Liz Fraser's voice was coming from, but no one was having fun there. Maybe this was the wrong musical tactic for me right now. I had postponed my university course for a year to concentrate on doing nothing. Perhaps there was an obvious argument for breaking out the Stax, punching a hole in the gloom. Or maybe I should have gone another route and played nothing but the most calmative, late Steely Dan, just let its fine spray play into the room.

But, typically, my concern was not what effect the music would have on my life so much as what effect my life would have on the music. I was familiar from childhood with the way that music heard while ill – lying in bed with a high temperature and the radio on – tends, whenever heard again, to be redolent of whatever you were suffering from when you heard it: hot eyes, clammy sheets, medicinal tangs, fever fuddle. It's another sense in which pop songs are catchy: they catch whatever you have. But, unlike you, they never quite shake it off. Even now, if I hear Laurel and Hardy's 'On The Trail Of The Lonesome Pine' I can begin to feel physically uneasy, simply because, during its peak period of prominence on the airwaves in 1975, I was stuffed away with Radio 1 and a middle-ear infection. Imagine, then, inadvertently tainting in this way some of the most important pieces of music you knew by playing them while under the influence of chemotherapy. Too risky, surely. I wasn't about to let this kind of associational virus loose among my entire record collection.

It wasn't that, during this grim period, I never used pop's optimism to lever myself out. A friend bought me a Walkman to cheer me up, the first one I ever had. It had struck me, even before I owned one, that the Walkman was, after the in-car stereo, probably the finest technical achievement of the twentieth century – about as refined as man was ever going to get. Without having to go in for bells on our fingers and bells on our toes (cumbersome and, let's face it, not all that satisfying, musically speaking), we could have music wherever we went. On my way to and from the endless clinics and surgeries, I played almost to ribbons an old cassette of Deniece Williams's ineffably joyful 'Let's Hear It For The Boy' (the way the words snap against the beat!) and sat there, clamped between the skinny plastic headphones, enjoying its friendly, life-affirming fizz. I could stare out of the windows of the bus and the world would turn into a video, which is not the kind of perspective you would want all the time, maybe, but which seemed wondrously absorbing at this point.

For the most part, though, upbeat and ritzy kinds of music weren't what I needed. Somehow they had the opposite of the desired effect. Let's say that, more often than not, directly after a lengthy injection of virulent and purgative chemicals, I wasn't in the mood for Donna Summer. Music that had seemed to be about a life which was excitingly unattainable now just seemed to be about a life which was depressingly unattainable. Hence the appeal of the Cocteau Twins whose music appeared to me to be about a life which was perfectly attainable – already attained, indeed – and utterly depressing. I gathered myself into its velvety folds. (And to listen to it now is to drag all that back, so I tend not to.)

I also played *A Walk Across The Rooftops*, a painstakingly miserable album by the Blue Nile on which the music has been scrupulously pared away to the noise of someone tapping despairingly on a radiator, while a voice just about gathers the energy to sing above it. It's an astonishing record, especially if you've got cancer. And *Hats*, which the band released an impressively reluctant five years later, was, if anything, even better. If Samuel Beckett had ever gone into the studio, he would have come out sounding like the Blue Nile. I cherished our moments together. (The Blue Nile I can still listen to: they proved too good, too resilient to be used and disposed of.)

I seemed to spend a lot of time listening, not to music but to my own noises, awake to every twinge and throb, wondering whether the uninvited guest in my system had kept a copy of the doorkey and was about to let himself in again. Illness centres you in yourself. For one determined on so many projects of self-escape and self-reinvention, this was a bitter set-back. It was hard to know what to do with the misery of it. There was nothing romantic about this cancer. Utterly arbitrary, it didn't have a narrative. It was just blank-faced and dutiful, a civil servant among diseases. So I went deep into some glum pop music and constructed what stories I could there.

That's not how it is for everybody, I concede. Some people, after brushing with a potentially fatal disease, burst forth from the clinic entirely remade. They come out of it in a hurry to live. They shine with purpose and commitment. They go straight to their K-Tel compilations and dance, dance, dance. Somehow, cancer failed to come good for me in quite this way, failed to act as a Brasso of the soul. Afterwards, I looked around me and it was still a toss up between *Songs In The Key Of Life* and *Innervisions* for my favourite album. I still couldn't see the point of jazz. I still couldn't play the guitar. But there was a new sheen on at least some aspects of my life: like friends and relations and a National Health Service. Especially a National Health Service.

Madonna

What shocked me about Madonna was not the pictures of her trussed in rubber, licking people and leaning over a wall with no knickers on. These and the other images in *Sex*, the metal-covered, ring-bound photo-album she published in 1992, seemed to me fairly inevitable, given everything else we already knew about her.

And I wasn't especially perturbed either by her repeated use of the word 'fuck' in the interview she gave David Letterman on American television in 1994, which got transcribed and quite widely reported in Britain. What was defended as the noise of a provoked shock-artist, a righteous disturber of our complacency, sounded to me more like the hum of a smoothly operating publicity machine.

No, what really shook me about Madonna was that sequence in the movie *In Bed With Madonna* where she got her dad up on stage. That took nerve. You've got to hand it to her. I could never have done that.

As my life in showbiz shaped up, I seemed to be taking my parents along for the ride. At primary school, I put them through utterly balls-aching school concerts – shrill-winded recorder orchestras, triangle bands, buzzing Stylophone combos, after which, feigning gratitude and pride – they limped into the car park with numb buttocks and tinnitus. As if that wasn't enough, at secondary school I unsparingly sought parts in terrible, unabridged productions of *Julius Caesar* and sat my parents on hard seats in draughty halls while kids wrapped in Alcan wandered around forgetting their lines. The only point of being in these things was so that your parents could watch you at it. If they had refused to attend that North East Essex Combined Primary Schools Celebration of Christmas gig at Essex University in 1971 . . . well, I would have been ruined.

But when I moved up to rock, something snapped. In the heyday of the Orphans of Babylon, and later with the Cleaners from Venus, I would have cancelled a show rather than put my mother and father on the guest list, assuming they had ever wanted to come, which they didn't. Even so, somewhere mid-adolescence it began to send a chilly hand up my spine to think they might witness me on stage – caught somewhere between what I was and some idea of what I wanted to be. The shame would have been all too much. I was quite ready, in the wake of my eventual success in the world arena, to secure them a luxury waterside home near Henley, parental relocation being one of the first commitments of the top-earning rocker. But, in the meantime, I didn't want them in the audience.

The Orphans of Babylon, take 3

A letter from Geoff:

I've got a tape of our performance Saturday last and it's OK. New songs needed? Yes. It's the 25th, and I'm listening through our old songs to find new live material, and there's plenty of it: e.g. 'Call Of The Mountain Sock', '(Not Surprising Really) She's Only Four Days Old' and many more. I think we should drop the lot and keep 'Teaching People To Fly (Ain't Easy)' and '30, 40 Or More' as encores, you?

As a final thought before he signed off, Geoff wrote:

I thought if you could play some of the numbers enclosed, we could become famous in Northants.

'The enclosed' were a few pieces of sheet music, stapled in a stiff, pale yellow cardboard cover on which was printed, in a rudimentary typeface:

A Collection of Scandinavian Folk Dances
Introduced at the English Scandinavian Summer School
of Physical Education
Published by the Nonington College of Physical Education

In the index, on the inside cover, Geoff had underlined in blue felt tip some of the titles: 'Knurrifas', 'Kliplev Marked', 'Heidilit, Kom Herom' and 'With My Hand I'm Clapping'.

The envelope also contained, without explanation, two black and white negatives (which, when you held them up to the light, were clearly portrait photographs of Geoff's mother and father) and a sizeable wad of fluff.

I think it was around here that I began to have serious doubts about the long-term future of the Orphans of Babylon.

Scritti Politti

I go into record shops a lot – any record shop, anywhere – sometimes to buy records, sometimes just to browse, but frequently to indulge in other, less readily comprehensible activities which have nothing to do with buying, or seeking things to buy, at all.

Very often I go into a record shop and look at records I already own. I actively seek out in the browser bins copies of albums which I already have and which I have no intention of buying again, and look at them. Normally I won't trouble to remove them from the rack or bin; I'll just flick to where they sit, open up a little viewing space and then pause, not really to think or anything, but as if seeking some kind of pointless confirmation: 'Yep, here's Scritti Politti's *Cupid And Psyche '85*. In front of the board saying Scritti Politti. In the S section.'

I don't find this behaviour easy to explain, though clearly there is wishfulness involved, that if only you didn't already have this record you would be able to buy it. Chiefly, though, I suspect it is descended from a piece of primary-school playground business wherein someone would skim through their bubblegum cards/football stickers or similar collectables while someone else stood at their shoulder announcing the relation of this collection to their own: 'Goddit. Goddit. Goddit. Haven't goddit. Goddit', etc. But in the playground, this performance at least served a practical purpose, as a prelude to swapping or some other form of trading, whereas my pop-fuelled adult version feels much more like the conduct of an addict, standing there in isolation at the browsers, reciting to himself a numb mantra: 'Goddit. Goddit. Goddit . . .'

Still more frequently, I go into record shops and look for records which I know do not exist. I comb the sections of the display devoted to favoured artists, with whose works I am completely familiar and from whom I well know there is nothing new due, as if, by an amazing warp of luck, I will turn up something of which I wasn't already aware – some extraordinary Norwegian import, some Chinese pressing of studio out-takes unwritten about in this country. This indulgence arises, I think because however much music you have by the artists you like it is never quite enough, and the prospect of cheating the release schedules or history and opening up whole new avenues for exploration is an enticing one. So it is that I will find myself in, say, the cubicle-sized branch of Our Price on Victoria Station in London, which doesn't stock all that many records that exist, let alone records which don't, trying to will into being a third album by the Bible, or some mysteriously unmentioned Take 6 recording.

From here, it's a short step to record fairs. If you've got the record thing, and you've got it bad, then eventually you reach a degree of craving that mere record shops alone will not satisfy and the next thing you know, you're pitching up at town halls and hotel function rooms where dealers congregate to flog their rarities and oddities and trash – the vinyl junkie's equivalent of the car-boot sale. In the early 1980s I got to be quite a swinger on the record-fair circuit. I was well placed to score: at the time, I had a girlfriend in Bristol, a university course in Cambridge and a family in Colchester. With a very simple piece of co-ordination involving my weekend arrangements and the small ads in the *NME*, I could get my attendance up around the three fairs per month mark, no problem.

Record fairs represent an alternative shopping experience and yet are as uniform as any branch of Our Price: the same trestle tables, the same preponderance of Bruce Springsteen bootlegs, the same poorly written section-dividers, the same people in anoraks sifting round-eyed through box after box of other people's junk. I used them most concertedly to expand on all fronts my collection of XTC records, which had fast become my central preoccupation. My commitment to this band had created an appetite which would not be content with straightforward albums and singles alone.

I picked up a copy of *Guillotine*, a Virgin label sampler on 10-inch vinyl which included the otherwise unavailable XTC track 'Traffic Light Rock', one minute and forty seconds long. I found an American radio copy of 'Generals And Majors' on 7-inch which had 'Generals And Majors' on both sides so that even the most cack-handed DJ could never accidentally play the wrong side. It joined the other copies of 'Generals And Majors' I already had, on the Black Sea album and on the British 7-inch double pack. I purchased an Australian pressing of 'Making Plans For Nigel'. I rootled out a bright red flexidisc, originally given away with *Smash Hits*, with 'The Olympian' by the Skids on one side and XTC's 'Ten Feet Tall' on the other – not the original album version but a different one, rerecorded for the American market and featured on the B-side of the single 'Wait Till Your Boat Goes Down', which I already had. I jumped like lightning at a copy of *Five Senses*, a 12-inch EP released in Canada, featuring five fairly hard-to-find tracks, all of which I already owned but, importantly, not in this form. And with a gasp, which had to do with both delight and incipient bankruptcy, I spent eight pounds on a 7-inch version of 'Statue Of Liberty' in original picture sleeve and *signed by all four members of the band*.

Record fairs plunged me into the grubby waters of the bootlegged live recording. Early on in my time as Lord of the Fairs, I happened on a cassette of Stevie Wonder in concert in Brighton – not the entire concert, just as much of it as would fit haphazardly on a C90. Unfortunately, as I discovered when I got the tape home, the bootlegger had been seated close to one of those people who release a loud, sentimental groan of recognition ('Naaah!') at the beginning of each number. 'Lately I have had the strangest feeling,' sings Stevie. 'Naaah!' says the man in the audience, and so on, for an hour and a half.

But I was undeterred. Needless to say, my bootleg-buying also took on a sizeable XTC dimension. At four pounds a throw I picked up various unlistenable-to cassettes of them in concert: at Marconi Youth Club in Swindon, at the Hammersmith Odeon, at somewhere unspecified in Holland. And I bought a vinyl double album featuring a recording made at a club called Hurrahs in New York in 1980 but manufactured in Watford. It came in an ugly thick cardboard sleeve, set me back twelve pounds and responded poorly to playing. Somewhere at the heart of its storm of hiss was a barely audible throb, as if the concert had been recorded by someone pressing a cheap dictaphone up against the venue's outside wall. I'm not sure I ever made it as far as disc two. I was, needless to say, delighted with it. Possession was the point, not listening to the thing.

Soon, not even record fairs were getting me to the place I needed to be. Shaky, lank-haired and bleached of face, I turned to mail order. I found in a fanzine the address of a dealer in Amsterdam and, having contacted him for his catalogue, arranged for him to send me no fewer than three C90s filled with Andy Partridge's home demo recordings and various scraps of bootlegs of XTC playing live in Sydney. I stored these alongside my own tapes of a Partridge appearance on the panel of *Roundtable*, Radio 1's Friday evening singles-review programme, and a set of recordings of him in a short-lived regular slot on *The Janice Long Show*, playing a spoof agony aunt. I'm not sure I've ever listened back to these tapes, but at the time it seemed a matter of some importance to have them.

Of course, this passion grows dim on you. It's too intense to sustain, perhaps. The last XTC single I bought on both 7- *and* 12-inch was 'Grass' in 1986. Then I missed a couple, settling, with a vague sense of deprivation, for the album versions only, before the singles side of the collection finally fizzled out with 'The Mayor of Simpleton' on 12-inch in 1989. But it still irks me that I never found the gatefold insert which accompanied the first 15,000 copies of *Drums And Wires* and which included the lyrics to that album and to the two that preceded it. It grates that I failed to find a copy of *Black Sea* that still had the plain green paper outer-bag in which the earliest batch of releases came. Nowadays I cannot imagine getting interested in any new band to the extent that I would track down ruthlessly and pay money I couldn't afford for a Sweden-only, limited edition, coloured vinyl 12-inch, in original picture sleeve with poster insert. If I'm feeling feisty, I will claim that this is a reflection on the indifferent quality of new bands but I know deep down that it's a reflection on me, not rousable to those heights any more, but not out of the game either: left instead with a dull ache that throbs, at a record fair or second-hand store, each time I see one of those XTC rarities again – they're not that rare, obviously – and wish that I didn't already have it so that I could buy it.

Then again, in other respects I'm in as deep as I ever was. The other day, I was in Colchester with my mother. We had gone into the town centre so that she could choose a birthday present, but as we were passing the George Hotel in the High Street, I noticed the placard leaning up against the door:

I gave my mother an apologetic look and said, 'Ten minutes?'. And she raised her eyebrows but said she would meet me in Marks & Spencer's. So I paid my 25p and went in. The usual scene: a couple of sad-looking people in anoraks doing the slow drift, boxes of junk, endless Bruce Springsteen live recordings. And, of course, the minutes flew and by the time I got to Marks & Spencer's, my mother was standing in the doorway, looking steamed up.

She said: 'If I'd known you were going to be that long, I would have gone upstairs.'

The conviviality rather drained out of our afternoon.

Still, I got a Carleen Anderson CD single in a broken case for two pounds, and a vinyl Minnie Ripperton album, completely wrecked, both outside and in, and utterly unplayable. Only three pounds, though. Where else can you find bargains like that these days?

The Cleaners from Venus

The word on the street about Martin Newell was that he was an anarchist and also the Colchester district's top-ranking songwriter. When I met him he was running a parallel career as a daytime washer-up in one of the Colchester district's top-ranking restaurants on North Hill.

I was at a loose end in that empty year between school and university which some people use for purposes both challenging and instructive but which I mostly spent wandering around Colchester town centre in a daze. Sometimes I wandered around the back of Newell's restaurant to visit a friend who worked on vegetable preparation. He introduced me to Newell, on dishes. I would walk up a dank side-alley and tap at the restaurant's back door, and there he was, at the sink, in skinny black jeans and a T-shirt. I leaned in at the doorway, midway between the smell of the hot suds and the stench off the bins. Radio 1 was always on loud.

Newell could cover more topics of conversation in half an hour than most people find breath for in a couple of months. He managed this by talking in torrents and by carefully minimizing the time in which he did any listening. Stroppy anti-Establishment rants mingled with outlandish tributes to the genius of the Beatles and the occasional smutty joke. Periodically he would break off to say, 'Now *this* is a good song', nodding up towards the radio.

He was eight years older than me, an unusual gap for members of a pop partnership, which is what we became, four years after these first meetings. When I joined the Cleaners from Venus, Newell told people we were 'pop's first father-and-son duo'. The distance between us wasn't unprecedented: Donny Osmond was eight years younger than Alan, the oldest member of the Osmonds, and Marie and Little Jimmy were younger still.

I have often wondered how different our relationship might have been if I had known Newell during the 1970s, when he was a fully paid-up, card-carrying glam-rocker and when his father, a gruff army man, who failed to share his son's delight in long hair and eye-liner, would eye the glad-ragged Newell up and down and remark, 'What are my friends going to say? Does it talk or does it bark?' Under-encouraged in his desire to make it as a spangly, pouting rock god, Newell had buried himself in his bedroom with his guitar. If he was still playing when his father returned from work, there would be a kick on the bedroom door – his father's way of saying, 'I'm home now. Let's have some peace.' Once Newell heard his mother protesting on his behalf.

'But he's composing,' she said.

'I don't care if he's *de*composing,' his father replied. 'He can shut that racket up.'

But he didn't shut up: he went on to become the Colchester district's top-ranking songwriter. In 1981, Newell was calmer than the teenager who ran around taking more amphetamine than was strictly necessary. Yet his hair was still long and dyed a startling aubergine and he still fancied the odd dab of eye-paint on occasions (just a lick of black along the lower rim). The glam clothes were long gone and he had taken to wearing a dusty top hat and tailcoat combo – Dickensian chic. Also, he was married, with two children from his wife's previous relationship, though family life didn't appear to have deposited the conventional load on his shoulders. His wife was a former doctor with an interest in the occult, who caused quite a stir in the village where they lived when she cured the family rabbit of myxomatosis by serving it some kind of leafy soup. She read Newell's tarot for him periodically, looked after his yin and his yang and discussed with him the possibility that the two of them had met in another life.

Newell no longer gigged in local bands. He was ex-Plod (yes, the same Plod that Relic supported at Lexden Church Hall, though, by then, sadly, Newell had left the band, to be replaced by a Marc Bolan lookalike). And he was ex-Gyp, with whom he had done his glam-rock best to come over like Rod Stewart, tarting himself up in a Transit van, squeezing himself into tight trousers in the unhappy confines of toilet stalls. Gyp played the kind of halls where the manager would come up before the band started and say, 'Can you play 'eavy?'

Now Newell spent virtually all his spare time in or around the sail loft he rented in Wivenhoe, by the river just to the east of Colchester, where he brewed his own beer ('Newell's Old Peculiar'), listened to the Beatles, tended the ducks and chickens in the garden and made candles, which he sold in bulk to restaurants. And on Mondays, his day off, he did pop music under the name of the Cleaners from Venus.

Just like the candles and the beer, the Cleaners from Venus were, before I joined, a kind of cottage industry. They didn't play live. The Cleaners from Venus was just a collective name for anyone who recorded music with Newell in his upstairs room on his four-track Portastudio – Newell's one concession to consumer materialism, to which he was otherwise vociferously opposed. (It was one of the ironies of the next four years that Newell had albums out but nothing to play them on.)

The Cleaners from Venus was Newell's beast – he wrote the songs, called the shots, dictated the pace – although originally he had a regular collaborator called Lol, who lived next door and played the drums. Similarly eclectic in his energies, Lol had once spent a weekend painting his Hoover. Eventually he moved to Bath, but not before the Cleaners from Venus had filled several cassettes with tunes and spread them about through a network to which Newell referred darkly as 'the cassette underground'. Newell would mail out tapes to his contacts and the contacts would copy the tapes up, sell them on and send Newell the money. Newell reckoned that some 250 people had bought mail-order-only copies of *In The Golden Autumn* (1983), many of them in Germany where there was already a hardcore postal Cleaners from Venus following. This was Newell's way of 'subverting the corrupt, inept and lazy music-industry system'. One day, he thought, all music would be made this way.

The point about these cassettes was, they were brilliant. They seemed to set themselves standards of songwriting which pop elsewhere had pretty much forgotten. You had to tune your ear to them – they were not like your other records. They weren't even trying to compete, made as they were on cheap, piercingly trebly instruments, passed through badly wired effects units. But they were bristling with snappy harmonies and jangling guitar lines and catchy melodies marinated in the sixties. Newell's lyrics painted wistful pictures of England in the past, and sour and racy pictures of England in the present. What you got on a Cleaners tape was a rare coalition between hippie whimsy and back-street wrath. I was a fan long before I was a Cleaner. I bought them all.

In 1985, the year before I became an official band member, one of Newell's regular mail-order clients in Germany took the cassette version of a collection of songs called *Under Wartime Conditions*, pressed it up as a vinyl album and distributed it to the stores. Newell was jubilant. This was, he reckoned, a real anarchist's triumph, a giant petrol bomb through the record companies' corporate windows. An album of songs made in his house in his spare time, using only a raddled guitar, an old piano with drawing pins in its hammers, a bass which was a barely modified plank, and a rusty xylophone, had gone down the system's blindside and made it right into the shops. 'And', he said victoriously, 'no one with a pony-tail and stupid plastic glasses came anywhere near it.'

So this was the Martin Newell whom I joined full-time in the Cleaners from Venus: an angered pop guerrilla with his own agenda, a one-man music-biz resistance unit.

Contrast these bristling principles with my own musical attitude at this time, which was, roughly, 'fame at any price'. For two people about to set out on a journey into the world of pop, matters on which Newell and I held conflicting views were, I suppose, dangerously numerous. For example:

Newell: big on artistic integrity; vehemently opposed to anyone from a record company imposing a marketing strategy upon his music.

Me: ready to talk.

Newell: firmly averse, on well-founded left-wing principles, to wasting time and money in expensive foreign recording studios, 'like the rest of those pampered nancies'.

Me: the Bahamas look nice.

Newell: angry that machines have taken over many of the performance aspects of pop music, replacing its flawed but vital heart with a brutal perfectionism; concerned to re-establish a sixties ethic – energy first, accuracy second.

Me: unhealthily obsessed with the clean lines of Scritti Politti's *Cupid And Psyche*, an album on which nobody does anything unless a computer says so.

Newell: strictly anti-producer.

Me: hoping very shortly to have Trevor Horn's home phone number.

Newell: strictly anti-touring, on the grounds that it is unnecessary in the age of television and video, wasteful of resources and endangers a songwriter's mental equilibrium by removing him from the life that inspired him to become a songwriter in the first place.

Me: looking forward to Wembley.

Newell: hostile towards partying, schmoozing, ligging, showbiz insincerities and 'all that "star" rubbish'.

Me: Rod! Great to see you!

Newell: utterly convinced of his moral responsibility, in the event of success, to remain unaffected by staying close to the normalizing influence of his roots at home.

Me: the Bahamas look nice.

As if this wasn't enough, we presented a striking visual contrast, too: Newell with his shaggy hair and Fagin kit, and me with my spiked crop and Oxfam suits, continuing a phase begun at university. (Newell frequently referred – satirically but with a hint of jealousy, I sometimes felt – to my 'sensible teaching trousers'.)

Then, again, consider what we had in common. Both of us believed in the sanctity of the three-minute pop song. Both of us were fundamentally pro-Beatle. Furthermore, though Newell was a Lennon man and could accurately ape the gritty disdain of his singing voice, neither of us hated McCartney. Both of us considered the theme tune for *University Challenge* to be the funniest piece of music we had ever heard. And both of us thought jazz was for tossers. This was, surely, more than enough cement for a musical relationship.

So the differences didn't bother me. Or not initially. On the contrary, they were a kind of guarantee. Most of the top rock and pop partnerships have depended on a chemistry of contrast, some attitudinal give-and-take to keep them sparky. Lennon and McCartney, Jagger and Richards, Simon and Garfunkel . . . I suspect even Donny and Alan Osmond had their points of departure, philosophically speaking.

As for Newell, he had his act and his attitudes sorted out well in advance of my arrival, so what he was looking for in our relationship I am hard pressed to say. Except that songwriting is lonely work. And, if you happen to be on your own, so is putting together anarchist pop albums and plotting the downfall of the music industry. Newell was a one-man group – which defeated the object, given that one's reasons for being in a band include a determination to escape the solitariness of one's experiences as a listener. Chiefly, I would say, he was looking for company.

But let me be clear: I wasn't just a sleeping partner here, I was by no means the Andrew Ridgeley to Newell's George Michael (if Newell could be said to have a George Michael, which is unlikely). I had my role. I could play the piano better than him. I also made a better cup of tea than he did. And though my creative input was destined to be smaller than his, I comforted myself that I was crucial to the partnership on another level. Temperamentally, my new partner was a Molotov cocktail, ready at the slightest prompting to break open in a puddle of flaming petrol. I was more level-headed, a diplomat. This was how I saw our pairing: Newell as inflamed visionary; me standing by as the Emergency Fire Blanket.

We didn't collaborate until I left university. It was 1985. I was at a loose end after graduation and, with an uncanny symmetry, was again spending my time wandering round Colchester town centre in a daze. I had no idea what I was going to do. I had an English degree certificate, which, in the shrivelled job market of the 1980s, was about as useful as a brass-rubbing. Torpor had set in. Just thinking about careers, I became tired. I found it hard to think of more than four or five jobs that anybody did. The university had said I could start another degree if I wanted to. But I was fairly sure I didn't. I wanted to be a pop star. I registered at the DSS and moved back in with my parents.

I figured it would solve my problems if I could just write a couple of chartbusters – get some songs out there to Whitney and Tina, look on as they hoisted them effortlessly into the Top Ten and then order a house with a pool and wave good-bye for ever to those post-graduate career blues. It was time to grab this songwriting business by the horns, or else face a life of indeterminate gloom. Starting as I meant to go on, early on a Monday morning, I set out on the bedroom floor my Crumar keyboard and my primitive beat box. There was just enough room left for me to wedge myself between them, cross-legged, with my back against the bed. In this position I doodled and plinked and awaited the muse.

The producer Quincy Jones has talked about feeling, at moments of creativity, the power of God surging down like lightning through his arms to his hands. After two hours of hunching awkwardly over the keyboard on that first day, I began to know what he meant. But it turned out to be recurrent tennis elbow and a touch of shoulder cramp.

In more than a decade of music, I had never written a complete song on my own. Instead I had amassed an extensive catalogue of bits: half a chorus, part of a verse, a nice bridge. I was always trying to bolt some of them together, but they never seemed to fit. As for lyrics, they were a nightmare. Where do you begin with lyrics? Occasionally a line for a chorus had flashed into my head, or something I could imagine as a song title. Going any further than that seemed burdensome. Part of the problem was, I knew what the desire to write songs felt like but I never experienced the desire to write a song *about* anything.

I can't say this changed on that morning when I sat down to write Whitney a hit. No sense of an irresistible calling drew me on but, for once, I could muster some determination and, after clenching and straining for five hours, I had at least written a song. It had a title. It had lyrics. It had a beginning, a middle and a fade. I was jubilant. I could already envisage the interview in *Rolling Stone*, some years hence.

"So, Giles, tell us about writing 'What's Going On In Your Heart?'"

"God, let me think . . . Well, I remember I lifted the drum pattern directly from Stevie Wonder's 'Uptight (Everything's Alright)'. Great drums on that track – they motor really hard. And the keyboard riff was just something I'd had knocking about for ages. Put it together in my bedroom at my parents' house, actually! [*Laughs*] And I wrote the lyrics on a sheet of A4 paper on a deck-chair in the garden there. The chorus line just sort of came to me, kind of a chant thing, 'What's goin' on in your heart?'. I was thinking about how most love songs are about wanting to get really close to someone. So what if you wrote a song that said, actually, I *don't* want to know you – turned that cliché upside down? So you get [*Sings*]:
> I'd be a fool to want to get to know you better
> And I'd like to think I didn't know you well

That kind of thing, with negatives. Anyway, I don't want to get too deep about it. It's up to the listener in the end. It's about whatever you hear in it, you know? Originally, I showed it to Whitney. But when she heard it, she said: 'You know what, Giles? *You* should do this song. Really. Keep it.' Whitney's great like that. Very giving."

I had the song, but I still needed to make a recording of it. I found my mind turning to Newell. He was the man to help me out. He had the right sixties pop sensibility. He would understand where the song was coming from. With his recording experience, he could realize my aims for the number artistically. Plus he was the only person I knew who owned a four-track Portastudio.

'I've written this song,' I blurted, from the door at the back of the restaurant. 'I didn't know whether you could record it for me.'

'What's it like?' said Newell.

'Kind of Motown-y.'

Newell looked sceptical. 'Well, come over next Monday,' he said.

I'd been to Newell's on several occasions, normally after evenings in the pub when we would return to his upstairs room so that he could play me his latest indictment of Thatcher's Britain, arranged for guitar and beatbox. Situated at the top of a narrow wooden staircase, the room had a scrubbed floor, a couple of stools, a few cushions – a friendly yet Spartan feel. It was by no means the usual musician's hovel with a spaghetti of wires on the floor, dotted with packets of strings, split plectrums and abandoned beer cans. The place was ordered and dusted, bohemian but tidy, suggesting a brisk efficiency. Newell kept his Portastudio under wraps when not in use.

But now I was in there as a recording artist. Newell, wearing a black beret today, busied himself at the miniature mixing desk, pausing only to roll cigarettes. He recorded the drum machine and made me play two layers of keyboards. Then he recorded himself playing bass guitar, bright and tuneful, which sounded just right. It was exciting, listening to the thing take shape, hearing it pick up speed and weight. Both of us seemed buoyed up by it.

'You'd better put the vocal on now,' said Newell.

The microphone was Sellotaped to an old metal music stand, which had to be placed on a desk to bring it up to head height. As you sang, you were staring directly into some bookshelves. Newell handed me a pair of headphones (Boots' own brand, possibly).

'Let's see what you're made of,' he said, and ran the tape.

The point was, although I had written this song I had never, until now, sung it. I had murmured it to myself and heard it in my head, but I had never attempted to belt the thing out at volume. This is one of the disadvantages of song-writing in your parents' house: you get all self-conscious about being overheard and end up whispering to avoid detection. As a result, the song was uncomfortably out of my range. Too late to go back now, with all the instruments recorded. By squeezing my throat, I could just about get up high enough, but only with an indignant squawk. After three lines of this, I coughed and dropped an octave. Down there I sounded like a monk at prayer. Two more lines, and I was glowing with embarrassment and uncomfortably hot.

'Let me have a go,' said Newell.

He clamped on the headphones and punched the Play button. Sitting dejectedly on a stool behind him, I heard the introduction fizz in his ears and the sound of Newell breathing heavily, waiting for his cue. Suddenly, with a sharp inhalation of air, he exploded into song. One hand held the lyrics out in front of him, the other pressed a headphone deep into his ear. His voice was high, clear, affectingly grainy. His knees flapped wildly and occasionally he brought a foot clean off the ground in the exertion of delivering this vocal. The words poured into the microphone as if he had had them on his mind for ages and was just dying to get them across. And suddenly I was sitting up straight. It sounded great. It sounded like a pop song.

As I would have added, in that *Rolling Stone* interview: 'I guess you'd have to say it was "What's Going On In Your Heart?" that got me into the Cleaners. And into everything that followed from that.'

Elvis Costello

The late 1980s and the early 1990s were years of great political and sociological shift. It was a period in which old orders began to fall away, yielding ground to the vital green shoots pushing through from beneath. There was the collapse of Communism and the troubled ascendance of new democracies in Eastern Europe. There was the transition, in Britain, from vinyl to compact disc.

During the 1970s it was impossible to imagine that anything would rise to challenge the single-party supremacy of vinyl. Cassettes came in, of course, and achieved considerable popularity although even their grass-roots loyalists would have conceded that this kiddy-scale format was never a serious candidate for government. Big, 12-inch square, cardboard-covered records: they were the law, they were what we had and what we stood by. And then in the mid-1980s – and in little more than a few months – we were shown new hardware, new product and the map was completely redrawn.

CD: it was always going to be a tough one. So many of us were rooted in the traditional way of things, bitterly resistant to change – vinyl-dependent. The record companies and the hi-fi manufacturers did their best to calm the inevitable popular unrest. (Given the money at stake, it was, of course, in their interest to do so.) We heard a lot in those early days about the stunning improvement in sound quality that compact disc was going to bring us; how the new format was capable of a glassy clarity of which our old vinyl records could only dream. We were fed copious propaganda about the discs' indestructibility, how they were scratch-proof, dust-proof, water-proof; how you could heat them up, roll them into little tubes, stuff them with prawns, serve them as hors d'oeuvres at cocktail parties and they *still* sounded brilliant.

Here, we were promised, was a music format that would not degenerate with use. A pet is for life but a CD is for ever. 'Play them as many times as you like,' they said, 'and no quality loss.' Of course, no one has really been around long enough yet to offer proper guarantees on this. Recently a few science wizards have expressed doubts about CD permanence, raising the dire prospect that one day, say in thirty years' time, all that encoded digital information will soak out of them and your entire collection will turn to blank plastic in a matter of hours. Just thinking about this now, as someone with major holdings in Compact Disc, I can sense the colour draining from my face. I have not come this far, I feel, to be left with a van-load of neatly boxed frisbees.

It would be a rich irony, though. Everything else about compact discs looks permanent enough, certainly by contrast with 12-inch vinyl. They are extremely difficult to snap. They don't turn into salad bowls if left in the sun on the back shelf of a car. And although they can jump, be jogged, get stuck, skitter and generally play up, it's unusual when they do. Whereas, with records, the prospect of a physical flaw, leading to major listening dissatisfaction, was a very real consideration every time you bought one, and every time you played it.

Naturally I was wary in those early days. I thought it was best to consider first the domestic implications and then work carefully outwards from there. It was readily apparent that compact discs were going to be an easier thing to bring home from the shops. Here was something in their favour. They wouldn't flap about wantonly in the wind like albums and you were far less likely to cause injury by jamming one between your knee and the handrail, coming down the stairs on the bus home, which happened with me and a vinyl copy of Heaven 17's *Penthouse and Pavement*. (A cosmetic wounding only, but still nasty. My knee didn't come out of it all that well either.)

And transporting CDs thereafter, taking them to other people's houses, was clearly going to be considerably simpler, too, the only plastic bags which fit a 12-inch record being bags from record shops, and if you happen not to have any of those knocking around the house, then you've got a problem, as you'll know if you've ever tried to wedge a couple of albums into a standard supermarket carrier-bag. (They go in just about OK – though at the risk of snubbed corners – but then you can't bring the bag's handles together.)

No, the durability and convenience arguments struck me as winningly solid. Mostly I was concerned about the sleeve situation.

To one reared on the open plains of the album cover, the images at the front of compact discs were comically cramped. They looked like snapshots of record covers; and, like snapshots, they had a mostly disappointing relation to the real thing. Plus that half-inch of thinly ridged grey plastic down the left-hand side was an ugly distraction. This wasn't how music was meant to look. Did they really mean us to stare at these things and solemnly pass them around while the album was playing?

And then there were those tacky plastic boxes, with their push-together fastenings and hinges. Tricky, too. I know people even now who own large quantities of CDs but who have yet to master the art of opening them. (As a rule, any approach that involves use of the nails under the right-hand edge is flirting with disaster in the shape of a possible popper

rupture up at the hinge-end. I myself go for a left-hand dominant, two-thumb manoeuvre, which was about eighteen
months in development. The left hand is spanned across the
front of the disc with the little finger clamped firmly against
the spine low down, the thumb parallel with it, working at
the opening edge. Meanwhile the right-hand thumb, cupped
round from the back in a mostly supporting role at the top
edge, woggles the back free of the front.)

And once inside, you've still got to get the disc loose from
its surprisingly cunning central mounting. (I'm a two-digit
right-hander on this one – thumb depressing the spongy
sprockets as the forefinger prises the disc forward from the
top edge.) I've looked on in agony at novices attempting to
claw them out with all five finger-tips, but what were any of
us meant to do? At least milk cartons came with operating
instructions – push back wings, pull forward, etc. With CD
containers, we were all on our own. In the dark. With raw
fingers.

As for the booklet, if it's an effort to extract the thing
(you've got somehow to slip it out from *under* the semicircu-
lar retaining tabs while getting it *over* the nobbles that hold
the lid shut) then this is as nothing compared with getting
it back in again, which requires the combined skills of a
watchmaker and a seamstress. (I would suggest rotating the
open case ninety degrees clockwise and easing the booklet
upwards with both thumbs from the bottom but, to be
honest, I'm fallible here.) All highly unsatisfactory.

So I chewed worriedly on these reservations for quite a
while before I bought into the CD dream. I would cast anxious looks at my shelved LPs and remember how much of
me was invested there. I didn't like the idea of them being
outstripped by time. I wasn't keen to see them go the way of
the oil lamp and the horse-drawn plough.

People would say, 'So, do you think you'll get a CD, then?'

And I would say, 'No, I don't reckon. Because of the sleeves. I'd miss the sleeves.'

And they would nod and say, 'Exactly, exactly.'

But then, at some point in 1987, a friend became the first person we knew to own a CD player and a group of us went ritually to his house one evening and clomped upstairs into his bedroom to give it an audition.

'Listen to this,' he said.

'What?' I said, hearing nothing.

'*That!*' he said.

It was the *nothing* he wanted me to listen to, the silence between the tracks. And it *was* impressive, the total absence of clutter: no swishing of needle in dusty groove, no ticks and spits from the encrusted grit, no soft lumping where the plastic arse-end of the stylus humped rhythmically against the vinyl, which happened on some of my more spectacularly warped singles. And here was the neurosis-inducing corollary: if all that noise was going on *between* the tracks, it was going on *during* them, too. It became apparent that everything you were hearing on vinyl was struggling to shrug off a thin coat of fuzz or hiss to reach you, its immediacy drastically diminished. CD – a miracle – offered sound in the nude, as the Good Lord intended it: hosed down, fanatically scrubbed, beautifully oiled, punching and popping out at you from this perfect digital hush.

If you're a genuine vinyl fetishist, this perpetual flawlessness is a mixed blessing. A friend's copy of the free single that came with the first editions of Elvis Costello and the Attractions' *Armed Forces* acquired, somewhere along the line (doubtless during some sort of late-night student gloomfest), a small glob of candlewax, which the record player's stylus either lodges against or slaloms over, depending on its whim. Far from being annoyed, my friend has been known to boast about this blip as though it was some kind of battle scar. That's how he knows it's his copy and nobody else's; and, more than that, it's his marker for how far he and Elvis go back.

And it's true: in a world where it often seems important to assert that you were in on some things right at the start (that, no, you haven't only just acquired *Talking Heads 77*, you got it when it came out, which is why the record is beginning to peep from a worn slit at the bottom of the inner sleeve), those blemishes – scratches, bits of old candle, staunched beer spillages – are a crucial historical index. Records left their mark on you, and, in the spirit of co-operation, you left your mark on records. What hope for this two-way relationship if CDs have the gift of eternal youth?

Yet I confess: on the whole I don't find it hilarious and touching that my copy of Aretha Franklin's *Greatest Hits* is so badly pressed (or so shockingly mastered) that the sound suddenly clarifies and swells in volume bang in the middle of 'Chain Of Fools', the third track on side one. Nor am I encouraged to shed tears of nostalgia over the two jumps which happen inside the first ten seconds of 'Rikki Don't Lose That Number' on my copy of Steely Dan's *Pretzel Logic* (grit inside the inner sleeve, I think). The music format which was going to rescue me from these mini-dramas couldn't come quickly enough.

So the combined weight of the industry propaganda and my own accumulated anxieties – that there was this format out there which was somehow *truer*, more *faithful* – built up and swung me over. Finally, grindingly, I chose CD. Not that my decision meant anything: the record companies in collusion with the hi-fi manufacturers had already decided long ago that we would all change to this new, more expensive format and they got their way by the simple expedient of slowing down vinyl production and drastically limiting our opportunity to do anything else (other than butt out altogether, and that wasn't an option). It was never a question of fighting. It was only ever a matter of how peacefully you would give yourself up. And after a brief, inconsequential paddy, I ran, gurgling, into CD's outstretched arms.

In 1988, I scraped the money together for a cheap Phillips ex-display model. It had a rather unsatisfying rubberized push-pad on the front, for stop, start, forward and reverse; and the disc-tray emerged with a creaky metallic rumble, like a train going slowly over points. But it was a CD-player none the less and its arrival excited me probably as much as the arrival of other key pieces of musical hardware in my childhood: the Phillips cassette recorder, the Amstrad cassette deck, the Garrard turntable. Waking up on the first few mornings after I had acquired it, I would cross the room and just look at it.

And, of course, I took the solemn oath that everyone takes when they first trade up to CD: that I would never waste money buying on CD anything I already owned on record. Because, though my new CD player was clearly crunchier to listen to and less troubled-sounding than my old record deck and though it gave me the promised silence between the tracks, it still had to pass through the rest of my battered hi-fi – my weary amplifier and baggy speakers – so the improvement wasn't exactly quantum. The sound was slightly smarter, as if freshly ironed, and that was about it. In fact, as I furtively admitted to myself in occasional moments of punishing honesty, some of the old vinyl sounded more lively for a few creases, a bit of air and static . . .

So, no pointless duplication of albums, no CD and vinyl overlap. My decision to go compact was, I avowed, a simple piece of company rationalizing in response to the new technology – but with no redundancies. The vinyl collection had its job to do and always would have.

Hollow words. Even as I was pledging, I was buying my first CD: *Characters* by Stevie Wonder, an album I had bought (and been quietly disappointed by) only six months previously on vinyl. The CD had two additional tracks, so I suppose I can justify this on some academic basis. But, even so, how easily I was lured in.

And ever since then, with increasing alacrity, I have shopped wildly for CD versions of records I already possess, prowled the browsers wide-eyed and tensed up, as if I was involved in some mad, self-generated game of Snap.

As a result, albums of which I own two copies include:

The entire 1970s and 1980s output of Stevie Wonder
Everything by Steely Dan
The first three Rickie Lee Jones albums and the mini-album
   (originally a 10-inch on vinyl) *Girl At Her Volcano*, the CD
   version of which cost me an absolute fortune on Japanese
   import
The first Blue Nile album
Meat Is Murder and *Strangeways Here We Come* by the Smiths
Rapture by Anita Baker
The first four Prefab Sprout albums
Everything by XTC except *Nonsuch* (CD only)
The Beatles double *White Album*
Little Criminals by Randy Newman
And many more

Albums which I currently have only on vinyl, but which I know – just *know* – that in the near future I'm going to be redundantly supplementing with CD versions include:

Love by Aztec Camera
Sign O' The Times and *Graffiti Bridge* by Prince
Goodbye Cruel World by Elvis Costello and the Attractions
   and *Spike* by Elvis Costello
Naked and *Stop Making Sense* by Talking Heads
Avalon Sunset by Van Morrison
I Feel For You and the first two self-named Chaka Khan albums
Partners in Crime by Rupert Holmes (only joking)

Album sales were in decline before the arrival of CD. When people like me started going out and buying our record collections all over again, well, blow me down if they didn't start surging back upwards. It's a perfectly legitimate ambition for any business in a consumer society – getting us to buy something we do not need. And long may it continue, because all of my favourite things are things I do not, under any serious analysis, need.

But only the record business – fabulously shameless in every stunt it pulls – has managed so seamlessly the ultimate marketing trick: getting us to buy something we do not need *which we've already got.*

The Cleaners from Venus, take 2

As well as being an anarchist and Colchester's top songwriter and the daytime washer-up in a restaurant on North Hill, Martin Newell was also a proxy landlord. The sail loft in which he had his studio and ate with his family was annexed to a large Victorian house, slightly crumbly and spooky-looking, with the kind of overgrown front garden that children's stories get a lot of mileage out of. The owner had gone to work in Australia indefinitely, leaving Newell to tend the place and collect rents from a small group of lodgers, students mostly, who occupied the giant rooms in the main house. Towards the end of 1986, one of these rooms fell free and, to facilitate Newell's and my rise into the upper stratum of the rock and pop songwriting greats, I took it.

It was clear that, given the two potential career paths open to me at this time – further university course leading, possibly, to academic teaching job; or major effort to hit the big-time rock-wise leading, inevitably, to major drug habit – by moving in with Newell, I was favouring the latter. I appeared to have reached one of life's crossroads and this was something I thought I should communicate to my father. It was time we had a pivotal exchange.

So far, my father and I had managed to skip pivotal exchanges. Nothing had occurred in my life so far that I had felt obliged to raise with him, in appropriately sober tones, when the two of us were alone together. For instance: 'Father, I have decided to go into the Church.' Or: 'Father, I am going to marry a Dutch masseuse and live in Santa Barbara.' Neither had he, for his part, ever felt the need to take me aside, sit me down and impart essential fatherly wisdom of his own: 'Now, pretty soon you're going to start having feelings. Feelings towards the opposite sex' etc. There had been none of that. Mostly we had just carried on, both of us quietly praying that nothing personal or crucial would arise that we would have to deal with, father to son, or, worse still, man to man.

There was more at stake in the conversation we were about to have than there might have been. For while my father had never shown the slightest interest in joining, say, the Who, he had always wanted to be an academic. Maybe he would have been one, except that the Second World War had intervened and his opportunities closed down around him. He drew consolation from the thought that, although this possibility had been denied him, at least it was open to me. And now I was about to toss it away.

I knew better than to thunder in and put it to him straight. I chose my words carefully from a selection of what I imagined were parent-sensitive phrases for this kind of thing. I tried to make it sound a matter of 'having a career as a musician', of 'trying to get into the music business'. Both turns of phrase seemed to me brisk, purposive, clean-shaven, crisp-shirted and, as such, preferable to phrases like 'go big-time', 'do the rock thing', 'make it mega', 'hit the road to Chick City', etc.

'Do you think there's any future in that?' said my father, responsibly, after a long pause.

'Yes,' I said, and I wasn't kidding.

My father's eyes were somewhere far away, unfocused. His bottom lip pushed up against the top one, and he nodded gently as if seeing my reasoning. Though clearly he didn't see it at all. As far as he was concerned, I might as well have announced that I had decided, after protracted negotiations with Nelly the Elephant, to run off and join the circus. Finally he said, 'Well, if you really think so. . .'

I really thought so.

Among other things, the move to Newell's represented the chance at last to emancipate my records, most of which had remained cruelly caged within their boxes since my return from university, the collection having expanded to such a degree that there was no longer room in my parents' house to spread it out and let it breathe.

There was no space problem at Newell's house. Mine was a large room with a giant bay window, through which it was impossible to see anything on account of a large over-grown tree in the garden which spread its branches thickly against the panes. The albums slotted in perfectly on the floor along the end wall: conditions there were dry, cold, no direct sunlight – virtually museum standard, but for a plinth. I had a bookcase, a bed that was bigger than a single but not as big as a double, a rickety desk and an acre or so of uncarpeted floor-boarding.

On a preliminary tour of the building, just after I had humped my boxes and bags of clothes up into the room, Newell showed me where a chip had been taken out of the woodwork on a doorpost downstairs. He said it had hap-pened one Saturday evening when a poltergeist entered the house, got bored with rattling the cups on the kitchen dresser, picked up a glass ashtray and flung it the length of the hall. Evidently Newell's wife, with her superior knowledge of the occult, had dealt with the matter swiftly and efficiently – shown the bastard straight to the door, or something. I asked if paranormal forces made themselves evident in the house very frequently. Newell said it had happened a couple of times last year, but it wasn't, like, a weekly occurrence. I nodded hard and tried to look reassured.

And then, as we got upstairs, he explained about the ghost. 'Entirely benign,' he said cheerfully. Evidently, the shape of a woman in a grey, hooded robe was sometimes to be seen about the place. Once or twice she had shown up in the kitchen, and occasionally she had been seen in the hall, but the real hot-spot for sightings, the place the old biddy liked to hang out the most, was on the landing outside the door to my room.

I didn't get a wink of sleep in the house that night. That's because I was back at my parents, getting a full set of winks there. I had returned early in the evening, mumbling to Newell something about 'letting the room air a bit' and 'sorting myself out properly first', and I repeated the same shoddy lie as I let myself into my parents' house and went sheepishly to my recently emptied room.

Still, I settled in eventually. Or sort of settled. The other tenants were a female Goth, who wore black leather and lace, had a mane of raven hair and an identically dressed friend with whom she listened to the Damned a lot; and a male drama student who had draped his room in sheets of silk, owned some surprisingly stripy trousers and possessed a large collection of albums by all-girl singing groups from the 1960s. (Of the hooded biddy, there was no sign the whole of my time there.) Our relations were never less than sunny as we brushed past each other on our way in and out of the kitchen and the bathroom, but I had the residual sense that I fitted here like a foot in a mitten.

I had the whole week free for songwriting, having found willing and largely undemanding sponsors for my lifestyle in the shape of Colchester's Department of Social Security. But Newell was only free on Mondays which tended to limit our output. We were looking to write the big one: a smash hit for Cliff or Tina. But, at the same time, we fancied ourselves as the kind of witty jokesters whose compositions you might hear on Radio 4's *Loose Ends* on a Saturday morning. We wrote a song called 'Hockney Paints The Stage', which was the title of a London exhibition at the time, a show of David Hockney's design work for the theatre, but which we interpreted literally and converted into a bouncy music-hall ditty in which a number of famous contemporary artists were forced to take menial jobs while they waited for their Arts Council grants.

On our second Monday, we wrote ourselves a press release, to mail out with tapes as yet unmade of songs as yet unwritten. It was headed: 'Smith and Newell: Songs? We Godd'em', a straightforward lie at this point, and underneath came a lavish assessment of our ability to deliver quality material, in any style, at the drop of a hat. We popped out to the local stationery shop and, at searing expense, printed up forty copies on bright yellow paper.

'These should keep us going,' said Newell.

Unfortunately, we'd written that day's date at the head of the master copy so, by the following week, the whole stack was useless.

We weren't entirely indolent, though. We wrote a song called 'Clara Bow', a sweet folky shuffle for which Newell had the chords already and whose lyrics we wrote together. Newell came up with a mid-tempo Motown pastiche called 'Stay On', a sort of musical riposte to my 'What's Going On In Your Heart?' Newell also pulled out a wedge of songs from his recent past, as yet unrecorded : 'Victoria Grey', a song picturing Mrs Thatcher as a haughty and uncaring Victorian *grande dame*, passing in a carriage, splattering mud on urchins; 'Illya Kuryakin Looked At Me', a fantasy song about the sixties, featuring Rita Tushingham, green electric trains and the blond one from *The Man From U.N.C.L.E.* We taped these too. After a while, we had an album's-worth of material, which Newell suggested would convert decently into a Cleaners from Venus tape. We had some copies made and Newell then pushed it out in the usual way through his contacts on the tape underground. We called it *Living With Victoria Grey* and, to cheer ourselves up, talked loudly and seriously in the pub about 'our new album' and 'the new material'. The note Newell wrote on the sleeve said, slightly forlornly: 'If you've enjoyed this tape, tell your milkman about it.'

This all happened over a period of weeks – weeks in which I had time to spare. I told myself that a shivering-in-the-attic phase was almost obligatory for musicians; it was not a sign that I was desperate but, on the contrary, a bright indication that I was on the right path. This helped me put up with the draughts in my room, where I commonly bunched myself up as close as possible to one of those free-standing, metal-box gas fires on wheels which, after about ninety minutes of constant use, cause your eyes to cloud over and soot to accumulate in the back of your nose. (Eventually I took to operating it for no more than fifteen minutes in any one hour because of a paranoid fear that its fumes were slowly destroying me from within.) I spent the days tinkering with my keyboard and beatbox or, ferocious cold permitting, fiddling at the piano downstairs. I tooled around with lyrics, without actually finishing any, and listened to records. I stared out of the window a lot. I wore a ragged mohair jumper. I thought of myself as strange and bohemian.

After working for a twenty-four-hour emergency car-accident service and as a lorry driver, my brother Simon and his wife Dorothy had become landlord and landlady of the Station Inn, Wivenhoe, a pub just a hundred yards up the street from where I now lived. Tiny, with a semi-circular bar, the Station took most of its trade in the evenings from home-coming commuters and at lunchtimes from the dockers who worked on the quay. On especially bleak days, I would escape the cold of the house in the middle of the day and go and sit in the pub's back kitchen and drink coffee. From their position at this epicentre of chat and gossip, my brother and sister-in-law were able to inform me – with some alarm for my safety, I felt – that the house I was living in was regarded by the more conservative elements of the village as a hippie commune and all-round drug haven. I laughed when I heard this and said that was all wrong. They didn't seem convinced. I had also told them that Newell and I were intending to make it as songwriters. They didn't seem convinced about that, either.

1985 passed into 1986 and winter became spring. We had heard nothing back from any publisher, manager, or song-hungry pop star. And we hadn't heard from *Loose Ends*, either. In March, I decided to go and live with my girlfriend in Bristol.

Aretha Franklin

There was never any suggestion, when I moved in, that we would combine our record collections. I can see how to do so would have obeyed a kind of cold-eyed logic: we did, after all, have a lot of records in common. Records had been the currency of our courtship, when I wanted her to have and like the music I had and liked, when I wanted her to hear words I could never have brought myself to say. I couldn't, for instance, imagine any circumstance in which I might have leant over to her and muttered, 'You make my soul a burning fire.' But I was happy to give her *Hotter Than July* by Stevie Wonder and direct her to 'All I Do', side one, track two.

I had often looked along her record collection and seethed at how much cooler it was than mine. It was smaller, but so much more perfectly formed. It wasn't bloated by any daft Nik Kershaw allegiance. There was no trace of a tedious 10cc loyalty. I had the mostly disappointing, Arista-period Aretha Franklin albums – *Aretha, Jump To It, Who's Zoomin' Who*, which did contain the stormer 'Freeway of Love', but not a lot else – while she had the very early live album recorded in a supper club which, though it comes from Aretha's unhappy period at Columbia, predating the great Atlantic years, does at least include a blinding version of 'This Could Be The Start Of Something Big' and is, in any case, a darn sight cooler than *Jump* bloody *To It*. The galling thing was, the trim, sophisticated triumph which was her record collection was to a large extent the fruits of *my research*. These were albums I had given to her or pointed her in the direction of. She hadn't had to truffle through the crap to find these pearls. She simply got to glass-case the prime specimens – my greatest hits.

But supposing we had, on the night of my arrival, pains-takingly sorted out the albums of which we had two copies and prepared a pile to take to the secondhand record shop (and, rest assured, there was no way that it would have been *my* copy we got rid of). What would we have been saying by doing this? That we were never going to split up? Possibly. But also – and more pressingly, I felt – we would have been saying that my records were now hers to call her own, to use as she wished. And I don't wish to dish the dirt, but this was a girl who had been known to leave records *out of their sleeves*. A girl who sometimes returned records direct into the card-board outer sleeve *without bothering to put them in the inner sleeve first*. A girl who laughed openly to discover records *inside the wrong sleeve*. Or worse, *in the right inner sleeve*, but *in the wrong outer sleeve*. A girl who had never in her life seen the need to buy *even one* clear polythene album sheath, so would almost certainly have scant regard for all mine. And alphabetical order? I don't think I need to say anything about alphabetical order.

There was a major hi-fi issue to resolve as well. I knew I could never be satisfied with her stereo. A secondhand, all-in-one music centre, it was subject to intermittent and utterly mysterious popping fits in the right-hand speaker. She calmly endured this, much in the way she calmly went out and bought the thing in the first place. For me, any new purchase – not just hi-fi but any domestic appliance – could take weeks of deliberation, with zealous scanning of the consumer literature: *What Answerphone, Kettle & Kettle Owner, HooverMart*. Not to become an expert – I've never been on some boffin-style quest to know these things inside out – but just to get a sense of what's out there and then to take some-body else's word about it. All the women I've ever known, if they wanted a hi-fi, they went out and bought one.

In the end, I got the spare room in the flat for my own stereo and my own records. We talked maturely about this in terms of the 'space' I would doubtless 'need', though it wasn't me who needed the space, it was my albums.

Needless to say, about two months after I moved to Bristol, things started to happen for the Cleaners. And when they did, it was the result of a connection forged long ago, bearing out the old rock'n'roll adage: it's not what you know, it's who you used to play in a band with.

When he was younger and singing with Gyp, Newell had shaken his spangly trousers alongside someone named Tony Phillips who went on to become a distinguished studio engineer. In time Phillips would work with Joni Mitchell and Prefab Sprout but for now he was employed as the engineer on the sessions for a new Captain Sensible album at a studio in Dorking. Captain Sensible had been the bassist in the Damned. He was one of the original punks. A friend of mine once claimed that Sensible had urinated on him mid-gig from the stage of the Town and Country club in London, which seemed perfectly likely. Post-punk, though, Sensible had big hits as a slightly more cuddly solo artist – 'Happy Talk', 'Wot', 'Glad It's All Over' – and got to spend a lot of time wearing a beret and round sunglasses, opening supermarkets and appearing on Saturday morning television. Now he was trying to make a new album for A&M, but struggling, as Newell's friend reported, for a lack of songs. At Tony Phillips's urging, Newell sent Sensible a copy of our tape.

What happened next was conveyed to me by Newell in a series of increasingly breathless phone calls between Wivenhoe and Bristol. First of all, Tony Phillips rang Newell to say that Sensible liked the tape. Then Sensible himself phoned Newell to invite him down to the studio. I experienced some fairly sharp prickles of jealousy here. Actually, 'prickles' isn't quite strong enough. Jealousy knifed me in the guts is more like it. I would have liked to have been swanning off to a residential recording study in Surrey to hang out with Captain Sensible. But I could hardly complain. I had rights in only one and a half songs on that tape. And I had moved to Bristol.

Newell travelled down on a train, taking his bicycle with him to cover the last couple of miles between the station and the studio. He wasn't the only lyricist summoned to Dorking that summer. Other songwriters had been called upon to help Sensible get round his writing block, including Graham Gouldman who, before he became successful as the bassist in 10cc, wrote 'Bus Stop' for the Hollies. In a richly significant piece of timing, Newell arrived on his bike just as Gouldman was leaving in a helicopter.

Newell described his days in residence at Dorking in glossy terms. In the morning one would descend from one's five-star-hotel standard bedroom for breakfast, spend one's days working undistracted in the air-conditioned hush of the lavishly equipped studio and enjoy home-cooked meals round a large dining table every evening, before adjourning to the pub. I thought this sounded like Eden.

The best news from my point of view was that Sensible had decided to record 'Clara Bow', which was a Newell/Smith composition. When he got back from the studio, Newell sent me a copy of the backing track, on which Sensible had yet to record his vocal. It was all tidy, clicking drum machines and neatly regimented keyboards – nothing like the home-made original, but crisp, even in this uncomplicated state, buffed to a high sheen. I tried to imagine it finished and playing on the radio. Just suppose Sensible chose to release this track as a single; just suppose it enjoyed popularity at 'Happy Talk' levels and sparked him off on another round of supermarket openings . . . Think of the royalties, the future commissions. It would be weekends in Dorking for the rest of my life. In all my fantasizing, it never once occurred to me what would actually happen: that Sensible would never get to put his vocal on the tape; that he would decide he was unhappy with everything recorded in those sessions; that he would ditch the lot; that his deal with A&M would close shortly after.

In the meantime, though, Sensible convinced Newell that the Cleaners from Venus should strike a deal of their own with the management company he used, to whom he would recommend us. He said there were people there who might put up the money to make a record and would maybe work on our behalf to attract some interest from the major record companies. I imagine Newell raised all his traditional objections to this notion: that the Cleaners from Venus were a thoroughly alternative organization who wanted no part of the capitalist construct which was the mainstream music industry, the very term 'music industry' itself being indicative of the extent to which the corrupt business stood in basic opposition to the fundamental freedom of all musical endeavour. But something here – perhaps that he was talking to a pop star in the context of a luxury residential studio – persuaded him in a way that I had never managed, or even dared to try. And so, shortly before eleven o'clock one morning in the early summer of 1986, Newell and I met in the Charing Cross Road in London and walked round the corner to our appointment with destiny. Or, rather, our appointment with two extremely young Scotsmen.

Sensible's management traded under the less than catchy name Ammunition Communications. The address we had was 22 Denmark Street. Once the centre of London's song-publishing world – London's Tin Pan Alley, indeed, where pianos had sounded from the closet offices of songwriters, working on hits, nine to five – Denmark Street was now a brash strip of guitar shops stuffed tight most days, but especially on Saturday afternoons, with just about everyone who ever wore denim playing the riff from 'Smoke On The Water' on instruments they had no intention of purchasing. A couple of the basements still contained studios and one contained an after-hours drinking club. The tide of litter from the Charing Cross Road seemed to wash up here and then get stranded – hillocks of wet and broken cardboard boxes, scattered hand-out leaflets for English-language teaching schools and all-you-can-eat salad bars.

Number 22 was fronted by what appeared to be a much-jimmied wooden door beside the entrance to one of the guitar shops. One of us pressed the buzzer. There was a long pause. We pressed it again. Another pause. Finally there was a crunching noise in the tinny speaker and the muffled voice of someone recently woken said: 'Gnar?'

'It's the Cleaners from Venus,' said Newell, unselfconsciously.

A remote lock buzzed and sprang and we passed through and walked up three dank flights of stairs to where the door to a flat was ajar. We stood awkwardly on the threshold until a tall figure in jeans, a T-shirt and bare feet emerged from a darkened room and led us through to the front, tousling his hair with both hands.

A close fug hung over the room as if a student party had raged in it for thirteen weeks and had only come to a gutted halt an hour before our arrival. The sole furnishings were a stained, clapped-out brown sofa and a matching armchair, both of which seemed to have been run over by a lorry. There was also a television and a video, and ashtrays were dimly discernible under mounds of ash and squashed butts. There was a small spillage of rented video cartons in the shadow of the television and, beside the sofa, a couple of gaping pizza boxes spotted with grease. Later, when we got to know our manager better, he would claim that he kept the flat that way to make it 'hospitable to musicians'.

The figure in bare feet was the manager's partner. He introduced himself as Pete, though he was known, for no good reason, as Pete the Bastard. Andy the manager entered from out of the darkness a little after, wearing a black T-shirt and the trousers from a cheap suit, black with little flecks of colour in it. (Over the next two years, those trousers and their matching jacket would become extremely familiar. I don't think I ever saw the manager wear anything else.) His hair was medium length and parted down the middle, framing a face whose pallor suggested a brief acquaintance with daylight at some point in the 1970s. There were some gruff hellos, some handshakes. On the train up from Bristol, I had fondly imagined this scene unfolding across a shiny black desk in some chrome-and-glass office environment, rich with the smell of fresh coffee. As it was, Newell and I perched warily on the sofa while the manager and the co-manager spread themselves on the crappy carpet and we all lit cigarettes.

They came from Edinburgh and they were younger than either of us. In fact, Newell would only have had to have been mildly precocious, sexually speaking, to have fathered them. The manager had married Pete the Bastard's sister at a young age and there had been a divorce not long after. But the manager and Pete the Bastard had stayed together.

There was some awkward chit-chat and a general awakening period while their eyes became used to the light. Needless to say, it was Newell who got down to business first. The pair of them lay there and listened as he set out, firmly and clearly, the limits beyond which, as a musician and composer of integrity, he was not prepared to go: he wasn't going to tour; he wasn't going to have a producer anywhere near any of his records; he wasn't going abroad, etc. And to my amazement, at no point did they burst out laughing. They simply nodded sagely and said things like, 'most certainly' and 'quite understand'. Then we went to a café over the road, ordered coffee and squeezed round a table where, finally, they did some talking of their own.

The manager spoke firmly and determinedly and without smiling very much. (His sense of humour, it turned out, was tremendously dry, at least until he soaked it in lager.) The pair of them had been appointed by the man who owned the property to run a studio in the basement at Number 22. They were doing a bit of band-management on the side and they were starting up an independent record label. They could offer us studio time in which we would make an album, using, they hoped, the songs from our tape. They could then put the album out on their own label. Naturally, their ability to distribute and promote the record would be limited. But the idea would be to impress the major companies with the finished product and then license it to them at a vast profit.

As I sat and listened to all this, they began to take on a romantic glow. Sure, they didn't exactly exude conventional business togetherness. And their flat was short of the trappings of success – furniture, for instance. But it was possible, without much effort, to imagine them as Colin MacInnes figures, young gunslingers chancing it. Didn't you hear about these kinds of people in the music business all the time? Guys who came out of nowhere, operating on sheer bravado, guts and pluck, people with a canny feel for what sells and what smells, muscling their way into the big bucks and never looking back? In any case, this pair had their own record company and a recording studio and they liked our music. And it wouldn't have taken us long to sift through our alternative offers at this point. Without having said so, or communicated it to each other by so much as a look, Newell and I were both already hooked.

After an hour or so in the café, we went back over the road, though this time the managers took us down into the basement where they had their office and their studio. In my imagination, the studios in which I would eventually make my début album had tended pleasingly to combine the décors of a sauna and an Alpine breakfast nook. Here, though, in a situation reminiscent of a million bad-package-holiday stories, the studio was still being built. The control room had been gutted and now waited the arrival of a new 24-track mixing desk. The door through into the sound room dated possibly from the 1840s, was the thickness of a tank's walls and clanked like the entrance to a meat freezer. The sound room was large, low-ceilinged and empty, but for a clutch of old plastic headphones and a battered grand piano, untuned. Water, seeping through from the pavement, had made the drum booth at the back an unusable hazard area. Sensing our unease, perhaps, Pete the Bastard tried to cheer us with the story that the Rolling Stones had made some early demo recordings on this very spot. (I was never able to verify this, though interestingly the studio over the road and the guitar shop next door made exactly the same claim for their own premises.) There was some more handshaking, some exchanging of numbers and some promises of phone calls, and we left.

It took several attempts to fix up a date on which we could begin recording. The completion of the building work in the studio took longer than anticipated and our starting date went back and back. Eventually we returned to Denmark Street in the early autumn. We had ceased to think of our-

selves as Smith & Newell: Songwriters. We were now, despite
our earliest intentions, officially the Cleaners from Venus, a
band on the hit trail.

Denmark Street was ours to use for three weeks. That's the
amount of time it takes a band like the Human League to
work up a bass drum sound that they're happy with. To us it
seemed luxurious. On the first day, Newell went up to the
guitar shop above the studio and took out a long-term rent
on a Rickenbacker guitar – the chiming, jangling instrument
you hear sparkling on Beatles records. We thought we were
making our *Revolver*, packed with shiny shards of pop. We
wondered briefly about calling it *With the Cleaners*.

John Parish, a friend from Bristol, played drums on a
couple of tracks. John was an avant-garde percussionist in his
own band, Automatic Dlamini. Newell had to talk him out of
using the rusty ploughshare which he had erected on a stand
in among the drums and cymbals, but otherwise things went
smoothly. Lol, Newell's friend and original partner in the
Cleaners from Venus, came up from Bath and played drums,
too. Captain Sensible arrived from Brighton one evening and
played some electric guitar on one of the tracks. He was
coming out of a depression at the time. He seemed quiet,
thoughtful, not about to urinate on anyone. The spiky perox-
ide crop he used to display on the telly was now a bowl of
black curls. The manager reasoned that an appearance by
Sensible on the record might attract some of his fans to buy it.
What appealed rather more to me about having him on our
album was that we would be able to write in the sleevenotes
on the back, 'Captain Sensible appears courtesy of A&M
Records', which seemed to me thrillingly professional.

We had an engineer, Nigel Haslam, to work the equipment
for us, but no producer, in line with Newell's laws. In truth,
we knew little about musical arrangement, about leading and

supporting, big sounds and small sounds, about directing the listener's attention to bring out the best in the song. We worked with the sketchy knowledge we had in the arrogant belief that it was all we needed to know. And as a result the album seemed to come together in a joyful rush. We had our punchy opener, 'Julie Profumo', and we had our big ballad, 'A Mercury Girl', all milky keyboards and sleighbells shaken softly at the periphery of the mix to give the whole thing a frosted edge. Well, that's how we felt about it.

Newell insisted that we work civilized hours with no wrecking ourselves by ploughing on into the middle of the night. This meant evenings tended to be free. As the recording progressed, I began phoning up friends that I hadn't seen in ages and arranging to meet them for drinks so that, when they asked me what I was up to these days, I would be able to say: 'Well, actually, I'm in the studio right now, just finishing off an album.' Afterwards we would go back to their houses where I forced my cassettes into their hi-fi's and bullied them into listening to mixes, snippets, outtakes. I wasn't especially after approval or constructive criticism: I was in pure display mode. Sometimes, it's true, I got opinions I hadn't asked for. I played a mix of 'What's Going On In Your Heart' to John Parish. He said, 'It sounds like Phil Spector's Wall of Sound remade in Lego.'

But my excitement was inextinguishable. And it was mainly the excitement which helped both me and Newell ignore aspects of the set-up at Denmark Street which would, I think, have been unacceptable to, say, Phil Collins. Our financial arrangement with Ammunition Communications was casual. Every now and then, the manager would take a slim wedge of banknotes from his trouser pocket and thumb off a tenner. 'Here,' he would say. 'Expenses.' We lived off tuna sandwiches from across the road and pizza from around the corner and drank coffee made with the kettle in the back room, which could probably have done with sterilizing or, better still, throwing away. Who knows what viral hell lurked in its calcinated tubes? At night we slept on the floor of the flat upstairs, selecting carefully the more acceptable items from a grubby and disquietingly stiff collection of sleeping bags and shredded blankets.

Newell and I were, in effect, living with our managers. Our relationships intensified fast. The manager became for us the topic of limitless fascination and speculation. Pete the Bastard seemed more easily understood: he was enthusiastic, energetic, a little naïve. He went swimming occasionally to keep fit. Whereas the manager was alluringly opaque, not prone to give much away – particularly if it was money. We were amazed by his ability to sustain himself, deep into the day, on a diet of instant coffee and Embassy cigarettes. He was a sixty-a-day man and his hands shook, but it never seemed to bother him or betray itself in his voice. When he wasn't on the phone he would tap the tips of his fingers on his desk and disappear into himself. He had authority, which was partly to do with the bark of his voice but was also in his demeanour. Because he appeared so unsurprisable, you assumed he knew what he was doing. Pete the Bastard was firmly under his spell. And so, in a very short time, were we. Whatever the manager said, we did. And always the same crumpled suit with, underneath it, a black T-shirt bearing the legend 'Voice of America', the name of a synthesized dance duo from Blackpool whom Ammunition Communications were touting at the same time as us. A box of these T-shirts was stored in the office. On one occasion, the manager sat at his desk and complained of feeling unfresh. Then he stood up, peeled off the T-shirt he was wearing, flung it into the far corner, plucked a new one from the box, pulled it on and sat down again. 'That's better,' he said, and picked up the phone to make another call.

It was impossible to think of him in a domestic context. In the tedious empty periods – and there are lots of those, waiting while engineers tinker and set up sounds and rig up effects – Newell and I sat with our feet up on the mixing desk, wondering if the manager had ever done anything normal. 'Do you think he's ever mown a lawn?' Newell said.

We pondered this for some time until the need to know overwhelmed us. We walked down the corridor to the office and stood just inside the door, shuffling like children going before a teacher. 'You ask him,' I said.

Newell cleared his throat. 'Um, can I interrupt?'

'Yes?'

'Um . . . we just wanted to ask. Er . . . have you ever mown a lawn?'

The manager blew out some smoke and narrowed his eyes. 'What is this about?' he said.

'Nothing. Really. Just – have you ever mown a lawn?'

'Of course I have.'

Newell and I nodded thoughtfully. There was a long glance.

'Where?' asked Newell.

The manager shifted in his seat and said nothing.

'Was it at your mother's? In Edinburgh?'

The manager sighed deeply. He pursed his lips. 'Maybe.'

There was another long pause.

'And what did you use?'

'Oh, for Christ's sake . . .'

'No, really. What kind of mower?'

'One of those electrical ones.'

'A Flymo, you mean?'

'Look, I'm extremely busy. Perhaps we can continue this

conversation at a later date. But for now – fuck off back to the studio and get on with your record.'

Around this time we posed for a publicity shot – a Walker-print, just like Pony's, with our name in tidy Letraset along the foot. It was taken by Geoff one weekend in front of a random piece of statuary in Wivenhoe. In the photograph I am wearing a black beret, pushed right to the back of my head where it forms a dark halo and a snug backdrop for my ears. Why am I wearing this? I had never worn a beret before and I have never worn one since. The other feature of this photo is a highly visible food stain in the centre of my jumper.

Paul Carrack

In order to be able to have the time to record with the Cleaners from Venus, I had had to change my circumstances. Before the band's deal came along, I had been as purposeless and unmotivated in Bristol as I had been in Colchester and Wivenhoe in the year before. I had had one short-lived job – editing the in-house periodical of the Bristol Industrial Archaeological Trust. The woman interviewing me had said, 'So, Giles, industrial archaeology. Does it grab you by the balls?' I confessed that it didn't and she gave me the job. I managed to get one issue out, containing a detailed report on the excavation of a nineteenth-century pin-making factory near Weston-super-Mare, before I packed it up.

And then things had begun to look tantalizingly possible for the Cleaners and all I could think was that this was my big chance, the opportunity I should put my weight behind. The thing about being in a band is, you're holding out for massive riches in the end but in the meantime it's time-consuming and pays you absolutely nothing. What I was looking for was something to go alongside the Cleaners, which guaranteed an income while allowing infinitely flexible free time. The only place you could really pull that off was inside a university. The place for me as a postgraduate was still open, so I took it: to ease my passage towards a future life as Sting. I signed up to do a PhD on Dr Johnson. I figured that if it turned out that I was in a recording studio more often than I was in a library, I was only reinterpreting my grant as an Arts Council award.

In September, I moved out of my girlfriend's flat and went back to Cambridge. Of course, when the band *really* took off,

I was going to return in triumph. The way she saw it, faced with the choice between our relationship and the Cleaners from Venus, I had chosen the Cleaners from Venus. Our relationship continued across the distance for a while, but looking back, there were many, many obvious signs that she had found someone else, signs I should have picked up. Like the weekend that she came to visit me with two new piercings in the rim of her left ear and a velvet hat. How come I didn't think that through?

But no. What it took in the end was the appearance in her collection of a Paul Carrack solo album, secondhand. Who had told her about that? Where had that come from? There was no way she could have gone through those secondhand racks and pulled out Paul Carrack and thought, 'Maybe I'll give this a try.' Hell, she was listening to Judy Tzuke before I met her. And now here I was, pulling from a scruffy, unalpha-beticized wodge of LPs, packed unsatisfactorily in the space beneath the side-table which supported her popping stereo, a copy of a hard-to-find solo album by the man whose voice you hear on 'How Long' by Ace. Someone had led her that way. Someone else had shared this with her. Not me.

The Cleaners from Venus, take 4

Going to England, the first album by the Cleaners from Venus came out on the Ammunition Communications label in February 1987. Catalogue No: CLEAN 1LP. *Harper's & Queen* described it, in a three-quarter-page piece accompanying a large black and white photograph of Newell and myself petting a cat, as 'an obsessive new addiction' and furthermore said of us: 'They have come to hoover your musical home and throw out all the junk.' But the article was written by a friend of mine.

Reviewing the album in the *NME* though (two and a half inches, bottom right corner of the page but, God, we were grateful), Campbell Stephenson wrote:

I've had it with nostalgia but I like this record. The references are 'Senses'-period XTC and the Smithereens playing *All Mod Cons* . . . Their ticket to the past is a return . . . 'You Must Be Out Of My Mind' is 'Imagine' for pessimists. Were it not for the thankful lack of clever dick trickery, the whole caboodle might end up close to 10cc territory . . . Quite what year their calendar shows it's unclear, but it's a fine vintage.

And I swear I have never met Campbell Stephenson in my life.

We were also reviewed in the short-lived alternative rock magazine *Underground* ('what we have here is an old-fashioned form of sampling known as imitation . . . at times uncannily reminiscent of the beat-age Beatles, choc-a-bloc with distant echoing harmonies, strumming guitars . . . Forget your fab four CDs, *Going to England* is period perfect') and in *Sounds* ('harbours plenty of well-crafted songs that would like to capture the essence of Squeeze's pop ditties . . . it's on the "Every Breath You Take" twang of "Mercury Girl" and the refined, jazzy shuffle of "Clara Bow" that they're most effective'). The London *Evening Standard* said we were 'Charming and idiosyncratic. The song "Illya Kuryakin Looked At Me" is the best yet evocation of the swinging sixties on record.' And the *Essex County Standard* said: 'Martin, from West Street, Wivenhoe . . .' etc. This was quite a good haul of press for beginners. But almost nobody bought the record.

At some point after the album was finished, the manager had issued us with a contract – thirty sheets of closely typed and intimidating legal jargon in which we were hereafter referred to as 'the artist' and the manager was hereafter referred to as 'the company' and the album was hereafter referred to as 'the album'. After the lax sixties, in which people like Pete Townshend would sign away vast portions of their life and earnings while drunk backstage after a show, it is now legal practice to insert into a recording contract a clause in which the artist acknowledges that he has taken independent legal advice before signing. Even here, record companies have found a loop through which to wriggle. If you lack independent legal advice and don't know where to find it, some record companies will set up and pay for 'independent' legal advice on your behalf, and these 'independent' lawyers will look through your contract and say they can see absolutely nothing wrong with it. Which gets that little problem out of the way in no time.

Feeling that it was imperative to employ the sharpest showbiz lawyers in town, but lacking the necessary money, I handed the contract to a friend's father who was a solicitor in Chelmsford. He was not, strictly speaking, an entertainment expert, although he had once told me that, had things worked out differently, he would very much have liked to be a violinist. Chiefly he did houses and divorces. This was probably the first record contract he had ever seen. But at least he was familiar with the language in which this document was written, a language in which even the conjunctions seemed to have been poorly translated from the Latin: 'whichsoever', 'heretofore', 'thereafter'.

It was, I have since discovered, an entirely standard arrangement between record company and artist, and yet it drew from my newly appointed legal consultant three closely typed pages of his own, explaining in words he thought I would understand why this deal represented a breathtaking constriction of our right to earn a living. We stood to receive twelve per cent of the income generated by our albums, once our albums had generated sufficient income to settle all the costs involved in making them, packaging them and marketing them. The cost of any videos and television advertisements would be borne by us in the form of a reduced royalty on records promoted by those means. The contract bound us up for six albums, without increase in this royalty rate in the event of our becoming successful. The company had, at any moment, the power to terminate the arrangement; we had no such power until we had complied in full with its terms. His advice was, Do not sign this contract. So I signed it.

Let me make something clear; I did not go into this deal blind. I had read my copy of *Expensive Habits* by Simon Garfield, a book about rip-offs and sad deals and swindles in the music industry. Indeed, I had taken notes on sheets of A4 as I read it, believing that the tales it told were tales I had better get by heart if I was intending to go anywhere as a musician. I knew how George Michael was still on fifty pound per week when Wham! were having No. 1 hits; I knew that Gilbert O'Sullivan had signed a deal of such medieval unfairness that his ability to make any money at all was shackled for years. I knew about Elton John and all the others who had put their names on dodgy dotted lines early in their careers and earned the right to be referred to hereafter as 'the complete saps'.

I didn't think I was like that. I was more modern. I was something like the chastened person that George Michael became after Wham!, one of the smart new breed of 1980s musicians who understood the business side, not like those sad old rockers of the 1970s, too blitzed on tequila and coke to notice that their managers were opening Swiss bank accounts and buying most of Oxfordshire. The point is, these transactions are often painted as instances of a greedy industry taking advantage of naïve musicians. But I was pretty genned up when that contract was passed over to me. And against my own better judgement and against the advice of an informed legal mind, I had signed it. Signed it, indeed, and initialled every crippling page.

I wasn't a victim of naïvety in this, or of the cruel machinations of a cynical business. I was a victim, not for the first time in my life, of the lure of vinyl. The truth was, I wanted simply to be able to have and hold a piece of vinyl which I had played on, part-produced, part-written – a record of my own. I wanted to scrutinize its sleeve, I wanted to slide the record from the inner sleeve. I wanted to read the small-print of the publishing details on the label and see my name in brackets after some of the titles. I wanted to put the album on the deck, lower the needle and hear *me* coming out – yes! Unbelievable! There I am! That piano bit, there! That's *me*!

And I wanted to know the bliss of seeing that record in a record shop. Consider the possible public culminations of other kinds of artistic endeavour: having your play staged at a theatre, say; having a painting hung in a gallery; having a book out. Can any of these things really hold a candle to being available in Our-Price? On record *and* cassette? On 7-inch *and* 12-inch? I don't think so. And why let mere contractual details threaten to retard a lifelong thrill like that? If the contract with Ammunition Communications had bound me to lead monthly karaoke evenings at the Basildon Young Conservatives Club, well, I probably would have signed it even then.

Perhaps I would feel differently about this if the whole thing had been a vast success and the manager was currently investing in his third Caribbean island while Newell and I were living in a squat off the Bayswater Road. But, as it is, I'm inclined to think the gamble paid off. First a small batch of test pressings with blank white centre labels arrived at the office, one of which I carried home gingerly and stored away. Finally there were finished copies and I went down to London to pick some up. The lettering on the sleeve wasn't really bright enough to show up against the illustration, which was a bit of a blow, but at least the sleeve was square and the object within was certainly round, flat and black, twelve inches across and with a small hole in the middle. There was no denying it: it was a real album.

Celebration collapsed into anxiety soon enough. After a neurotic testing-session in the privacy of my own room – quick bursts of the Cleaners, followed as closely as possible by quick bursts of big-selling albums – I managed to work myself into a fit of childish resentment. Why, when heard back-to-back with Scritti Politti's *Cupid And Psyche '85*, did out album sound so much flatter, so much duller? Why didn't its top notes gleam like that? Why didn't the bass thump out at you as if determined to free itself from behind the speakers' gauze? Why was it so much quieter? Why did it sound as though the needle was having to press down through a layer of wet bread to get to the music? A simple answer: our album had cost, maybe, four thousand pounds in studio time and expenses. Scritti Politti's had probably cost something in the region of a quarter of a million and I suppose it's only fair that they should have got an increase in quality for that kind of spend. Even so, a new ambivalence entered my feelings about our record. It was at once, it seemed to me, the real thing and a cheap imitation.

There were consolations, though. We had a cardboard record divider with our name on in the Virgin Megastore in Tottenham Court Road. We were under 'C' in Cambridge Our-Price. And we were under 'B' in Andy's Records, Colchester, a mistake that I hastily rectified. In fact, whenever I was in a record store over this feverish period, I made sure to move our sleeve to the front of the rack, for maximum browser temptation. (I should add that this kind of in-store meddling is not just the preoccupation of the sad wannabe. Much later, as a journalist, I interviewed Neil Tennant who arrived a little late, confessing that he had just promoted the Pet Shop Boys video to the No. 1 slot in the Our-Price at Notting Hill Gate.) Eventually – after about two months – I would know the indignity of happening upon our album in the Notting Hill Record and Tape Exchange. Three copies of it. For now, though, I was a blissful innocent.

Late that spring we played our first live shows. This, of course, was something Newell had vowed he would never do. He would later claim it was the slow but consistent erosion of the principles he held dear that finally forced him to go mad and leave. When the possibility of a gig was first floated, he fought off the manager, saying, 'No, absolutely not,' his mouth tightening. But the manager talked him round, saying it would benefit the album. And it wasn't like he was asking him to *tour* or anything, just to do one or two shows . . . And I began to see how subtle they had been in that first meeting in the flat with their nods and their 'indeed's and 'quite understand's, initially accepting any condition Newell laid down, with a view to changing his mind about it later or letting circumstances overtake.

We picked the two best musicians we could find in Colchester. On bass, Nel, who had already played on the album and who would later become involved with New Model Army, and on drums, Ichiro Tatsuhara, who would later become involved with the immigration authorities. We rehearsed where nearly all Colchester's bands rehearsed – in the tiny sideroom of a nightclub in Priory Street. Nel and Ichiro were disciplined and fast. Somewhat alarmingly, they seemed to know the songs better than we did. We had three days to prepare a forty-five minute set so there wasn't time to go in for finesse, let alone to programme lasers, explosions or video sequences. We ripped out most of the fiddly stuff from the recorded versions, squared the songs off at the edges and prayed we would get away with it on the 'gutsy' ticket.

We played at Dingwall's in Camden Town, London, on a special Ammunition Communications label night, organized by the manager and Pete the Bastard. They hired a barge with a bar on it, filled it with people from record companies, and set off up the canal to get everyone drunk. An hour later, the boat docked outside the club, everyone staggered ashore and those still capable of standing and watching came in to see live performances from us (bottom of the bill owing to a bad call by me in the coin-tossing that afternoon), Voice of America (the synthesizer duo from Blackpool) and a trampy glam rock band called West End Central, featuring Rene Berg, who was a former member of Hanoi Rocks.

It was hot and crowded. I wore a white shirt and a tie

in the hope of affecting a kind of mid-eighties stylish-but-businesslike look and mostly because Green was wearing one in the photograph on the inner sleeve of *Cupid And Psyche*. Much like the beret in the publicity shot, I never wore ties. Newell, meanwhile, was in bus-conductor's hat and a sleeveless T-shirt. These were things he wore all the time. We were somewhat under-rehearsed, but we were at least refreshingly loud. I know this because John Parish was in the audience and I asked him afterwards: 'What did you think, John?'

He thought long and hard, his brow creased. Finally he looked up and said: 'It was very loud.'

Later came our big outdoor appearance. 'We've got you on to an open-air festival,' the manager said. I had visions of something sun-drenched, possibly Italian. 'It's in Scunthorpe,' he added. It took place on a Saturday afternoon and we were supporting Furniture, who were a year on from their solitary hit with 'Brilliant Mind'. A giant white van was hired, with two rows of seats to accommodate the four of us, a pile of drums, guitars and keyboards, Pete the Bastard, who was on minder duty, and Captain Sensible, who was also on the bill, singing and playing guitar over backing tapes of his greatest hits. It was raining and cold. We played, without a soundcheck, from a large scaffolding stage to a small wind-whipped crowd in kagouls. Quite badly.

Afterwards, Newell was approached by a girl of around fourteen.

'Which band are you in?' she said.

He said, 'I'm in the Cleaners from Venus.'

She said, 'I've only just arrived. How did you get on?'

He said, 'I don't know, really. Seemed to go OK.'

And she said, 'I bet you were crap,' and walked away.

Gigs like this were a test of one's digestive system as much as anything. On the way back in the van, as I was opening a can of lager, I paused to reflect on what I had thus far consumed that day:

> One cup of tea with sugar
> A Star Bar
> One stick of Wrigley's Spearmint Gum
> Two cans of Special Brew
> A hot dog with onions from a van
> Another cup of tea with sugar
> A Kit-Kat

All interspersed with three-quarters of a packet of Benson & Hedges. I was aware that, next to what hardened, night-after-night bands consider an on-the-road diet, this was positively nutritious. (High in smoke and sugar, it's true, but some encouraging roughage there in the form of the onions.) But if it only took a one-night stand to reduce the contents of my stomach to a hot zone of fizzing acids, how was I going to stand up to a tour?

Further on in the journey, I made an important discovery about Newell: he had a bladder like a fishnet stocking. We had already made two unscheduled stops and Pete the Bastard, who was driving, refused a third, muttering something about how it would be nice if we could be home before Wednesday. So Newell stood up in the back of the van, with one arm outstretched to steady himself against the side wall, and as the van continued to lurch and sway down the M1, he relieved himself into an empty beercan. I made a mental note not to put my beer down. I made another mental note never to go in a van with Newell again.

Everyone got drunk, but Newell got drunkest. Which was amazing given that the liquid was only fleetingly inside his body. At his feet sat a squadron of slowly cooling beer cans.

Every time I saw brake-lights flare red on the road up ahead, it occurred to me that, in the event of an emergency stop, I was in danger of being crushed from behind by numerous weighty instruments in flight cases, a former member of the Damned and several tins of piss.

I wanted to be at home, in bed.

It was hard to know whether this limited live exposure was advancing our career. But back in the office, the manager was clearly doing his utmost to broaden the operation. One day I got a phone call in Cambridge. 'You'd better let your tutors know you're leaving,' said the manager. 'We've got the Enigma deal.'

This was staggering news. Talk of 'the Enigma deal' had rumbled on for some time. Enigma was an American independent company intending to set up in Britain and looking for a lively British act with which to launch their new operation. They would have money to promote our records and money to pay us wages. To secure 'the Enigma deal' was to become, finally, after these years of struggle, a professional musician.

I phoned Newell and we gibbered feverishly at each other for a few minutes. Then I went out for the evening to celebrate.

Lager was ordered. Friends toasted my future and wished me well. The lager mixed with my uncontainable excitement. More lager was ordered and there was more well-wishing. I tried to respond to this decorously, thinking of the feelings of those, less fortunate, around me. I tried to bear in mind what Nietzsche said about there being no feast without a tragedy. I fought to remember that, though I was now free of gloomy academe for good, liberated to make my way in the glamorous world of pop, my friends would not be coming with me. They were still prisoners here, good-naturedly enjoying the salvation which had come my way. But the next weeks, months and maybe years would find them trudging to the university library rather than jetting out to the Miami beach house, carefully supping a grant-stretching pint in the pub of an evening rather than slipping from the limo and heading, with a dark grin, through the thrilling flash and jostle of the paparazzi and into the nightclub.

So when I said my few words of thanks and farewell, I was suitably meek and reassuring. Although I was leaving them, I said, they weren't to think of me in any real sense as 'gone'. I wasn't the kind of guy to be changed by superficial things like fame and money. I wasn't the kind of guy to forget where he came from. Depend on it. They were my friends. If they needed me, they would always know where to find me. (And failing that, they could always ring the switchboard-operator at the record company, who might be able to put them through to a secretary or a publicity officer or someone who might know where I was, although, of course, a busy schedule is a busy schedule.)

Outside afterwards, I mounted my bike. The air was cold and clean, and on the way back to my room, in the middle of a wide common, I paused and turned dizzy circles in the night, fit to whoop into the silence, 'Free at last, my Lord, free at last!'

Waking late the next morning, dry-eyed and with a stripped tongue, I thought immediately back to that cycle ride. And I remembered that I didn't have a bicycle. So I wonder whose bike that was. And then I realized that the phone was ringing and I got out of bed and crossed the room.

'Hello?'

It was the manager.

'Forget the Enigma deal,' he said. 'It's off.'

Two Hymns

My father's illness came on him very fast. We didn't know at first that it was a brain tumour. It started with him having strangely calm fits, moments of absence in which his left hand would shudder. He would recall nothing of them afterwards. One Christmas Eve, his left side seemed to give out altogether, just briefly, and he had to hold himself up against a kitchen cupboard. The fits increased in frequency and duration, and eventually his doctor sent him to a specialist in London. I went with him that day, up to Liverpool Street by train, round on the tube. Afterwards, he tried hard to look untroubled, unfrightened. Sitting opposite me on the train back, he had another attack.

The operation to remove some of the tumour was radically debilitating. He started with a clock and a calendar beside the bed until he remembered about time and days. It wasn't too long before he could speak. Then he began to think about learning to walk again.

When he was convalescing at home, I made him a tape of a Spike Jones record I had borrowed from the library because I thought there was nothing that could prevent you laughing when you heard Spike Jones. Actually, though, there are plenty of things.

He lived for fifteen months after the operation. Sometimes he seemed fitter than he had ever been. Other times he could not stand. When he died he had been in a coma for a week. I was on a train back from Bristol and I wasn't with him.

At my father's funeral we sang 'He Who Would Valiant Be'

and 'Lead Us, Heavenly Father, Lead Us', which were his favourite hymns. No pop songs, obviously. Because my father didn't like pop songs. And because there isn't a pop song written that could have been played there.

The Cleaners from Venus, take 5

The manager triumphed in the end. He got us our dream. He secured, for the Cleaners from Venus, a deal with a major record company. But only in Germany.

The deal stemmed from a meeting the manager had at MIDEM, the record industry's trade fair. Held annually in Cannes, MIDEM is an excuse for music-industry people to get drunk and pretend to be in the film industry. When the manager and Pete the Bastard announced that they were flying out for three days at MIDEM '87, Newell and I were sceptical. We had seen how they behaved outside office hours. Older than they seemed when behind their desks, both of them regressed rapidly, under the influence of lager, to become archetypal, on-the-town Scots lads. Over the course of an evening in the pub, they would pass from being garrulous and charming in the first hour to dangerously oversexed in the second, and finally incoherent and doing impressions of a pirate ('A-HARRRRRGGHHH!') by the third. I was the victim of a night out with the manager which had started quietly at 7.00 p.m. in the pub along the road from the studio and had ended at 4.00 a.m. the next day over a plate of something disgusting upstairs in a Chinese café in Soho. My memories of what happened in between are inevitably patchy, though I dimly recall a record-industry party, an after-hours club just north of Oxford Street and a lot of walking and shouting. I then caught an early-morning train back to Cambridge, one that stopped everywhere. At one point I was jolted awake to find that the carriage had filled with schoolchildren, a number of whom were looking at me with round eyes and open mouths, silent and terrified at the drooling state I was in.

From Newell's and my point of view, there was no reason to believe that, for the manager and Pete the Bastard, MIDEM would be anything more than a thinly disguised, expenses-paid brewery tour. We pictured them laying waste to the duty-free trolley on the plane out, and again on the plane home. We thought it highly likely that at least one of them would come off the plane at Heathrow without his trousers.

We weren't entirely wrong: a story they returned with involved one of them ending up naked in a hotel corridor. But they found time to do some business. They passed our tape to a German music publisher called Ulrika Schoen, who owned publishing rights in Latin Quarter and The Bible. Ulrika returned to Hamburg and discussed us with RCA. And now RCA were making us an offer. They would release and promote *Going To England* in Germany. They would contribute to our recording costs for two further albums. In short, this was our opportunity to be big in Germany. Some bands are years ahead of their time. We would have to settle for being an hour behind ours.

Why had Germany gone for what England had thus far refused? For one thing, perhaps, over there the name of the band didn't seem immediately duff. Perhaps it even had a ring of the exotic and funny about it rather than a naff tang of the wilfully surreal. For another thing, we sounded – or we thought we sounded – like the Beatles, only more commercial. And in Germany at that point Beatle-alikes remained a viable business proposition, as indeed did anything redolent of 1960s British pop. We would have preferred to have been big in our own land but, with the way things appeared to be going, we would have settled for being big in Turkey.

On the day our deal was announced, we went to a Mexican bar in the Charing Cross road where the manager called for tequila slammers and a horrifying quantity of lager in large glass jugs. Inside a week, he and Pete the Bastard had managed to secure not just our deal, but also a contract for Voice of America to record two singles for Virgin Records. Virgin Records in England, indeed. They looked extremely pleased with themselves and I began to believe our faith in them was well placed. The ship had come in and it was loaded with American beer.

How do you get on in the music industry? My personal step-by-step guide would have to read something like this:

You send your music to a former member of the Damned.
He plays it to a twenty-four-year-old Scotsman in a cheap suit.
The Scotsman flies to Cannes and gets drunk.
A German woman picks up the tape in Cannes and flies with it
    back to Hamburg.
The German woman plays it to a Beatles fan at RCA Germany.
A major record company awards you a three-album contract.

It's easy when you know how.

RCA pressed up their own copies of *Going To England* and released them in the summer. We received some samples in London. The sleeves were bright and glossy, and this time the lettering stood out boldly. I enjoyed the fact that the album now had an authentic bar-code on the back. High-quality printwork on the spine, too. But it was the label I was most proud of, with RCA's angular block capital logo, exactly as it appeared on my copy of the Al Stewart single 'Year of the Cat'. It was a better quality pressing, too – or so I was told. It didn't really sound any different.

In September 1987, RCA invited us to Hamburg to play a

promotional showcase gig, and here another of Newell's early stipulations crumbled into dust. He tried to make himself feel more comfortable about it by holding out for unusual treatment. He wanted to travel by ferry. And he wanted to stay in a bed and breakfast outside the city. Neither of these requests was met.

On the day of our flight, we assembled at the office in Denmark Street at 7.00 a.m., myself and Newell, Nel and Ichiro, the manager and Pete the Bastard. I had never seen the manager ready for work this early in the morning. But, despite the hour, he had all his business wits about him. To save money, we travelled to Heathrow by tube.

We were met at Hamburg airport by Ulrika, the publisher. She spoke English perfectly and with a hint of the aristocrat, like a woman who had been educated at Roedean. This was because she was a woman who had been educated at Roedean. Alongside her was a photographer from a Hamburg evening paper, who started snapping at us as we walked into the Arrivals lounge. One photographer is not exactly the paparazzi treatment, but even so it was one more than I had expected and strangely flattering. Not even members of my family have taken photos of me arriving at an airport.

The photographer wanted to do some posed pictures, too, and led us outside to a sort of playground area near the viewing deck where there was a large hardboard cut-out of a cartoon plane with smiling eyes and puckered red lips. We poked our heads and arms through the windows and waved. Then we posed in front of a highly polished airport truck with a sign on its roof which read: 'Follow Me'.

A taxi took us to our hotel, which was sensitively located in the heart of Hamburg's extensive and explicit red-light district, just a condom's throw from the notorious Reeperbahn. Anything less like a bed and breakfast outside the city it would be hard to imagine. Newell and I shared a small square room, three flights up, with orange curtains and one double bed. We felt like Morecambe and Wise. Directly below our window, a prostitute stood waiting for tricks. We watched her for a while until she moved on. I flipped through the television channels: a news programme, a daytime game-show, some children's cartoons, an overweight man inserting an enormous vibrator between the splayed buttocks of a . . . 'Hang on a minute. What was that?' said Newell. I flipped back. It was our very own, twenty-four-hour hardcore porn service, piped into the room by the thoughtful Swedish hotel owner, who later explained to Newell that he 'thought English rock bands liked that kind of thing'. Maybe English rock bands like that kind of thing, but not nearly as much as their managers. Pete the Bastard christened it 'the pink bits channel'. Later that night, from our room, Newell and I would hear him and the manager down the corridor, thoroughly refreshed, singing, 'Bring out the pink bits!' and shouting 'A-HAAARRGGGGHHH!'

That first evening we had an appointment with our man from RCA, the person responsible for signing us to the label. He met us in the hotel lobby and took us to a bar along the street. He was not the leather-jacketed, pony-tailed berk of record-company legend. He was softly spoken and talked seriously about our music and how much he liked it. He said he thought we could do very well in Germany. He said he didn't want to force anything: he wanted to develop us slowly and patiently. He didn't see us as a flash-in-the-pan singles act; he thought we were an albums band, in it for the long run. *Going To England* was all about getting the ball rolling. Our second album would establish us firmly. Our third would push us over the top into the big league. After an extremely comfortable hour and a half, he left us, saying he needed an early night and that he would see us at the gig the next day. We stayed on in the bar a while longer, talking about how solid and straightforward our A&R man seemed, hardly believing our luck.

It was still fairly early when we finished our drinks. Newell went back to the hotel, Nel and Ichiro went off to do some exploring and the managers took me out for a quiet drink in a live sex club. Pete the Bastard was insistent that we should find a place where you could see people 'actually doing it', so we scouted Hamburg's bleary streets for some twenty minutes, weighing up the various implausible claims writ tall on hoardings beside neon-lit doorways. All Action Sex Show. Full Frontal Non-Stop. Real Male–Female Live Viewing.

Inevitably, the one we plumped for turned out to be a bar the size of a railway buffet with a small stage at one end on which a bored woman in her forties lay naked on a revolving deck-chair while another woman, slightly older, sat nude on a seat beside her. When we walked in, joining the four or five other dupes nursing absurdly pricy beers and disappointed expressions, the woman on the chair stood up and danced – or, at least, moved her arms like someone jogging very slowly. There was no music for her to dance to anyway. After about twenty seconds she sat down again and resumed her conversation with the woman on the electric garden furniture. We finished our drinks, the manager called to arrange a mortgage to cover the tab, and we left.

Back in the hotel bar, we found Nel and Ichiro in a state of excitement. On their walk, they had found what used to be an underground car park where men now went to pick among the prostitutes who stood themselves on sale against the concrete. In that crowd they had bumped into a familiar, friendly, though now rather sheepish-looking face. It was our man from RCA, getting an early night. Like they say in Hamburg: if you're not in bed by ten, come home.

I had never played anywhere as big as Hamburg's Grosse Freiheit ('The Freedom Hall'), a giant ballroom with a high stage, directly opposite what used to be the Star Club where the Beatles played. And I had never played a gig where the equipment was set up before you arrived. It was waiting for us when we turned up in the afternoon to soundcheck. And the dressing room was huge and warm and well-lit, and along one wall was a table stacked with fruit and meat and salad and chocolates and there was more beer there in crates than even the manager and Pete the Bastard could have seen off in one sitting.

And that night, we stood in the wings, skipping from foot to foot, until we saw the lights go off in the hall, and Newell said, 'Right, then' – no pre-gig prayer routine for us, no intra-band hug session or feel-good basketball huddle, just Newell saying, 'Right, then' – and we ran out on to this spacious stage in the dark, hearing the whistles from the audience, feeling, as we went on, that swift switch in temperature, from the cool of the corridor to the heat from the hall. And a single light came up and Newell said, 'Good evening' – not 'Good evening, Hamburg' which would have been naff, but just 'Good evening', which was cool – and Ichiro rapped his sticks together and shouted the count-in, which never sounded like numbers the way he did it, but was just 'An! An! An-an-an-an . . .' And we clattered into 'Julie Profumo' – *Going To England*, side one, track one – with Newell's high, lazy Essex voice clearing the racket:

> I'm going to England
> I'm leaving to-dzay . . .

And I was on guitar for this song, with space to skip around in, room to run to the microphone for the backing vocals in the chorus:

> And one day soon, I will forget this junkyard,
> Take you with me if you're going that way . . .

And from the stage, against the lights, you couldn't really see the audience, just silhouettes and glow, but you could sense that the place was packed and heaving in time with the beat. And it was one of those rare times when the noise the four of you are making gathers a momentum which doesn't seem to be running away from you, but instead carries you aloft. I felt us bowling down the runway. I felt our wheels lift off the tarmac and fifteen hundred people raised their hands up at us and cheered us into the air.

Packing up afterwards? Pah! We had roadies to do that for us.

Our flight home the next morning was punishingly early. The plane arrived at Heathrow at 10.00 a.m. As we pushed our trolleys through Customs, a man in a uniform beckoned Newell over to a table and asked him to open his guitar case. Newell promptly went into a fit of shivering. It was strange and frightening to behold. He had nothing to worry about. He wasn't carrying any drugs. He wasn't over the limit on his duty-free. He didn't even have any money they could steal. But, at the very sight of someone in authority, some sort of hippie gene woke up inside him in a hurry and sent him into a dizzy paranoia. The fuzz were on his case and he didn't like it. I tried to say something to calm him down but he was just a blur of anxiety. It was over in seconds: the Customs officer took one look at the guitar, shut the case and that was that. But on the tube train back into London, with the time now approximately 10.30 a.m., Newell had to quieten his jangled nerves by consuming an entire bottle of duty-free cherry liqueur.

One other thing: we later learned that tickets for the Hamburg show had cost the equivalent of eight pounds. For eight pounds we had given the audience a skinny, forty-five-minute set, RCA having informed us in advance that forty-five minutes would be 'perfectly adequate'. Our night of glory in Germany was also a stunning rip-off.

In all about ten thousand copies of *Going to England* were sold in Germany. This wasn't enough to make us household names (except in those particular ten thousand households), or even to allow us to figure in a bestselling chart. But RCA seemed happy enough. They talked about it as a base to work from. In the late autumn of 1987, we started to record our follow-up.

Buoyed up by our experience on stage in Hamburg, our continental sales success and the imminent global breakthrough that I felt sure these things portended, I was keen that we should step up to another, better studio. I wasn't after a state-of-the-art 48-track place in the South of France. I just thought something with a window or two might be nice. But we were locked in with Ammunition Communications, who could only advance us studio time on their own premises and not money to use in other studios. It was back down to Denmark Street again.

Except that Denmark Street was not quite the same. A year on from the recording of *Going To England* and cracks were beginning to appear in the empire of the manager and Pete the Bastard. They may well have managed to get two of their acts on to the books of major labels, but neither of these deals had generated much in the way of cash. Commercial business in the studio was next to non-existent: that side of things had been run down to keep the studio free for our use and for Voice of America. It was clear that the money was running out.

It was also obvious that some of the money had never actually existed. Certain bills for the hiring of instruments and studio equipment had not been settled. Certain hire companies were no longer dealing with the studio. The company had ceased being able to afford the flat upstairs. The manager had moved in with his girlfriend in Notting Hill and Pete the Bastard was now living in the office. Every night he made a bed up in the windowless, stuffy back room. Everything he owned was wedged into a corner, which might have presented a problem for the day-to-day workings of the company, except that everything he owned was a pile of T-shirts and jeans, a pair of trainers and some underwear. Also a badminton racket, which grew to look like a symbol of some long-forgotten golden age. After recording, Newell and I now slept in the studio, one of us under the mixing desk, one of us under the piano, both of us under a selection of the same crusty items of bedding that had been available to us in the flat. We slept clothed, for fear of what those blankets might do to our skin.

Under pressure of its use as studio, office and doss-house, the basement grew lank and more than commonly airless. Occasionally Pete the Bastard, admirably unfazed by his predicament, would pass the office Hoover over the carpeting and for half an hour or so the place would fill with the smell of freshly heated dust. The manager tended less and less to peel off a tenner and say, 'Expenses.' There was an acute cash-flow problem during which, across one desolate weekend, the studio was without coffee and loo roll – but having only an absence of coffee and loo roll to complain about would come to seem like luxury. One day the phones were cut off until some money was hastily drummed up from somewhere and they were reconnected. We expected the hi-fi and the pair of Captain Sensible silver discs off the wall to go at almost any time. In the most symbolic event of all, the unwashed bedding finally rebelled. There was an outbreak of scabies.

In order to have more flexible time to devote to the band, Newell had left his washing-up job and had started a gardening round in Wivenhoe. I had my 'Arts Council' grant, so I was OK, but clearly Newell could not earn any money while he was recording, so the company had put him on a tiny weekly retainer. There were weeks when this money didn't appear, bringing Newell close to destitution. At one point during the recording, he went home to Wivenhoe and was briefly stranded because he had no money for the train fare back. I don't imagine it was ever like this for Duran Duran.

We thought we had some strong songs for our second album – 'Blue Swan', 'Let's Get Married', 'I Wasn't Drinking' – but when we came to record them, Newell and I were pulling the material in different directions and it stretched and split on us. I wanted to proceed cautiously, build the album gradually. Newell wanted to get the songs down in a burst, let them keep some energy and some rough edges. These approaches were not designed to complement one another. One afternoon, after a tedious bout of retakes, he and Ichiro ended up shouting insults at each other through the control-room window.

In an ill-judged attempt to make the album sound ritzy and shimmering, like Prefab Sprout as produced by Thomas Dolby, I started ladling rich keyboard sounds all over the place, like chocolate sauce. Newell wasn't interested enough to insist that they be scrubbed off. The whole process took about two months. When the album was finished, we were united at least in being dissatisfied with it. The tapes went off to Hamburg for mastering.

Newell was also subject at this time to a slow but relentless campaign of persuasion from the manager who was bent on getting him to go on tour – which Newell had said from the start he would never agree to. Evidently RCA were talking confidently of a German national tour in the spring of 1988 to accompany the release of the second album. The manager's feeling was that Newell had now shown that he could go on a stage and that he could go abroad, so what was the problem? Newell gamely reassembled his arguments about the absurdity of touring and the danger it posed to anyone's, but particularly his, mental equilibrium. The discussions lasted over a period of about a month before Newell finally gave in and said he would go, thus binning the last of his major scruples.

In between the completion of the album and the scheduled date for the start of the tour, I went back to Cambridge and Newell returned to his gardening round. I kept in touch with the office in London but Newell didn't. Later he explained to me that two months' living underground and sleeping between potentially scabrous sheets had damaged him more than he realized at the time. He had gone sour on the whole business. He felt he had been manipulated into precisely the position he had intended to avoid. He had been cajoled into going on a tour he didn't want, to support an album he didn't like. And he wasn't getting paid. He called the manager at the office. With two weeks to go until the start of the tour, with rehearsals and musicians booked in, with RCA plastering tour-date stickers all over our new album, Newell decided he wasn't going.

I got on a train that afternoon and went down to Wivenhoe to see him. He was in a bad way – shaky, tense about the jaw.

'If I was a baker,' he said, 'and I baked a really good loaf of bread . . . well, you wouldn't send me all round the world, baking it in a different city every night.'

I said I wasn't sure the analogy held.

He said he couldn't believe he had ever been talked into touring. He said he was lying awake, panicking about it. And when he slept, he had nightmares involving Transit vans full of musicians. He looked at me plaintively. 'I don't want to be a pop Messiah,' he said.

My initial reaction was selfish. All I could think was, This is a bit bloody previous. If he had cracked up after the pair of us had enjoyed a couple of weeks of blazing fame – hell, if he'd cracked up after a couple of *days* of it – I could have coped. But to have the breakdown in advance of the pressure seemed to me slightly joyless: the cold turkey without the drugs, the clap without the groupie.

But then there surfaced in my mind the image of him tugging energetically on that bottle of cherry liqueur at 10.30 a.m. on a tube train from Heathrow and I softened. He wasn't faking this: it was no prima donna tantrum. Newell wasn't the touring type and he had never pretended to be. He was a songwriter and a bag of nerves. He deserved protection. He deserved support.

Back in Cambridge, the phone rang. It was the manager. He said he had been talking to RCA. They were too far down the line with the plans to cancel the tour. They thought it should go ahead without Newell.

'That's impossible,' I said. 'He sings. He's the frontman. He writes the poxy songs. It's Newell's band, for God's sake.'

'Well, Brian Wilson gave up touring with the Beach Boys. He stayed at home and the rest of them went out and performed his songs. So why not you?'

I said, 'I don't believe this.'

'Listen,' he said, and his voice seemed suddenly more ominous. 'There's an opportunity to salvage something from this. RCA are being very patient. What I'm saying is, your career is in the toilet. But they haven't flushed it yet.'

I went on that tour. I had to. It was too late to pull out. To ditch the tour was, in the elegant metaphor of the manager, to pull the chain. Nobody stood to benefit from that. And, yes, the Cleaners from Venus without Newell would probably be like Starsky without Hutch, or Peters without Lee. But if Newell eventually came out of his depression and we were still signed to RCA, I thought it would come to look like a fortnight well spent. It wasn't an agreement to tour that I was entering into, so much as an undertaking to bandage a haemorrhage.

Now I had to front the band. I could impersonate Newell up to a point, but in the end my voice was dull, inexpressive. I could see that we were flirting with disaster. But I can't pretend that some part of me didn't thrill to the prospect. An open stage! A chance to shine! And I can't deny either that I didn't, in some respects, feel happy at the prospect of not having Newell around – much like when the person you sleep with has to get up earlier than you and you get the whole bed to spread out in for a while.

We hastily recruited Dan, a friend of Captain Sensible's from Brighton. He was a balanced and calm person who did forty minutes of yoga every morning. He had a long, black, curly MTV hairstyle, he could play guitar and he could sing, too. He did about a quarter of the songs and I covered the rest. Ichiro the drummer came, but Nel the bassist refused, as a show of solidarity with Newell. Nigel and Dave from Voice of America were coming as a support act. We used their bassist, Winston, and their guitarist, Tony, and gave them Ichiro in return. In other words, in a complex musical time-share scheme, three of the touring party had to play twice each night. Needless to say, this arrangement was developed by the manager to save money. He evoked history to justify it. 'That's how the old Motown tours used to be in the sixties.'

A white tour bus was rented with a large hold at the rear in which to stow the instruments. A set of secondhand aeroplane seats had been bolted into the back. They were peppered with cigarette burns, but high on comfort, at least while the van was stationary. In transit, the shot springs flung themselves about drunkenly underneath you, launching you towards the ceiling at various random, jaunty tangents. It struck me, as we pushed through London towards the motorway, that we were about to drive half-way across Europe in what was, to all intents and purposes, a motorized Kiddy Castle.

If you were of a superstitious cast of mind, you would possibly read some significance into the fact that we were nearly arrested on the way to our opening show in Berlin. Our driver was from Manchester and he'd never driven to Berlin before. Indeed, as I discovered in a confidence-sapping conversation with him on the ferry, he had never driven abroad before. Still, he seemed to be coping fine, driving us through the night across Belgium and into Germany, speeding us down to the border controls on the East German border and lining us up on the corridor route which, before the collapse of Communism in the East, took you directly to isolated West Berlin.

That was when it went wrong. The journey seemed to go on too long. I remember looking out of the window, noticing a surprising drabness in the architecture, a strange absence of neon and people dressed in leather, and many of the other things one might have expected from West Berlin. I also noticed that the people we passed on the pavement tended to stare after us very hard. Also, that all the other cars on the road seemed to have shrunk.

Eventually, the driver conceded that he couldn't find the club we were heading for and we stopped by the kerb. Pete the Bastard got down and crossed the road to talk to a soldier. We watched their exchange from the van, Pete the Bastard pointing to his map, the soldier looking very doubtful and shaking his head.

Pete the Bastard ran back and got in beside the driver.

'This is East Berlin, you fucking idiot.'

Somehow, the driver had managed to turn off the corridor and sink us deep behind the Iron Curtain. Without visas.

'I'll go back,' said the driver.

'Too fucking right you will,' said Pete the Bastard.

As we retreated, the van was tense and silent. I could envisage us needing the assistance of a British consulate very shortly. But I wasn't even sure if East Germany had one. At last, though, we began to see signs again for the corridor and shortly after that we were rounding a bend and heading joyfully up a sliproad back to the motorway and safety. At which moment, four soldiers stepped out of their checkpoint booth and pulled us over.

This time we all got out. The soldiers walked round the van, opened up the back, got inside, trying to work out why this foreign vehicle was attempting to pass out of the East, stocked with foreign electric equipment and a collection of pale, T-shirted British youths, some with pony-tails, none with adequate paperwork.

One of the soldiers said, 'We will have to take you to Potsdam for interviews.'

I said, emotionally, 'But we have a show to do', which would have sounded fine in a movie, but sounded pretty pathetic at a military checkpoint by a motorway in East Germany.

I felt a strong desire to weep. I had come to rock capitalist Germany and here I was about to become a prisoner of the Communist East. And they hadn't even heard the album. Remembering the Heathrow Customs incident, I was relieved that Newell wasn't with us. It is quite likely he would have attempted to sprint for the woods and been shot.

At this juncture, Pete the Bastard came good. Awesomely good. He produced a roll of Deutschmarks from his back pocket and said, 'Can we pay a fine?' The soldiers deliberated in silence for a few seconds, until the one who had done the talking stepped forward, removed the entire roll from Pete the Bastard's hand, and said, 'OK. You can go.'

As we pulled back on to the corridor, there was a barrage of cheering and whooping and much congratulating of Pete the Bastard for his audacity. We took it in turns to lean through from the back, ruffle his hair, clap him on the shoulder, flick him on the ears. He calculated that the incident had cost us in the region of sixty pounds. We reckoned this was a small price to pay to avoid disappearing for ever into a Communist slammer.

In Berlin, we had just enough time to set ourselves up before the club's doors opened. We were playing upstairs in some sort of converted office space and there were about six hundred people in the audience, most of them terrifyingly fashionable. A handful near the front seemed to know the songs, and were mouthing along with the words, which was hugely inspiring, though I wasn't about to swing the microphone out to the audience, Bono-style, shouting, 'C'mon, *sing* it', cupping a hand to one ear. Personally, I always hate it when rock stars do that, but I can imagine it must be pretty gratifying to hear the lyric you dashed off in ten minutes one night on a sheet of hotel stationery passionately echoed back by ten thousand fans.

Afterwards, the woman who owned the club – a deep-voiced Dietrich figure, in her fifties probably, in thick make-up and swirling black gown – took us to a restaurant and passed round a small black box filled with neatly rolled joints. Ichiro, wasting no time at all, went home with the waitress.

We had most of the next day free to sightsee. Nigel, Tony, Dave and I went to the Berlin Wall and, under a low sky, climbed one of the sets of wooden viewing stairs which enabled you to look over across the mined sand, past the military control tower to the grey apartment buildings on the other side. We stood silently for some time, staring out across this division, each of us doubtless pondering the fate of nations and planning the meaningful pop song we would write on our return.

At each destination the RCA press office had set up interviews for me, with fanzines and rock magazines called things like *Ya!, Rockfest OK!* and *Boom!*. The first question was always: 'Where is Martin Newell?' (except on a couple of occasions when the interviewer assumed I *was* Martin Newell). To which my stock response was, 'He's at home doing the garden.' Then I would go into a few details about his problem with touring. Then we would talk earnestly about the Beatles. In the afternoon before we played at Heidelberg University, a cable television station filmed an interview in a disused concrete auditorium in the hills above the town. In the car on the way back, I asked the producer what this building had been. He said it had been built by Hitler for rallies.

In an unlikely concession to luxury, the van had an onboard video, but a strictly limited supply of films. The definition of boredom is sitting in a traffic jam between Dortmund and Munich, watching *Airplane* for the ninth time in a week. We sustained ourselves through the longer journeys by drinking warm vodka and orange mixed in plastic cups.

This was only a fortnight's touring, but it wasn't without its insights into what a life like this might be. Every move on every day was routined. I passed from hotel to van to venue to hotel . . . At no point did I have to think or make any decision for myself. Rather like the Queen, I didn't even have to carry money around. Whatever I drank or ate was silently settled for in my absence. I felt removed from the world, cosseted, rigorously overseen. It reminded me most of all of that stay in hospital when I had my spleen removed. This is what it would be like to be Phil Collins. It would be like being in hospital.

In the window of a large record store in Munich, we spotted our album sleeve, mounted right there beside Prefab Sprout's *From Langley Park To Memphis*. Tony the guitarist, who had a strong instinct for the impermanence of our condition, took a photograph.

In a converted railway building in Dortmund, a huge, bare-shouldered skinhead eased himself out of the crowd and on to the stage. At the microphone, I could see him coming out of the corner of my eye. I wondered about dumping my guitar and leaping over the monitor into the audience. But the next moment, he was upon me. I felt his hot arm go round my neck. And then I felt the smack of his lips on my cheek as he kissed me. With that, he bounced away. It was the best sex I had all tour. There had been a distinct absence of screaming girls under our hotel windows when we arrived. There still weren't any as the fortnight went on. A couple of the shows went well, but mostly we were just getting away with it. We arrived in Stuttgart to find our gig had been cancelled without explanation.

In Hamburg, on the tour's penultimate night, we were booked into the Grosse Freiheit again, scene of our former triumph. That afternoon taxis sped me smoothly from radio station to newspaper office ('Where is Martin Newell?') and then to a café in a park where I recorded an interview for use on the radio that evening. It was here that the press girl asked me if I needed a drink. I said an orange juice would be very nice. She returned from the counter carrying not one orange juice, but two. It wasn't as if they were uniquely small orange juices. This was Germany: the orange juice came in a giant frosted tumbler, slopping tidally on a bed of ice and sprigged to the hilt with innumerable, deftly origami'd orange slices. But she brought me two anyway, just in case. And in this absurd over-provision, I glimpsed the pampering that must accompany real rock stars all the time.

I wasn't aware of the precise moment that the chairman of RCA Germany walked out. I learned afterwards from our publisher that it was during the third number. This was always interpreted afterwards as a sign of his contempt although, of course, it may simply have been that he had an urgent appointment in an underground car park. I'm not sure what my reaction would have been if I had seen him leaving, but I suspect I would have left my guitar on the stage, jumped down and run after him across the room towards the exit, shouting, 'No! Stay! It gets much better towards the middle. Really! We're just warming up! Please!'

His leaving so early was a shame for many reasons (not least for the future of the band's career), but it did mean he was spared the sight of me dealing ineptly with a small crowd disturbance half-way through 'Follow The Plough'. A fight started at the front, right below me – nothing too nasty, just two blokes who had grown tired of colliding as they leapt about and had decided to thump each other a bit instead. If I had been a pop star in the Messianic tradition I would have handled this much better than I did, perhaps by raising my hand to silence the band before leaning into the microphone and saying, in a low, yet resoundingly contemptuous tone: 'Our music cannot be the soundtrack to your violence.' Cue gargantuan applause and appreciative roaring and whistling from the audience and an immediate outbreak of lighted candles.

As it was, with the music continuing to rage, I broke off from singing and, more than a little panicked, shouted, in a voice which chose this moment to go strangely high on me: 'Don't!'

They ignored me, hit each other a few more times, got bored and went back to dancing.

I didn't think the gig that night was too bad. It would have been better if Newell had been there, but we were tight and loud, and people jumped about and we were called back three times. Maybe at the Grosse Freiheit people don't feel they've had a proper night out unless the band plays four encores and, at the conclusion of the last, induces a large-scale religious vision and announces a peace process for the Middle East. Because in the dressing room immediately afterwards, slumped in a chair trying to get my breath back, I received a visit from Ulrika the publisher and someone I didn't know from the RCA office, walking behind her as if he was on his way to a funeral. Ulrika stood solemn-faced directly in front of me and said, 'Can it be any better?'

The room swam slightly. For an instant it occurred to me that, exhausted and partly deafened as I was, I had misheard her and what she had actually said was, 'That was the single most shuddering musical experience I have ever had. You took me to places I had no idea rock could go. I love you, and I want you to live with me here in Hamburg and have my children.'

But, as I continued to look up at her, the mist cleared and her face came into focus again. She was saying, 'Can it be any better?'

And I thought hard about this question before I answered.

'Er . . . no. It probably can't be.'

And I was right. It couldn't. It didn't. It wasn't.

Back in Cambridge, I talked excitedly about the tour – about the skinhead in Dortmund, the sight of our album sleeve next to Prefab Sprout's in Berlin, the orange-juice incident. Especially the orange juice incident. I dined out on that orange juice. What I tended to leave out were the stories of the chairman's desertion and of my backstage confrontation with Ulrika. I felt too sore about them. And I knew what they foreshadowed.

I calmed myself down by listening to a lot of records that I really loved. It may be one of the definitions of true greatness in a pop song that you cannot even begin to think about emulating it while it is playing. It's the last thing on your mind. I began to wonder whether my problem wasn't that I had listened to too much bad music, but to too much mediocre music, music which was only half good and so encouraged you to believe you could do as well – that maybe on an exclusive, high-fibre diet of Aretha Franklin, Otis Redding and the Temptations, I would never have begun to evolve the appetites I did. Maybe there's a case for stickering albums – in addition to the Parental Advisory stickers, which warn that a recording contains strong language, an Emulation Discourager sticker reading: 'Don't Try This At Home'.

I went down to Denmark Street a few more times, fiddled around in the studio to no particular end, talked to the manager and Pete the Bastard. Newell wasn't in touch with them, and they weren't in touch with him. The studio was more run-down than ever, close to the brink. One day, the manager called me through to his office.

'They sold four hundred copies of the CD,' he said.

'Brilliant!' I said.

He looked at me sternly. 'No,' he said. 'Not brilliant. Forty thousand would have been OK. Four hundred is piss poor.'

And, shortly after that, the manager quit – walked out and was gone. Pete the Bastard hung on grimly for a while, long enough to receive the call from RCA cancelling our deal.

Not long after this, the owner of the studio appeared to assess the damage. The company was run down so far that he had little choice but to close up and sell. A middle-aged man in a nylon shirt turned up to write an inventory. I had to have a meeting with him and the owner to ask for permission to keep the master tapes of the Cleaners, which were now in danger of being flogged for scrap.

The man in the nylon shirt sat back in his chair and said, smugly, 'I do not believe some of the things I have found in this building. It will be very interesting if any of this ever goes public. Very interesting indeed.'

I wasn't sure what this veiled threat could refer to, other

than an old pair of Pete the Bastard's socks. But at least he agreed to hand over the tapes.

Occasionally, I get asked, 'Did you see any money from the Cleaners from Venus?' and yes, I am still seeing money from the Cleaners from Venus. As many people know, the big bucks in music are made from publishing and performance royalties, the fees paid by radio and television for the use of your work. My royalty statements from the Performing Rights Society arrive twice a year, regular as clockwork. Last summer I received thirty-two pence.

The last I heard of Pete the Bastard, he was involved in exporting videos to war-torn Yugoslavia. The manager went into music publishing. Not long ago, I received in the post a tape containing a remixed version of 'A Mercury Girl', a song from our first album. A cheery letter from the manager informed me that he was intending to punt this number towards the publicity people at Mercury Communications in the hope that they would notice the striking similarity between the lyric and their corporate name and begin using the song in their advertising. 'If they accept it,' he wrote, 'it's Milky Bars all round.' But they didn't.

Phil Collins

When the Cleaners collapsed, I tried to reconcile myself to the fact that a position in the rock aristocracy would lie for ever beyond me. I had to realize that Bob Geldof would not be a guest at my wedding, that Annie Lennox's daughter would not be a bridesmaid, that confetti would not be thrown by an elegantly morning-suited and broadly smiling David Bowie. I had to realize also that my grant was about to run out and I needed to earn some money. I started writing about pop music, which I suppose had the consolation that it was one of the few other occupations in which you might get to hang out with Bob and Annie and David.

The truth is, in the 1990s, 'hanging out' is something pop journalists don't do a lot of. If you were Nick Kent in the 1970s, or Lester Bangs, or if you were a *Rolling Stone* staff-writer, hanging out was the centre of your craft; you would get to hang out until you could hang no further. Covering the Who, say, would have involved spending a couple of weeks with them in the studio, just sitting around, watching, gassing, taking notes and drugs in dangerously unequal quantities. Or maybe you would join them on tour, be on the bus with them and in the hotel and under the table. You had access to all areas. You got to know how it looked, how it sounded, how it smelt.

Typical that by the time I started interviewing pop stars, journalists were down to an hour (if you're lucky) in a London hotel room, rented specially for the occasion – probably the same London hotel room in which you interviewed some other rock star on the PR treadmill just the week before – outside which would be a queue of other journalists, all waiting to get *their* hour (if they were lucky) and all carefully marshalled by the record company PR (who might wish to sit in on an interview with you, just in case you asked the question about the little boys). In the 1980s, record companies learned the meaning of Public Relations, and they learned it principally from Hollywood, which taught the virtues of controlled exposure, of doing your utmost to obstruct and cajole and boil journalism down until you had it right where you wanted it, until it was little more than an extension of the industry's PR arm or marketing department, another selling tool.

Typical of the modern way of doing things would be the day I spent in Rome with Phil Collins. This was for a piece for *Q* magazine. I got two hours each way in a four-seater Lear jet from Gatwick (paid for by Atlantic Records, Phil's overseas label) with Phil, Phil's assistant and Ken the photographer. And in between, a hectic dash by limo round Italian TV and radio studios for Phil to plug his latest album. Spot the fish-with-its-tail-in-its-mouth aspect of that and win a Genesis boxed set. This is how self-contained the public-relations machine has become. Record companies can now set up situations in which you watch the artist doing interviews that the record company has set up. This grants you the illusion of access, but really only makes you play the PR game at one remove – seeming to observe how Phil lives and works, but only observing how he lives and works while he's doing publicity.

Still, I had a high old time, especially the bit where we came out of the side-door of the TV studio surrounded by bouncers who had to manhandle us through the thronging fans (Italians have got a bit of a thing for Phil) and duck us down into the limo. I'd always wanted to do that.

Some eight months later, drifting stupidly round a record

company party after the Grammy awards in New York, I bumped into Phil on his way out. I know that pop stars meet many journalists in the course of their business. I knew that the odds on Phil Collins recognizing me were not great. I wasn't expecting any high-fiving, any mutual clapping of our suited shoulder-blades; I didn't think there would be a grateful hug, from which he would pull back, still holding me firmly by the elbows, and say, 'Giles, boy, long bloody time, my friend! Jesus, but I've missed you!'

And given that any other outcome would have been disappointing, the obvious thing to do was to walk on by. Who needs a stilted and embarrassing exchange of hellos with Phil Collins?

Me, clearly.

'Er, Phil? Giles Smith? I went with you to Rome?'

Collins gave me a suspicious squint. I could see his mental Rolodex spin and come up blank.

'And now you're here,' he said.

Well, it was true. He couldn't say fairer than that. I was, indeed, there.

'Gotta go,' he added. 'Very tired.'

You have, of course, to retain your perspective somehow. The interviewer/interviewee relationship is a temporary arrangement for business purposes. It will not lead to your being asked to join Simply Red on congas. But it doesn't help when the interviewee pretends to befriend you. My interview with Lionel Richie took place in his dressing room at the *Top of the Pops* studio. He was eating a King Cone, which had melted badly, forcing him to sit forward in his chair with a wastebin on the floor between his knees to catch the drips. At the conclusion of the forty-five minutes for which Lionel was prepared to share his thoughts, he and I shook hands – his was rather sticky by now – and suddenly he had an arm round my shoulder and was wagging a finger at his assistant. 'I want you to make sure', he told her, 'that this person becomes one of my *special* people.'

But does he ever write? Does he ever call? Does he hell.

What dies hard is the conflict between your duties as a reporter and your instincts as a fan. It wasn't, for example, exactly *professional* of me a minute and a half into an interview with Paul McCartney in 1989, to come over all faint. (I was a bit overexcited and I hadn't had any lunch.) He was extremely nice about it and covered for me during my confusion by chatting amiably until I'd recovered strength enough to ask him a question. But it was always going to be hard for me to conduct a deeply probing inquisition after that.

And what were the odds on me nailing Stevie Wonder to the wall? I did get to meet him eventually, in 1991 on the top floor of the Chelsea Harbour Hotel, just after the release of the *Jungle Fever* soundtrack album. I was more nervous than before any Cleaners gig: worried about not liking him, worried about him not liking me, which is perhaps not something an interviewer should care about, though how could I not? And, yes, I asked the photographer to take an extra picture or two of us together – the only time I've done this, I swear. (There used to be a pop columnist on one of the tabloids whose walls were practically held together by pictures of himself at parties with his arms around the famous. But most of these images of chumminess had been acquired by subterfuge – him and the photographer jumping out simultaneously, snatching the shot and leaving – so what you saw was the columnist with a shocked Cher, an amazed Seal, a frightened Kylie, etc.) That first meeting took place in a cramped annex to his hotel suite and lasted for all of twenty minutes with, for the last five of these, an intrusive press woman from Motown America hovering behind him making wind-it-up signals at me, helping to render the experience about as intimate and unstressful as a prison visit.

Yet, at the end, Stevie took me through to the room next door, where various members of his entourage were draped on the sofas, sat down at the set of keyboards which travel everywhere with him and played and sang me a new, speeded-up version of 'All I Do', which made the hair on my arms stand up. These were precious and powerful moments. They were moments I will never forget. But it's not as if he's been pestering me at work ever since.

Say what you like about Lou Reed, at least he's honest. The second time I interviewed him, his assistant showed me in, saying, 'Lou, you remember Giles Smith.'

'No,' said Lou, a block of ice in shades. 'No, I do not.'

So, pop journalism as vicarious star-mingling? It doesn't work out. You get closer to them than in your wildest dreams. And further away from them than you ever imagined you could be.

The Orphans: still alive

I'm at this wedding in Oxfordshire in the summer of 1991. It's midway through the evening, quite a long time after the dinner, and people are loosened up, many of them dancing in large, well-dressed clumps to a surprisingly good reggae band. Holding a glass, I step outside the marquee for some air and there, in the half-light, a tall, expensively suited man in his early twenties comes up.

I don't recognize him at first, because he's the youngest brother of a friend from university and the last time I met him he was a small boy with a high voice. And this in itself is a startling moment for me, because for the first time in my life I have to stop myself saying that thing which I thought only aunts were supposed to say, 'Good Lord! Haven't you *grown*!'

But I just manage to swallow those words and we get the reintroductions over, and just as I'm readying myself to go in on some kind of so-what-are-you-doing-now? angle, he drops the big one.

'I am the Orphans of Babylon's biggest fan.'

I narrow my eyes slightly, because naturally I'm thinking, This is a wind-up job. Someone here has put him up to this. The Orphans of Babylon didn't have fans: we had curious onlookers. And, anyway, that was about six years ago, somewhere else. I offer a wary smile, waiting for the catch, the punch-line, but it doesn't seem to be coming.

'*Pinch Me, I Think I'm In Kent*!' he says. 'What an album!' And then he tells me how, along with a friend, he broke into his brother's bedroom one day, years ago, looking for tapes to steal.

252

'We read the title, put it on and thought, Now, *this* is what we want.'

They took it back to school with them, he says. They introduced it to their friends. It became a shower-room singalong, a dorm classic. I am agog, confused, suspicious.

' "Ray Reardon",' he says. 'Great song!' And suddenly, and utterly without embarrassment, he starts singing.

> That was a helluva break by Ray Reardon
> That was a helluva break by old Ray
> That was a helluva break by Ray Reardon . . .

And on the fourth line, I join in, very quietly, just mouthing the words really, in disbelief.

> Green, yellow and blue.

Second verse, now, and his voice is strong and proud:

> That was a helluva break by Ray Reardon
> When he potted them down that lucky day . . .

And my voice is rising in volume to meet him:

> . . . He potted, he potted the lot
> Green, yellow and blue.

Into the middle section and we're starting to motor, eye to eye.

> Down he went for a little old red
> And he potted it, he potted it, it went down the hole
> Followed by a yellow and a green and a blue

And it made up a hundred and two
It made up a hundred and two!

And then round the bend into the final verse, snatching little handfuls of the air in between us, pointing home some of the lines with our forefingers, heads tipped back, elbows out wide, wriggling on the spot in a version of the twist . . .

That was a helluva break by Ray Reardon
That was a helluva break by old Ray-ee-ay-ee-ay
That was a helluva break by Ray Reardon
Green, yellow and blue
GREEN, YELLOW AND BLUE!

. . . until we hit the endnote, shouting with laughter, hooting into the darkness.

It all goes a bit quiet after that. There's a rather difficult period where we both rock gently on the balls of our feet and I look down into my empty glass, which is now hot and misted for having been held too long. Finally I lift my head. 'So, how *is* your brother, anyway?'

And he says, 'Fine. Yes. Very well. Fine.'

There's another pause and he says, 'Well, nice seeing you again.'

And I say, 'Yes, nice seeing you, too,' and he goes back into the marquee.

Grace Jones

Just recently, I've been thinking about upgrading my speaker wire. Evidently the wires which come as standard on most factory-fitted speakers are inferior sound carriers by comparison with the posh, furiously expensive copper cabling available from specialist stores. The copper stuff, they say, sends the noise down a treat. This is what a friend told me. So I've been stooped behind the sofa, thoughtfully fingering the ridged plastic shoelaces, brittle with age, which currently transport the music from my amplifier to my speakers and speculating on what might be getting lost along the way.

It's a little alarming to find oneself worrying in such detail about the performance of one's hi-fi, but I console myself that I am not alone. In 1993, a lot of people seemed to get caught up in the excitement which followed the revelation that CDs performed better if, before playing them, you placed them for a while in the freezer compartment of your fridge. Somehow this crisped them up. The fad briefly gave a new dimension to the old joke about the contents of the sad bachelor's Indesit: one carton of milk (half empty), one hazelnut yoghurt (off) and a Led Zeppelin boxed set.

What kind of person originally thinks of these things? To whom does it suddenly occur: 'I wonder what this CD would sound like if I put it in the fridge for a while?' Someone, I would speculate, for whom pop isn't doing quite what it used to. Someone a bit like me.

Not that I was ever tempted to experiment with disc-chilling, partly because it was so nerdy, but mostly because it would have involved me defrosting the fridge, the freezer compartment of which would have been, as usual, bulging with accumulated ice, to the degree that I would never have got a CD in there other than by bashing it home edge-wise with a mountaineer's mallet.

Anyway, my resolve on this one was never tested. The fridge-as-CD-rack notion didn't take off, chiefly, I suppose, because, short of finding room to freeze your entire collection, you would be forced to select and cold-store your CDs some hours in advance of listening to them; and in the end you can't reliably plan ahead with music the way you can with, say, food.

Just like the disc-chillers, though, I find I am increasingly drawn to think about hi-fi in more peculiar, microscopic terms. If you are *genuinely* interested in music systems, you can make an appointment with one of the top-notch, perfectionist dealers. Some kind of woofer consultant or tweeter expert then comes round to your house and performs a thorough investigation of the acoustics in your living room and at the end of this advises you what system to buy, where to place the speakers so that they function most gloriously, how to house the amplifiers to avoid unwanted interference from other electrical sources like lights and televisions (inaudible unless you're a gnat, but there it is), and at what volume to operate the system for maximum joy. If you're serious about this, he may come up with a list of recommended acoustic adjustments to further enhance your listening pleasure: line your curtains with egg boxes, cut all the pages out of your books, wrap the cat in tin foil, etc.

And I am desperately, desperately drawn to this as a concept: that you would tailor all of your domestic arrangements to the construction of the ultimate stereo, the perfect system, from which the sound would zing around you, massaging every pore. (I like to imagine that in some of the more volatile set-ups the listener isn't even allowed to go into the room, because to do so would screw up the minutely refined sonic balance.) Costs a fortune, of course. So, in the absence of that, perhaps those copper speaker wires . . .

I think I first became aware of my increasing commitment to nearly pointless hi-fi tweaking in 1992, when I bought a pair of speaker stands. Speaker stands are not, by most people's reckoning, essential items. In some respects, they are to hi-fi what the manager and trainer figures and the TV tower were to a Subbuteo football set: nothing to do with the game, and yet, once the initial excitement of owning a pitch and players had died down, utterly crucial. (True, you're less likely to snap your speaker stands by kneeling on them when going up for a corner, but I think the analogy holds firm.)

In the flat I had at the time, my speakers were positioned against the wall on a low shelf. I was perfectly happy with them there until a friend came round and explained the principles behind stands: how they allow the air to circulate round the speakers, how they minimize the amount of sound being soaked up by whatever the speakers rest on or against, and how you might just as well dump your speakers in a lead casket and bury them in the garden as not sit them on stands.

A certain kind of neurosis takes over following conversations like this, the same kind of paranoia that originally induced me to buy a CD player. Even before the friend had left, I had managed to convince myself that 50 per cent of the sound generated by my hi-fi was passing through the wall into the house next door, 40 per cent was dropping through the ceiling to the flat downstairs and that I should count myself lucky if I could catch the remaining 10 per cent by pressing my ear to the gauze.

The stands I bought were tall, a fusion of matt black metal tubes and plates, with steel needles for feet – the kind of thing advertising executives in the early 1980s bought to sit on. They were, needless to say, not an impulse buy, but a completely pre-scripted purchase, based on about a month of in-store reconnaissance, yet informed, finally, by no genuine, purposeful knowledge whatsoever. I had dismissed the smaller ones on display because . . . well, because they were smaller.

From an interior design point of view, the effect of the twin towers I chose was to make the speakers rather dominant. You could now see them from anywhere in the room. In fact, you could see them from almost anywhere in the street. Impressed, I subjected the whole revised arrangement to what was then, and remains, my standard test when any new piece of equipment arrives, or when any aspect of the existing set-up changes position: playing, at volume, the 12-inch version of Grace Jones's 'Slave To The Rhythm', perhaps the most sonically gorgeous record I know.

Actually, I prefer to think of it as Trevor Horn's 'Slave To The Rhythm': he produced the track and it's he who casts its parts and creates its drama – the film-score strings and wind, the tremendous tambourine, the little flute theme that suddenly lifts out of the track's booming core and skips along the top for a while. The arrangement is clearly intended to glorify Jones, to make a big, glossy fuss of her as she sings, but for me she's just doing her usual, one-dimensional, draggy cabaret act and she's way down the bill here.

The minute 'Slave To The Rhythm' started to take off – that bright 'ching' from the finger-cymbal, that little huff of synthesized breath underneath it – the improvement in sound quality was startling. Startlingly small, that is. There was perhaps a touch more at the top end, a touch more at the bottom, maybe a touch more in the middle too, I don't know. Was that a more chingy 'ching' I heard? A more huffy huff? Possibly. But how much of the increased immediacy was down to the fact that speakers which were once neatly tidied to the side of the room now had me forced back in my seat with my nose squashed? It's hard to say.

The point was, *something* was different, and when the initial disappointment about the scale of the difference subsided, this small betterment began to look welcome and important even. Indeed, that the stands had made a minor improvement rather than a giant, ball-bustingly obvious, major one, seemed appealingly professional of them. I felt they flattered me with their precision. I was the kind of person for whom these almost incalculably minute distinctions mattered.

I imagine the effect of attaching new copper speaker wires would be similarly imperceptible and similarly gratifying. It might afford me some of the pleasure I got late in 1992 when I upgraded my Phillips CD-player to a Marantz 'Bitstream' model. I had no idea what 'Bitstream' was, but the word sounded good – nubby and computer-related and at the same time sexily fluid – and the machine came with a hand-held remote control, so you can make the disc-tray go in and out from the other side of the room, which I enjoy doing enormously. (You still have to get up to load it, of course, but what the heck.)

Cables, stands, remote controls . . . it seems clear to me that this twitchy hi-fi business is a displacement activity. It is one of the ways in which I attempt to settle with my conscience over this continuing commitment to pop. It's my way of grounding it – however spuriously – in science and at the same time making it seem a bit more like work, a bit more like a proper adult preoccupation. Which is to say that, at my age, I might feel a little self-conscious in the newsagent queuing with the *NME*, but I kid myself I can escape from this if I wrap around it a copy of *What Speaker Wire*.

Blur

Back in Colchester for Christmas Eve in 1992, I went to a very civilized, early-evening drinks party at the house of a close friend's family and was startled to find myself in the same room as Damon Albarn of Blur and his parents, Mr and Mrs Albarn. Incredible: you spend the best part of your childhood looking out for pop stars in Colchester and then, when it no longer matters quite so much, they start wandering into your friends' parents' homes. Damon was sporting a punky rug and had a bootlace knotted round his neck. Mr and Mrs Albarn were wearing casual Christmas evening wear and, just briefly, all four of us were involved in one of those parents-plus-son-combination Christmas conversations.

'Damon has had rather a good twelve months,' Mr Albarn told me enthusiastically, as his son fidgeted with slight embarrassment beside him. 'We're just hoping he can keep it up next year.'

And, of course, he did keep it up, next year and the year after, going from strength to strength, touring like a fiend, recording the *Parklife* album, narrowly missing the Mercury Music Prize and generally getting written about everywhere as a fine thing.

Later, when carols were sung around the piano, Albarn (all credit to him) joined in unashamedly and I found myself looking on at a unique Christmas tableau – an impromptu choir featuring the parents of some of my oldest school-friends, my mother and the lead singer of Blur.

Utterly predictable, of course, that when someone from my family finally got to duet with a chart-topping pop hero, it was my mother.

Sisters With Voices

1993, autumn. I am on holiday in America with my girl-friend. We've heard a song we like on the radio in the car; we've picked it up at least three times but without ever hearing the DJ say what it is. We are determined, though, that we will hunt it down and own it, in the knowledge that in the future, played in any car, anywhere, this song will now summon effortlessly to mind this particular hired car and whole portions of our journeying, complete strips of road and landscape and weather, better than any roll of film or video camera.

So the next time we're in a town we find a record shop and I lead the way cockily over to where the cassette singles are, an entire wall of them, and begin looking.

'What are you doing?' she says.

I say, 'I'm looking for that song.'

'But we don't know who it's by. Or what it's called.'

'Well, it had the word "weak" in it a lot. It's probably in the title. We're just looking for a title with the word "weak" in it.'

There is a pause. I am standing on tiptoe, running a finger very slowly down a towering stack of shrink-wrapped cassettes. I already sense the next question and I don't want it to come.

She says, 'Why don't you ask the man behind the counter?'

'No!' I squeak, in a voice suddenly high with panic. 'You can't do that.'

'But he might know it straight away—'

'No! He won't. Well, he might. But don't.'

No, I would rather stare until I am squint-eyed at this wall of some seven thousand thin cassette spines in search of a song of which I know neither the name nor the performer. It seems to me that permanently impaired vision would be a small price to pay for not having to go and talk to the man behind the counter, for not having to confess my ignorance, for not having to make myself vulnerable in that way. And I may well be in my early thirties and capable, more or less, of mature, balanced behaviour in relation to some of the clutter (bills, tax, insurance) which comes with an adult life but *I will not ask a question in a record shop*. (And this despite the best efforts of the music-retailing profession worldwide to make record shops *safe for people like me*.) Because of the risks. Because what if this song turns out to have been at the top of the American chart for the last seventy-three weeks? What if it is this giant, phenomenally naff item, and somehow we don't know about it? What if, what if . . .

There's another pause and suddenly she's not standing beside me. And I'm worried, because I think I know where she's gone.

Next thing, I hear her at the counter saying, 'I wonder if you could help me. We're looking for this song, but we don't know what it's called, or who it's by . . .'

At this point, I have to put out a hand to stop myself collapsing face first into the display module. The room swims slightly and I'm thinking, This is terrible. But it's OK, I'm not going to pass out.

And then . . . and then she starts *singing* it to him.

I can't believe this. Singing in a record shop! Where does she think she is?

He, though, immediately bounces out from behind the counter and leads her back over to where I am, crouched now with my neck bent sideways through ninety degrees, somewhere in the 'Fs', teeth clenched, breathing hard, having absolutely nothing to do with this. And he leans into the rack above me, with a light 'Pardon me, sir' and pulls out the single we're looking for. (Which is, we now learn, 'Weak' by Sisters With Voices, so nothing to panic unduly on the non-recognition front, although, for some reason, I still feel that I really ought to have known.)

The two of them trip happily back to the counter and settle up. I straighten slowly, pull myself together a little and follow her out of the door a short while after.

'I knew it was called "Weak",' I say, trying lamely to salvage something from this. But she is a long way ahead of me and doesn't hear.

The Cleaners from Venus and then some

Since the Cleaners from Venus, Martin Newell and I have got on just fine. There are no outstanding legal cases, no undignified fights for rights, few personal recriminations. Ours is not a Roger Waters/Dave Gilmour situation. As at the end of any relationship, there was a cooling-off period in which neither of us was particularly bursting for each other's company until finally we realized we could be adult about it and see each other again.

Newell came out of the whole business intact. For a while he did no music at all, just buried himself, as it were, in the gardening. Then he got the urge again, as musicians are cursed to, and he became involved with Nel in a kind of folk/pop busking duo called the Brotherhood of Lizards. This was, I suspect, a project through which Newell hoped to wash the mess of the last three years right out of his hair, to forget all the delusions of grandeur and the spent hopes and get back to his roots. The Brotherhood of Lizards did a tour of Britain by bike.

And then Newell cut out the music again and started writing poetry. He wrote comic verse, much of it about pop music, and he got himself on to the poetry gig circuit in a sort of John Cooper Clarke role. And finally, in the autumn of 1993, he signed another record deal with a small independent company and was given a budget to make an album on his own.

And who agreed to produce it? Only Andy bloody Partridge of XTC, that's all.

Newell rang me up to tell me about this. There is a whole range of emotions you run through when your former musical partner ends up making an album with one of your all-time heroes. And not all of those emotions are charitable. 'I can't believe it,' Newell said. And neither could I. In fact, I was hoping, right at that minute, that I would wake up and discover he had never phoned me at all with this news. My first reaction was to shimmer at the injustice of it. Sure, Newell admired XTC, but it was me who had all the singles in plastic slip covers. It was me who could accurately mime-drum any Terry Chambers part you cared to mention. It was me who had the back numbers of *Limelight*, the XTC fanzine, to which I had once contributed an eight-hundred-word article on XTC's sleeve designs.

But then I began to see that this was precisely the reason it was Newell, and not me, who was about to be sitting in Andy Partridge's home studio for a month. Because Newell was first and foremost a musician, and I was first and foremost a fan. There was still room for Newell's relationship with Andy Partridge to become a professional one, whereas I'd have been getting him to autograph things all the time.

Those initial pangs of jealousy soon made way for another kind of anxiety: what if the fruits of this collaboration between Newell and Partridge made Newell exceptionally famous? What if, now free of our relationship, he thundered into the Top Ten and I started seeing his face everywhere and hearing his music in shops? I care about Newell way too much ever to wish him ill. I care about him enough always to wish him well. But not *that* well. And once again, I'm forced to use the boyfriend/girlfriend analogy. I felt uneasy about Newell's possible future in the way in which you would feel uneasy about your ex-girlfriend going on to marry Hugh Grant. I wasn't that keen to end up a Pete Best figure: Giles

Smith, Colchester's nearly man, interviewed briefly for the 'Martin Newell at 50' celebrations on BBC2.

It was Newell himself who nursed me through the worst of this. In a small but significant way, he cut me in on the deal: he invited me to visit him during the recording sessions in the green shed at the bottom of Partridge's garden in Swindon. I arrived in the afternoon and made myself comfortable at the back of the room. Partridge had just put down a soaring, Mott the Hoople-style guitar solo. Now he was recording Newell playing some rhythm-guitar parts. If you had told me in 1986 that I would one day sit in Andy Partridge's shed, watching him recording a track by Martin Newell, and that later all three of us would go up the pub, I would have laughed in your face. I felt strange and uneasy for most of that afternoon and evening, as if I was about to be exposed as the victim of some elaborate practical joke. It didn't make it any easier to swallow that Partridge was just as funny and clever and approachable as we had always imagined he would be.

When the album was mixed and finished, I went down to Newell's house in Wivenhoe and he played it to me on tape all the way through, the two of us crouched in front of a ghetto blaster (still no hi-fi round at Newell's). He had named it *The Greatest Living Englishman*, after one of its best tracks. As we listened, Newell glazed over with pride and was clearly, from time to time, trying to control smiles of pleasure at what he had achieved here. This might strike you as insensitive behaviour but it is normal and acceptable conduct for musicians. Writers tend to be much more guarded and shifty about the way they expose new work. Musicians whack their tapes into your machine, crank the volume high and sit down right there with you while it plays. I've been in this position with musicians countless times and I have never known someone wear a look which says, 'I'm a bit unsure about this: what do you think?' On the contrary, music seems to fill its makers with a prickly excitement about themselves.

Of course, this wildly compromises your critical responses as a listener. I once interviewed Janet Jackson and midway through the interview, to my stomach-sinking horror, she passed her Walkman across the table to me, saying, 'Here, take a listen to this. It's my new single.'

And I had to sit there, under a pair of expensively padded headphones, while she sat opposite, picking at a packet of Crackers and wearing one of those 'I'm about to laugh, I'm so pleased with this' looks. I, meanwhile, went into a flat spin. How was I supposed to respond? Toss my head from side-to-side, with my eyes closed, smiling blissfully? Whoop at some crucial moment – like where the verse slotted into the chorus? Talk to her during the song about the bits I liked, shouting embarrassingly, as people do when they're wearing headphones? In the end, I settled for a steady nod and an expression of eager pleasure from start to finish, at which point I took off the headphones and said something excruciating like, 'Just *sensational*', though I had been concentrating way too hard on how I was reacting to listen to the music.

I had no problems like this auditioning Newell's new album. At the end of it, I was able to tell him – and I really meant it – that his album was great, the best piece of work he had ever done, infinitely superior to anything the two of us had managed. I thought Partridge had brought out things in his voice that Newell himself probably didn't know were there, and had filled the music with all kinds of lovely touches. The album was crisp and professional-sounding, yet retained something of a warm, home-made feel – which was the balance Newell had always been after, the whole time I'd known him. And the songs were as fluently melodic as ever. It was Cleaners from Venus and then some.

And every night for about a month when I went to bed, I prayed to God that it wouldn't be a hit.

Tony Blair

'Language', wrote Ben Jonson, 'most shows a man. Speak that I may see thee.' Failing that, he might have added, let me have a quick flick through your record collection because if anything else is going to give away the kind of person thou art, that is.

Shortly after he succeeded the late John Smith as leader of the Labour Party, Tony Blair was asked in an interview what kind of pop music he liked. (As the 1960s generation ascends to positions of political prominence, this is a question we're going to be hearing a lot more.) Mr Blair came up with REM, Seal and Annie Lennox. I'm prepared to believe he fired these names off the top of his head, that these are indeed the three acts whose tapes are in ceaseless rotation on Mr Blair's in-car stereo. Yet if the party had commissioned an expensive advertising agency to spend seven months in collaboration with a public-relations firm researching this declaration, it's hard to believe they would have come up with anything so beautifully poised. REM, Seal and Annie Lennox: an American rock group and two British singers, one black male, one white female, with fingers in pop, soul and dance, an ample musical spread, economically achieved.

Note how the balance tips in favour of the British artists, to avoid the suggestion that Mr Blair might be somehow in thrall to American culture. All the chosen ones are alive, commercially active, high profile: there's no dust on Mr Blair's taste. And he manages the supple feat of bowling right down the middle while appearing to be coming in from the outside edge. None of these acts is obscure – you'll find all three of them in Woolworth's – and yet the selection does not have the giant, gallumphing obviousness of, say, Phil Collins, U2 and Whitney Houston. We read Mr Blair as sincere and involved enough to have at least scraped off the surface, and yet there is no alienating specialism here, which would have been the risk of declaring a fixated passion for grunge core or for some of the obscure cuts of the legendary but little-known Delta bluesman, Otis B. Stankmeyer.

There's something for all of us there. Better still, even if you don't especially care for one or two of these artists, it would be next to impossible for you to take exception to anyone who did. 'Can you believe that Tony Blair? He likes *Seal, REM* and *Annie Lennox*!' It is beyond the capacity of the human voice to make that sentence ring with scorn.

But let's not be fooled by this. It's a self-editing trick that each of us plays with our record collections every time we clear the naff ones away before people come round. This is my pre-university purging tactic, writ large for the world stage. Seal, REM and Annie Lennox are unlikely to be the whole story; they are only the publicly acceptable version of the facts. Until we can peep into the corners of that record collection, we will not know the man whole. All of which opens up the possibility of a completely new kind of political scandal:

BLAIR IN RICHARD CLAYDERMAN SHOCK
Secret album was 'for his mum' claims Lab leader

Todd Rundgren

I've liked Todd Rundgren ever since Geoff played him to me and talked me through the best bits – the 'la-la-la' section in the middle of 'Can We Still Be Friends?', the key changes at the end of 'Marlene', the live version of 'A Dream Goes On Forever', the way he screams 'if you need a friend' at the end of 'Love Is The Answer'. These were moments at which Geoff would screw his face into a wince, point at the speaker with his forefinger and let out a clipped 'Ah!'

The difficult thing about Rundgren is, he's a musician of no settled mood or style. One minute he's the Beatles, the next he's an acid-rock casualty, and the next he's Rick Wakeman. On the worst albums, he's all those things at once. The records of his that interested Geoff and me were the pop ones and we hated it whenever Rundgren rocked out or, as he was prone to do, filled entire sides of albums with turgid guitar odysseys. There was only one thing to recommend his eclecticism: it made him the perfect artist for home-made compilation tapes. Friends – if they have any opinions about Rundgren at all – will tend to denounce him as a dope-sozzled 1970s weirdo, or as the producer of Meatloaf's *Bat Out Of Hell*. At which point, you slip away to your stock of Rundgren albums, tweezer the gorgeous pop ballads out from between the stomach-churning synth epics, line them up on a C90 and hand this over with a smug smile, saying, 'I think you'll be surprised.'

But Rundgren has bequeathed me more than just this. The Rundgren records that Geoff nudged me towards tended also to be the ones on which he played and sang everything himself, even operating the studio. Both of us would have liked to try that. Though we were attracted by the gregariousness of bands, these demonstrations of solitary prowess appealed to us powerfully. For all that Geoff and I shared the music we liked, there were still whole areas of our experience as listeners that were inward and private and which – other than through a wince, a pointed forefinger and a clipped 'Ah!' – we did not communicate to each other. Music that was itself the result of self-absorbed labour seemed especially resonant.

An image on the sleeve of the *Something/Anything?* album shows Rundgren in what looks like a surburban front room, cluttered with musical instruments and tapes and one man's debris – the scene, we're to presume, of the making of the solo portions of this record. Rundgren has his back to the camera. He's standing on a coffee table with a guitar round his neck. His arms are aloft and his fingers point victory signs at the ceiling, the gesture a rocker might make to a large crowd at the end of a gig. Except he is facing not an audience but the light coming dimly through the closed curtains.

The first time I saw this image it was lying on the floor of Geoff's bedroom where it formed part of a clutter similar to the one it depicted – of guitars and guitar leads and scraps of paper and records out of their sleeves. When I got my own copy of the album, I was struck by the image again and pored over it frequently thereafter. It suggested a musical hermitude which spoke directly to my own adolescent broodiness, to the sense I had that my moods were something I would like to hole up with and dwell on alone.

Even after adolescence, this was a feeling that I never quite shook off. I have a tendency to be sullen and self-absorbed in the face of adversity, as if there is no personal dilemma I could not work out, given a solo recording deal, six months to myself and a home studio. Geoff is like this too, so I am forced to conclude that our predicament is largely the result of listening to Todd Rundgren records – to Stevie Wonder records, too, though Wonder's one-man-band recordings, in which I have steeped myself more deeply even than Rundgren's, are different. Wonder, even at his most self-involved, seems always to be working towards some kind of release; release is the last thing a Rundgren solo record finds, or wants.

I have kept in touch with Todd Rundgren in the intervening years. I got excited in 1986 when, quite out of the blue, he produced the XTC album *Skylarking*, in the same way that I had got excited a year earlier when Scritti Politti worked with Arif Mardin, one of Aretha Franklin's producers. I'd introduced these people to each other years before in my record collection, and here they were getting together in real life. (As it happened, Rundgren and Andy Partridge of XTC bickered throughout the making of the album. So much for my social engineering.)

And intermittently, I have bought Rundgren's new albums. Buying a Todd Rundgren record unheard is about as big a risk as you can take in a record shop. It could be good, or it could be the worst thing you've ever acquired. You just have to hand over the money and pray. It worked out OK in 1985, with the album *A Capella*, on which Rundgren uses nothing but his own voice, layered into thick harmonies in the studio. A heart-stopping piece of falsetto at the end of 'Pretending To Care' showed he still had an amazing enthusiasm for his own company.

The Ever Popular Tortured Artist Effect (1984) was, though, the worst thing I had ever heard. Until I got *2nd Wind* (1991). Yet between those, in 1989, I gambled on *Nearly Human*, gritted my teeth as I lowered the needle to the deck and found it contained no twenty-minute epics and two pop songs as sweet as anything Rundgren has come up with – 'The Waiting Game' and 'Parallel Lines'.

Not until 1994 did Todd show any sign of losing me. It was the year he placed himself on technology's frontline. He rechristened himself TR-I, meaning Todd Rundgren – Interactive. He released a CD-ROM called *New World Order.* Given the right computer hardware, you could toy with the music's constituent parts and mix the album for yourself. There was also a primitive version for conventional CD players, allowing you to use your machine to sequence brief chunks of *New World Order* in the order you desired. So much for Todd the hermit. Now he was asking us *all* to get involved.

In the race to establish CD-ROM, David Bowie and Peter Gabriel were quick off the blocks too. But Rundgren went a stage further and extended the principle of interactivity to his live show. On his 1994 tour, members of the audience were free to come and go on the stage and influence the course of the show by pressing a button here, playing an instrument there. He told Andy Gill in the *Independent*: 'At one point in New York, the audience got so enthusiastic they pushed me off the stage, and I wound up in the crowd. I was just wandering about while they were geeking around on the stage.' Not content with participation from ticket-holders, Rundgren even managed to involve people who had stayed at home. In Amsterdam, he contrived a show to which people could contribute from their computers on the Internet.

This is the future. This is what our relationship with music will become – challenging, involving, interactive. But I'm not ready for interaction. I've yet to exhaust the possibilities of reaction. The ambition of the new musical technology is to stir us from our passivity as listeners. But as listeners, how passive *are* we? When Geoff first played me Rundgren's 'I Saw The Light', I suppose I was passive in the sense that I just sat there on the floor in his bedroom listening to it. But when that beautifully curly guitar solo finally spiralled up into the last verse . . . well, I've rarely felt more active in all my life.

It's possible that my generation will consider itself lucky that it can remember a time when you could pay to see a rock show without having to perform in it; when you could buy an album and play it without having to mix it yourself first. In the past, Geoff might ring up and say, 'Come round and listen to the new Todd Rundgren album.' Geoffs in the future will be saying, 'Come round and listen to me mixing the new Todd Rundgren album.' We will become a nation of self-appointed George Martins.

I didn't go to Todd Rundgren's 1994 Interactive shows in London. I couldn't face it. Something about that audience participation aspect put me in mind of the nightmare of pantomime-going as a child. I imagined I would spend the entire show feeling sick with the imminent prospect of being hoisted on to the stage. Call me old-fashioned, but if I go and see Todd Rundgren, I want to see him at the piano playing some of his tunes; I want to hear him sing 'Hello, It's Me' and send the hair up on the back of my neck; I want to see what he does with that 'if you need a friend' line. I don't want to see some geek get out of the audience and noodle around on Todd's synths. I can see the radical thrill of this idea, as political philosophy: deconstruct the 'star' system, eliminate the controller, empower the audience, throw the process wide open. But I'm quaint enough to believe that, while geeks are everywhere, Todd Rundgrens are few and far between. The democracy advocated here seems to me illusory. The message is: we can all of us be creative. If only.

The Cleaners from Venus . . . finally

There's a scene at the end of the movie *This Is Spinal Tap* where the estranged guitarist, Nigel Tufnel, suddenly shows up backstage at some disastrous Spinal Tap show. The band have been spiralling downwards ever since he left and the meeting is a tense one, all bruised pride and wounded ego. But Tufnel brings news. He chews hard and says, 'I bumped into Ian [the manager]. Seems that "Sex Farm" is in the charts in Japan. It's No 5 last week, actually, so he asked me to ask you – Tap – if you'd be interested in reforming and doing a tour.' Bingo – a reunion back on the road again, the road that never ends.

So it was hard, at first, to suppress a laugh when Newell phoned the other night, He, too, was chewing hard. And he, too, was talking about Japan. 'My solo album is selling quite well over there. They want me to go out and play a few shows. Nothing too strenuous – just for a week or so. But I have to get a band together and . . . well, do you want to be in it?'

I've got to hand it to him – he tried to sell it to me very gracefully. It wouldn't be the Cleaners from Venus, it would be Martin Newell, which would be nice for me because I would have no responsibility, other than to sit somewhere to the side of the stage and play the keyboards on his splendid songs and enjoy myself. And then there would be all the peripheral fun – the flight, the mucking about, the hotel, the funny things that just inevitably happen if you set out somewhere with a pop group. And all on expenses. (Probably.)

I didn't know how to tell him that obviously I couldn't.

How to put it in words? Because I am thirty-two now. Because I have a girlfriend with whom I live and a cat and a mortgage on a proper house with its own front door and stairs and a garden. Because I have a job and a car. Because last weekend I had my first ever bonfire. Because the weekend before that I found myself in Sainsbury's Homebase buying a lawn-mower (after consulting one of those 'Tried and Tested' articles in the Sunday paper, of course). Because there are unnerving signs that I might, after all, like jazz. Because if it was going to happen to me, if I was really going to have a life in pop, it would have started by now, and all that stuff is dreams and wishfulness and bloody brilliant sometimes but absolutely agonizing and a pain in the arse most of the rest, and there just comes a time when you've got to say no, put the whole thing behind you and simply – for God's sake – grow up.

'When are the rehearsals?' I said.